Teaching Religion Using Technology in Higher Education

This edited collection helps those teaching religion in higher education utilize technology to increase student learning both inside and outside of the classroom. Recent times have seen major technological shifts that have important implications for how religion is taught at a post-secondary level. Providing multiple perspectives on a range of topics—including social media use and interactive classroom learning—this book presents a series of original case studies and insights on how technology can be used in religion classes in higher education to improve student learning.

John Hilton III is Associate Professor of Religious Education at Brigham Young University, USA.

Routledge Research in Religion and Education
Series Editor Michael D. Waggoner,
University of Northern Iowa, USA

1 **Religion in Education**
  Innovation in International Research
  Edited by Joyce Miller, Kevin O'Grady and Ursula McKenna

2 **Civility, Religious Pluralism, and Education**
  Edited by Vincent F. Biondo III and Andrew Fiala

3 **International Perspectives on Education, Religion and Law**
  Edited by Charles J. Russo

4 **Philosophies of Islamic Education**
  Historical Perspectives and Emerging Discourses
  Edited by Nadeem Memon and Mujadad Zaman

5 **Comparative Theology in the Millennial Classroom**
  Hybrid Identities, Negotiated Boundaries
  Edited by Mara Brecht and Reid B. Locklin

6 **God, Education, and Modern Metaphysics:**
  The Logic of Know "Thyself"
  Nigel Tubbs

7 **Migration, Religion, and Schooling in Liberal Democratic States**
  Bruce A. Collet

8 **Teaching Religion Using Technology in Higher Education**
  Edited by John Hilton III

Teaching Religion Using Technology in Higher Education

Edited by John Hilton III

NEW YORK AND LONDON

First published 2018
by Routledge
711 Third Avenue, New York, NY 10017

and by Routledge
2 Park Square, Milton Park, Abingdon, Oxon, OX14 4RN

Routledge is an imprint of the Taylor & Francis Group, an informa business

© 2018 Taylor & Francis

The right of John Hilton III to be identified as editor of this work has been asserted by him/her in accordance with sections 77 and 78 of the Copyright, Designs and Patents Act 1988.

All rights reserved. No part of this book may be reprinted or reproduced or utilized in any form or by any electronic, mechanical, or other means, now known or hereafter invented, including photocopying and recording, or in any information storage or retrieval system, without permission in writing from the publishers.

Trademark notice: Product or corporate names may be trademarks or registered trademarks, and are used only for identification and explanation without intent to infringe.

Library of Congress Cataloguing-in-Publication Data
A catalog record for this book has been requested

ISBN: 978-1-138-08722-4 (hbk)
ISBN: 978-1-315-11061-5 (ebk)

Typeset in Sabon
by Apex CoVantage, LLC

Contents

Preface   vii
JOHN HILTON III

Series Editor Introduction   xii
MICHAEL D. WAGGONER

PART I
Technology in the Classroom   1

1 Third-Screen Teaching: Enhancing Classroom Learning With Mobile Devices   3
   RICHARD NEWTON

2 Student-Created Podcasts as a Means of Knowledge Assessment   18
   DAVID KNEIP

3 Who Do You Vote That I Am?: Using Student Response Systems in Religion Courses   34
   RENATE HOOD

4 Teaching Religion With Clickers   44
   KRISTY L. SLOMINSKI

5 "Seeing" the Sacred Landscape: A Digital Geographies Approach to Contextualizing Ancient Sites in Religious Education   57
   KYLE M. OLIVER

PART II
Leveraging Technology in and out of the Classroom 77

6 "If You'll Tweet Along With Me": Effectively Using
Social Media in Religious Education 79
ROB O'LYNN

7 Social Media in Higher-Ed Religion Studies 92
BROOKE LESTER

8 Blended Learning in Religious Education: What,
Why and How 109
ANTHONY SWEAT

9 Character-izing Gameful Learning: Using Student-Guided
Narratives to Motivate, Engage and Inform Learners 127
CHRISTOPHER HEARD, STEVEN V. ROUSE

PART III
Using Technology to Expand Your Classroom 143

10 Technology Twist on the Visiting Professor 145
GERALD L. STEVENS

11 Taming the MOOS: Massive Online Open
Seminars in Religion 157
PHYLLIS ZAGANO

12 Welcoming the Stranger to the Conversation 173
CHARLOTTE HEEG

13 Comparing Spiritual Outcomes in Face-to-Face Versus
Online Delivery of a Religion Course 186
JOHN HILTON III, KENNETH PLUMMER,
BEN FRYAR, RYAN GARDNER

Contributors 207
Index 208

Preface

Throughout the past decades, technology has played an increasingly important role in society. I remember my parents purchasing a computer when I was ten years old; it used a 5.25-inch floppy drive and could do little apart from word processing. Within two years, we had upgraded to a computer that had a 40-megabyte hard drive—much more space than we knew what to do with. Shortly before graduating from high school, I began to hear of something called e-mail, and I knew a few people who had access to "the Internet"—whatever that was.

As I have grown older, the pace of technological innovation has rapidly accelerated. By the time I received my undergraduate degree, some of my peers had their own computers and cell phones. When I returned to graduate school for a master's degree three years later, both were ubiquitous. Four years later, when I began my PhD program, one of the first courses I took was called "New Media," which explored blogs and social media, and demonstrated how to create websites and upload videos to YouTube. When I consider the fact that my ten-year-old can do all of these things and more (compared to where I was with technology at that age), I am amazed at how technology permeates nearly every part of society.

Advances in technology have influenced all aspects of our lives, including education. Opportunities for online learning, such as iTunes U, open educational resources and Wikipedia have proliferated, influencing the way learners consume information. Students today approach classes with expectations about technology's integration in education that are dramatically different from those of their counterparts from previous generations. Distance learning, which once required a heavy use of postal services, is becoming increasingly common and is even mandated at some universities.

Changes in technology have led to many educational innovations, including massive open online courses (MOOCs), blended learning, learning management systems, podcasts, student response systems and others. These changes provide instructors with a range of new opportunities: they can use online services to host expert lecturers, create online forums where students can collaborate or conduct digital field trips using virtual reality. Methods of learning for students now extend beyond writing papers or taking exams.

With the increasing opportunities come many difficult questions. For example, when access to factual information is just a few clicks away, do learning outcomes change? Given the questionable veracity of online information, what role do educators play in helping students become critical receivers of information? What type of emphasis will there be on the ability of students to create learning resources? Will advances in technology lead to learning opportunities that are more advanced or simply result in students who lose focus while multitasking in class?

This book examines several facets of using technology to teach religion. The present volume is divided into three sections. The first section, Technology in the Classroom, explores a variety of ways that the Internet, along with a variety of digital devices, can influence processes of learning, teaching and assessing. In Chapter 1, Newton describes the role of mobile devices, such as smartphones, in the classroom. He provides context for discussions of "digital natives" and "learning styles," and suggests ways smartphones can be used as learning tools. Newton focuses on pedagogical innovations in classroom practice (e.g., providing a backchannel for conversation) and other strategies for successful preparation for exams (e.g., using collaborative note-taking).

In Chapter 2, Kniep focuses on podcasts and their use in teaching religion. He claims that, while assigning students to *listen* to podcasts can be beneficial, instructors might consider assigning students to *create* podcasts, by which instructors can assess their knowledge. Drawing on his personal experience with this approach, Kniep describes how student-created podcasts help overcome the common difficulty of working both with students who are verbose and those who remain quiet, particularly when discussing sensitive topics such as religion. Kniep provides both technical and pedagogical suggestions for meaningful student podcasts and argues that this approach helps educators grade more efficiently and interact more deeply with students.

Chapters 3 and 4 focus on an increasingly important topic: that of student response systems. In Chapter 3, Hood defines student response systems and explains several benefits that stem from their use, including increased student motivation and participation, and relief from some of the anxieties that may attend religion classes. She details the approaches of several response systems and explores their relative advantages as effective technological resources in religious education. Hood provides a strong case that when properly implemented, student response systems offer multiple pedagogical benefits in teaching religion.

In Chapter 4, Slominski focuses on clickers—a specific type of student response system. Clickers allow students who are uncomfortable raising their hands to express themselves, and they provide variety from traditional lecture formats. Slominski outlines some further benefits of this approach, including the way it encourages students to take stances on complex religious issues and to acknowledge the diverse religious perspectives within a classroom. She explains how instructors can use clickers to receive instantaneous feedback and customize the class as necessary. At state-funded institutions, where professors might be cautious about students sharing personal beliefs in the classroom, clickers can transform deeply personal viewpoints into indirect data, providing distance and a level of anonymity that aids critical analysis.

In the final chapter of the first section, Chapter 5, Oliver describes how instructors can use digital technologies to contextualize ancient sites that are vital to a deeper understanding of religious issues. While most students will not have the opportunity to travel to distant sacred sites, the Internet can help students visualize such places. Using a lens of digital geographies, Oliver offers ways to use media to help students explore religious sites through online videos, online picture repositories, Google Earth and virtual reality content.

The second section of the present volume describes how to leverage technology both in and out of the classroom. The first two chapters in this section focus on one of the most important technological developments of the past decade: social media. In Chapter 6, O'Lynn introduces social media and its applications in the religious education classroom. O'Lynn offers practical advice for implementing social media practices in religious education using Facebook, Twitter, Instagram and Snapchat, among many other social media outlets.

In Chapter 7, Lester explores how to use social media to create community when teaching religion and describes both positive and negative aspects of its use. Using social media in the classroom can help students form connections and communities; however, social media is not a panacea. Its use limits anonymity and, in some cases, subjects users to online abuse. Lester describes how to ameliorate problems with social media in the classroom and how to use it successfully in both traditional and distance-based religion courses.

In Chapter 8, Sweat discusses blended learning, a relatively recent form of learning that has been heavily discussed in educational technology circles. Blended learning combines face-to-face instruction with electronic learning, delivering content outside the classroom via technology. Theoretically, a blended-learning model helps students achieve lower-order, knowledge-level outcomes outside of class so that in class they can focus on higher-order participatory outcomes, such as analyzing, evaluating and creating—outcomes that are vital in many settings where religion is taught. Sweat defines blended learning and its relationship to flipped classrooms, briefly reviews its research literature and explores potential applications in religious education.

In the final chapter of the second section, Chapter 9, Heard and Rouse focus on ways computer games may or may not inform, motivate, and engage students learning about religion. Drawing on theoretical considerations relating to learning and games, the authors replaced 6 of 18 homework assignments with interactive fiction stories on a computer. Although empirical results from other contexts suggested this approach could benefit students, data from students' survey responses showed otherwise. Students indicated that they felt no more motivated by the experimental mode than by the standard mode, and a significant number of students learned more from traditional homework. These results indicate that not all types of technology adaptation will improve learning outcomes.

The final section of this book describes how to use technology to expand the classroom. In Chapter 10, Stevens describes how to use the Internet to increase, dramatically, the opportunity to host guest lecturers. Stevens argues that a visiting expert in a field can infuse students with interest through his or her live and spontaneous remarks, and that students gain significantly more when they can interact with such an expert in a question-and-answer period. While instructors used to need to maneuver multiple logistical obstacles to invite guest lecturers, technology eliminates most of these obstacles. Stevens narrates a case study in which technology allowed students to bridge the distance of time and place, and learn directly from a specialist on first-century Roman roads, an experience that would not have been possible without technology.

In Chapter 11, Zagano touches on another recent phenomenon in educational technology: MOOCs. Zagano describes her foray into this genre of education by creating an open online seminar related to a specific topic in religious studies. More than 300 people from five continents registered for the seminar, and 292 remained until the end. Zagano explains how she created this course, providing a template that others can follow. She also shares survey responses that indicate that most participants had very positive experiences.

In Chapter 12, Heeg describes how some specific Google Hangout videos, originally created for an open online "Introduction to the Old Testament" course, were repurposed in a small Bible study group to integrate neophytes into scholarly discourse concerning texts of the Bible. By viewing informal conversations between biblical studies professors, Heeg's learners were better able to integrate academic vocabulary and concepts within congregational Bible study discussions. This approach demonstrates one of many ways that online technologies can be used to journey beyond formal classroom spaces on campuses into broader learning environments.

In this book's final chapter, Chapter 13, Hilton, Plummer, Fryar and Gardner report on the results of an experiment that compared the spiritual outcomes of students who took an online religion course with those who took a face-to-face version of the same course. Using an instrument that measured affective outcomes, they surveyed 789 students—both on-site and online—enrolled in a general education religion course at a private religious college. Some educators have argued that distance learning could negatively affect students' religiosity, but researchers observed no significant differences between groups. These results indicate that even when focusing on affective outcomes, distance education may be a useful tool for teaching religion.

Taken collectively, the chapters in this book offer fresh perspectives on using technology in the context of teaching religion. The educators and researchers in this book effectively argue that both students and faculty can benefit from using technology in the classroom when teaching religion. While technology is not a panacea for concerns religious educators face in the classroom, it does afford many new opportunities to enhance learning and teaching.

John Hilton III

Series Editor Introduction

The opening years of the twenty-first century brought increased attention to religion as an important dimension of culture and politics. The dramatic multipronged attacks of September 11, 2001, came as a jolting reminder of the potential for violent action that can have bases in religious motivations. Over the same period, we came to see an increase in religious group activity in politics. In the United States, this may be seen as an evolution most recently from the Moral Majority movement led by televangelist Jerry Falwell that emerged as a force in the late 1970s as the beginning of the New Religious Right. On further reflection, however, we can see the involvement of religion extending much further back as a fundamental part of our social organization rather than a new or emerging phenomenon. We need only recall the religious wars of early modern Europe through to the contentious development of US church and state relations as evidence of the long-standing role religion has played as a source of competing values and beliefs with consequences for our life together in a democratic society. That said, there has been a significant upturn in research and scholarship across many disciplines relative to the study of religion in the last two decades. This is particularly the case with issues at the intersection of education and religion.

While religious education—study *toward formation* in a particular faith tradition—has been with us for millennia, study *about* religion as an academic subject apart from theology is more recent. Whereas theology departments proceeded from religious assumptions aiming to promulgate a faith tradition, the religious studies field emerged as a discipline that sought to bring a more disinterested social scientific approach to the study of religion. The origins of this approach date back to the European research centers that influenced US scholars beginning in the eighteenth century. The formalization of this trend, however, is a fairly recent phenomenon as illustrated by the 1949 formation of Society for the Scientific Study of Religion with its own scholarly journal and the creation of religious studies departments across the US in the wake of the US Supreme Court decision in 1963 that allowed teaching *about* religion (rather than *for*) in public education institutions. It was also that same year that the

American Academy of Religion was born out of a group of scholars that had since 1909 been meeting under the various names related to biblical study.

It is out of this increase in scholarly attention to religion and education that this book series arises. Routledge has long been an important presence in the respective fields of religion and of education. It seemed like a natural step to introduce a book series focused particularly on Research in Religion and Education. My appreciation extends to Max Novick at Routledge for working with me to guide this series into being, and to Stacy Noto, Christina Chronister, Karen Adler, and now Matthew Friberg for continuing Routledge's oversight.

In this eighth volume in this series, Professor John Hilton III brings together 17 scholars to explore multiple uses of technology in the teaching of religion. The challenges and opportunities inherent in the use of technology in teaching explored here apply to both religious education in faith-based formation and to education about religion in the secular academic teaching about religion. Technology changes rapidly and continually, so the target of understanding what is out there and mastering its use will also change and move as will the students with whom it is intended to be used.

There is a wide range of experience with technology currently in college classrooms. Current students, Generation Z, born in the mid to late 1990s to the mid-2000s, are the students in college who grew up with the smartphone. Many baby boomers are still faculty teaching these students and many of those faculty members may be found everywhere—from basic to advanced—along the tech-savvy spectrum. Of course, generalizations are just that, broad and often misleading. There are also many millennials that are beginning to take their place in faculty and administrative positions and, therefore, are bringing greater technology experience with them into the classroom. Nevertheless, there is arguably wide variance in acquaintance and comfort with technology that may be used to advantage in teaching. It is this challenge that this volume and collection of authors address.

Michael D. Waggoner

Part I
Technology in the Classroom

1 Third-Screen Teaching

Enhancing Classroom Learning With Mobile Devices

Richard Newton

> Its continuing mission: to explore strange new worlds, to seek out new life and new civilizations, to boldly go where no one has gone before.
> —Intro to *Star Trek: The Next Generation*

The future of education is now. We may not have distilled its best practices or mandated evaluative rubrics for it, but humans are always at work, teaching and learning to make sense of the world around them. We have even euphemized its processes and politics with the term *culture*.

Our histories can scarcely imagine a time when we were not cultivating the know-how to nurture the next generation. The root agricultural metaphor testifies to our dependence on this life-giving act. Our aspirations are predicated on improving what we have already witnessed. Thus we should not be surprised by the way our educational fantasies expand on our present reality.

You need not be a science-fiction fanatic to see the resonance of *Star Trek* with today's classroom. Gene Roddenberry's brainchild follows the galactic adventures of an intrepid crew. Though equipped with interstellar vehicles, laser weapons and plasma shields, the characters' martial adornments are rationalized in subservience to a larger educational enterprise. It is a story about cultural expansion.

In *Star Trek*, the tools for cultivation are as familiar as they are fantastic. Since its 1966 premiere, viewers have tuned into a three-screen future.[1] There is the large televisual screen that frames the galaxy, other ships and strange celestial bodies. There are the computer consoles from which the crew performs complicated operations. But it is the third screen that communicates the focus of this dramatic metacommentary on the human condition.

The mobile, trifunction recorder—or "tricorder"—provides the means through which individual characters can sense, analyze and record data around them.[2] With a tricorder, a person can communicate the information collected to other crewmates and consoles. The integration of these technologies has remained a sight to behold, but the possibilities of the tricorder are a poetic reminder of the wonder of an individual's freedom to think.

Of the three devices, the tricorder was once the furthest from a real-world analog, though eventually life imitated art in what has come to be known as the "smartphone." According to NASA, "Your cell phone has more computing power than the computers used during the Apollo era."[3] It combines cellular telecommunication, Internet connectivity and an application-based operating system. Early twenty-first-century style has kept Roddenberry's three-screen artifice largely intact. Televisions have never been clearer and computers never faster, but phones—and, thus, their users—have had a chance to be smarter.

Not surprisingly, education is a controversial site for adopting emergent technologies such as smartphones. In the late 1960s and 1970s (before government regulations on child-friendly programming), television's ability to mesmerize young audiences earned the device the slanderous title of "the idiot tube."[4] And while learning software played a key role in the rise of the personal computer, parents of the 1980s and 1990s were concerned that overexposure to these machines would "rot" children's brains.[5] These fears seem quaint, even archaic, in a time when television and computer consoles are inescapable from "first-world" life.

Pundits resort to similar hyperbole to decry the "zombification" of society.[6] The concern is born out of an observation that mobile device users (especially youth) increasingly focus on life as presented on their screens with little regard for the outside world. As we increasingly engage the world through the third screen, gatekeepers of culture call for the resurgence of paper and pencil, the printed book and vocal conversation.

To be certain, the concerns are serious. As humans increasingly depend on mobile connectivity to the Internet, our brains develop a compulsive addiction to the potential dopamine release from positive online interaction—giving added currency to the stars, hearts, likes and happy faces of social networking.[7] Educators fear that this cybernetic feedback loop can give way to distracting and detrimental obsessions—from attention-deficit concerns, to "fear of missing out," to harmful psychiatric disorders.[8]

Also decried is the digitization of educational resources such as e-books, dictation programs and search-oriented applications. The argument goes that these learning aids stimulate the brain less than reading physical books and manual note-taking.[9] The visceral reading and writing experience leaves a sensory impression on students to the extent that our brains construct a mental map of the text. Electronic versions of these activities—less bound to the smells, textures and displays of the page—do not engage our senses in that way, leaving us subject to the orientation of a device's cursor. By banning devices such as smartphones from the classroom, teachers hope to create a healthier, more stimulating learning environment.

But this exclusivistic approach to the third-screen technologies betrays some assumptions that the history of religion would have us qualify. Kelly J. Baker, a historian of American religion, would prod us to unpack the discourse on zombification in the new millennium. The fearsome creatures are symbolic "agents of the end of the world, often visualized as an end of the American nation as we know it."[10] Zombies embody a fear that the tools we received in the past to grapple with our present will be inefficient in helping us survive in the future. Hence the metaphor has been applied to "anything from consumerism to terrorism to mindless politics/politicians to banking to epidemics to smart phone users."[11]

In the case of third-screen devices, educators feel ill equipped to help students manage this powerful technology. We are out of our authoritative comfort zones, not unlike clergy at the cusp of the Gutenberg era, when some of their flock began reading the Bible for themselves for the first time. We have had centuries to hone bibliocentric pedagogy and millennia to master the lecture format, but third screens open up a classroom window onto an exciting world that we sometimes wish students—and we ourselves—would rather not see. It is hard to remember that even in the last 200 years, the word *bookish* was used to deride students who had checked out from the world around them. Our failure to do so should give us pause.

In working out my own digital-age teaching philosophy, I am reminded of Donald Kraybill's sociological studies of the Amish. The plain-dressed Christian community is famous for resisting technology. Kraybill has argued that this is a misrepresentation of the Anabaptist group's piety. The Amish are not antitechnology, he has frequently commented, just more thoughtful.[12]

With the advent of a new contraption, Amish elders have asked what this tool will say about their community's dependence on God and commitment to the way of Jesus Christ. It is in that spirit that they decide between asceticism and acculturation. And that is the point. Rational usage is determined by the possibility of community enrichment, not having the latest and greatest thing (whether it is technology or pedagogical ideology).

Our approach to mobile devices in the classroom should exhibit a similar discernment process. Somewhere between being a Luddite and being tech tethered is the possibility of cultural creativity (cf. ludics) upon which humanity is ultimately dependent.[13] As teachers, we are in the vocation of intellectual transformation. So how might we use the third screen to transform the flow of information in the classroom so that students not only consume knowledge but also produce it?

In this chapter, I invite you to find out. We will begin by theorizing about the function of third screens in our classrooms. Then rather than trying to survey the ever-changing landscape of apps or devices, we will look at four types of educational tasks where third screens might enhance teaching-learning as well as sample activities for you to consider.

Retheorizing Digital-Age Myths

We are grappling with the reality that smartphones mediate Millennials' sociocultural interactions in a way that exceeds their predecessors. The 2015 Pew Research Center's Teen Relationships Survey projects that 73 percent of American teens (13–17 years old) have smartphones.[14] Gallup reports that text messaging (either through Short Message Services (SMS) or an app equivalent) has supplanted aural/oral conversation as the preferred means of distance communication.[15] Teenagers use mobile-based applications such as Instagram are used not only for describing experiences but also for soliciting visitor feedback (e.g., "hearts") to inform clothing decisions, eating choices and interactions with peers.[16] The question is not whether third screens are affecting the classroom experience. It is how.

Teachers often fall back on two pedagogical *myths*—the "digital native/digital immigrant" divide and "learning style" preference—to inform their response to Millennial technology use. I use *myth* in the technical sense to question these explanations' historical-critical validity and to provoke deeper thought about what we want them to be.[17]

The digital native/digital immigrant divide comes from a discourse popularized by Marc Prensky to highlight the impasse between "old-school" analog teachers and their computer-savvy students.[18] The idea is that the proliferation of personal computing, the centrality of the Internet and the primacy of digitized media ushered in a new information age. Those born in this epoch speak in a native tongue marked by hypertextual communication and multimedia exchange, modes largely foreign to those born in the predigital world. Prensky opined that many of our educational problems stem from the shaky assumption that "digital immigrant" teachers are equipped to prepare digital native students despite their own culture shock. In turn, our society has been quicker to critique Millennial idiocy than to acquire competency in the field of digital pedagogy.

Heeding Prensky's call, institutions of higher education have heavily invested in retrofitting brick-and-mortar classrooms in an attempt to cater to prospective digital native students. These efforts coincide with the consumer-oriented mentality of college students who have fluency in the language of "learning styles," a framework that suggests that student brains have varied preferred avenues for knowledge acquisition in accordance with one of many rubrics with a host of categories (i.e., kinesthetic, visual learning, auditory, reflective, theorist, activist).[19] In practice, these models help teachers to differentiate instructional techniques to a student's learning style in order to increase performance. Upon this premise, the generational preference for digital technology makes educators negligent for not using the latest electronic tools.

Despite the popularity of the digital native/immigrant and learning style theories, researchers in education and social psychology have heavily criticized both. For instance, Prensky's 2001 argument does not wholly take into account that many of the social media technologies used today were developed by pre-Millennials.[20] Similarly, the theory does not account for the social factors that determine a student's access to technology and the means for building digital literacy.[21] And at this point, the case for discrete learning styles remains thin. There is little evidence to suggest that one can meaningfully register learning preference in a way that matches up to effectiveness measures.[22] Once we are aware of the limits of the two aforementioned pedagogical presumptions, we can free ourselves to imagine the truths to which they may otherwise point.

When I started reflecting on third-screen teaching, I quickly realized that while my students have smartphones, they hardly make the students smarter. They were still asking me what certain words meant, how to calculate their grades or when assignments would be due. All of this—and more—was available to them through their mobile devices, but they hardly use them as such. When I asked them why, they said, "I never thought about using it that way," or "Because we're usually not allowed to use cell phones in class. I never thought about what I'd do if I was allowed to." There is a digital divide here, but I would characterize it differently than Prensky did.

The 1980s and early 1990s saw a reconceptualization of what it means to talk about digital technology. Those living during the period came to understand *digital technology as a tool*. Each new device and app could help you do something you could not do as easily before.[23] My students (generally born after 1995) know a world where *digital technology is furniture*. It is there to be used with little reference to a manual analog or frame of reference. They do not know what to make of a card catalog, slide rule, telephone book or bound encyclopedia because they never had to cultivate anything with them. This is not a bad thing but rather the circumstance of an increasingly singular technological environment. They do not know to see mobile devices as an enhancement to life. They are a part of living.

Yesterday's avant-garde is tomorrow's routine, but in the liminal discomfort of today, classroom culture must come to terms with this key difference. It is to answer with students the unexamined question of what they could do with the smartphone that they were not doing before.

Backward design helped me isolate four tasks central to the teaching-learning process in my praxis. I knew I wanted my classroom to use mobile devices more effectively, but I needed to determine areas to focus my implementation. From student centered to teacher centered, the tasks I arrived at include (1) personal study, (2) cooperative learning,

(3) external referencing and (4) information production. A "problem-centered" approach also removes the temptation to fetishize any particular application or device. Accordingly, any mention of a particular technology should be read as an example rather than as an exemplar of a task. Selection is always a negotiation between function, cost, availability, learning context, device/operating system/platform compatibility and personal preference.

I used Jim Collins's notion of "good to great" to build on my pedagogical strengths as a means of addressing teaching-learning deficiencies in the classroom.[24] So with each task, I discuss the particular issue I wanted to resolve along with the important step of naming what has worked thus far. As you reflect on your own praxis, you may find that you have different strengths and needs. I encourage you to approach the list with a "growth mind-set" to inspire your own creative third-screen solutions.

Third-Screen Teaching in Practice

1. Personal Study

First impressions make a difference. By definition, new material is bound to make students uncomfortable, but those who lack confidence in the act of learning will struggle no matter what material is being covered. How might we ameliorate the early transmission of logistical (e.g., due dates and study recommendations) and content knowledge? Because students are already tethered to their mobile devices, we can cut the distance in places where students might otherwise find themselves lost.

Note-Taking

I like to begin classes by emphasizing that there is a difference between dictation and note-taking. Dictation is the mere verbatim representation of information as presented by someone else. It lacks the intimacy of making that information one's own. While recording information is a key part of the latter, the ability to do this more efficiently should free up a student's time to appropriate the material for him- or herself. As I put it to my students, "If your technology can save you time, what are you now free to do?" Third screens can remove the apprehension of missing out on information, freeing them to focus on reengagement of the material. I make clear that they have not studied unless they are doing both.

When I do board work, I have students develop the board with me as they go along. During dense presentations, I may provide a worksheet for students to fill in the blanks. Otherwise, they are creating their own copy of what I am doing, step by step. I model for them that we are putting pieces together—not just preparing a single product to regurgitate. I assure them that at the end of the presentation, they may snap a picture of the board but only after having gone through the process with me. Their homework is then to go back over the process of putting the pieces together, consulting their image as needed. Similarly, one could have them record lectures on their own devices. In any case, make the student responsible for getting the final product on his or her personal device—even if you are providing slideshow handouts or your own media files.

This is not a novel idea. Versions of these techniques have been used in language paradigm instruction for decades. By explicitly incorporating the mobile phone, you can backward-engineer tethered students to "hide your word in 'their' hearts," to borrow from the opening of Psalm 119. They now have a picture or audio file always near them to consult along with the memory of having put it there. In some cases, this is enough to build students' confidence to revisit the material on their own.

Office Hours

A theme of my pedagogy is matching personal responsibility with expert guidance (aspirations on both ends). I strongly encourage students to take advantage of my office hours in a purposeful manner. Some students will do this on their own and others only when I personally invite them. And then there are students who will, for whatever reason, pass up the opportunity for advisement. Regardless, I want to make it as easy as possible to help as many students as I can have an effective session. For me, the key is making them work for it.

I require students to make an appointment using an online, mobile-friendly booking service (e.g., YouCanBookMe.com). Students must sign up and tell me their contact information (i.e., name, e-mail address, course) and the area in which they need assistance. My times are limited to thirty-minute blocks (rather than an hour or some less-descript period). This trains students to set goals and use their time wisely. Students can link to the appointment service through a short URL, a QR code, our class learning management system or my personal website. For those students who want to drop by for an appointment, I have them register at my office door. The student and I then receive an e-mail and calendar notification of the expectations for our meeting. They are building good professional habits and helping me help them.

Talk to Yourself

For all the wizardry of smartphones, students forget that they are telephonic devices. When I encounter students who are "stuck in their heads" or have trouble getting ideas down on the proverbial paper, I remind them to talk it out *with themselves*. They can use their phones to ask themselves the questions they are already asking cerebrally. The device can create that Socratic distance necessary to see the problem from a different point of view.

Have the student locate the voice-memo app (or even call their own voice mail). Their job is to talk through ideas, read aloud drafts or lecture on the problem subject. When they have exhausted themselves, have them take a brief break and listen to the show while taking notes on what is working and not working. Have them record another "show" that improves upon the previous one. Students will quickly become adept at the process of drafting.

2. Cooperative Learning

Mobile devices can siphon student attention away from the people, places and concerns around them. But under the right circumstances, the hyperfocus and groupthink we associate with zombification could become the traits of an interactive classroom. It requires us to change the terms of engagement. Cooperative learning is about leveraging the third screen to facilitate this kind of interaction toward your student learning outcomes.

Collaborative Note-Taking

I have spent many semesters encouraging students to form study groups with little avail. When they did form groups, they either used the opportunity to complete homework assignments together before spending time on honing their skills individually or waited until just before an examination to review burning questions. I know that these groups can be successful, but I realized that I had to teach students how to work together.

Within my seminar and midsized courses, I had begun incorporating cooperative learning strategies. I regularly used quick lower-stakes assignments to insist students come to class having completed either formal study guides (in lower-level courses) or substantial review (in upper-level courses). Then I guided students through "think-pair-share," create and teach a group infographic and other such classroom activities. It habituated them to the idea of working together to turn their individual notes into an intelligible form for another person. Students grew accustomed to addressing each other's questions while working out a mutual understanding. That is when I stumbled on another development.

At the end of the semester—in both a seminar and a midsized course—I found that students maintained an ongoing "chat" that ran parallel to the class.[25] They exchanged phone numbers and e-mail addresses, and posed questions to each other as they worked. Strangely, the students did not admit doing this until the very end of the semester during our course debrief. I suspect they were anxious about whether I would consider this plagiarism. I had to assure them that this is called studying.

With their permission, I probed their conversations. Students shared that they would raise questions either during their regular individual note review or in preparation for major assessments. These were the points that would usually concern me. But I noticed that the chat worked under the self-governed presumption that participants had tried first and were to reciprocate assistance. Peer pressure was their ally, and then there was the extra step of having to go to the phone during personal study (rather than doing personal study in a group). When done, they had created a study guide that I could hardly have devised for them, and they were near it at all times.

Backchanneling Class Films

Backchanneling, or "live-tweeting" as it is commonly known, is one of my go-to activities. Sometimes the most efficient way to present course material is to show students a relevant film. I have students use their mobile devices to answer a single guiding question while watching a film. The question can be conceptual: "How do you see theories of mythmaking being acted out in the following film?" Or you can ground the question in a direct task: "Identify ten vocabulary words connected to the activities on-screen without repeating each other's submissions." Make the prompt challenging enough to keep students so busy that they do not have time to get off track. This is a relatively easy way to enhance an otherwise pedantic activity. A few additional considerations, however, are in order.

For this activity to work, students need to be able see the film, their input field and their classmates' responses at the same time. If you do not have access to a program that lets you do this, you can adapt this activity. The film can be shown on a large communal screen or wherever and whenever students are allowed to stream the film. The input field will be on the third-screen device. To run all of the responses, students can either be tasked with consulting the response feed on their own individual devices (with the possible drawback of having to switch back and forth between input and output fields) or displaying the response feed on another screen. I have seen instructors bring in another screen dedicated to the response feed. I myself have just adjusted window sizes on the computer playing the film so that I can have a window scrolling the response feed or acting like a chyron.

You will also need to determine how you want students to share their responses. Generally using a hashtag on a microblogging social media app like Twitter is the easiest way to do this. However, this requires insisting that students sign up for an account and make their responses open to the public. Out of concern for student privacy, I used an inward-facing, third-screen polling service called Poll Everywhere to do this. There are many services that boast such capability, but be on the lookout for services that work with your own assessment workflow. I chose Poll Everywhere because it syncs with my school's learning management system—a key consideration when I scaled it up to large-class usage. Others I know have used Kahoot because they enjoy the gamelike interface and its compatibility with streaming media sites.

3. External Referencing

In the early days of the Internet, educators latched on to the "World Wide Web" tagline to highlight the worlds of information students could connect to with the help of a computer. With third-screen devices, students bring those worlds with them into the classroom. The following activities remind students of the resources at their fingertips.

Help-Less Teaching

In smaller institutions, students may be prone to take advantage of faculty—relying on them to become corporeal dictionaries, syllabi and library databases. Junior and contingent faculty may oblige these onerous requests out of fear of negative teaching evaluations. The politics of higher education as a consumer market cannot be underestimated. But there is something to be said about teaching a person to fish rather than fishing for him or her.

Use these requests as teachable moments. Going back to the technology-as-furniture concept, many students do not think about using their phones as a resource. Take a moment and see if they have a mobile device on their person. If so, prompt them to find the appropriate resource via web browser or app. At the end of the conversation, make a sell for the value of professionalism (e.g., "resourcefulness is a virtue in the workplace") and initiative (e.g., "You have space-age computing power in the palm of your hand. You are cheating yourself if you don't use it"). Even this basic use of third-screen technology can be a game changer in the classroom.

Virtual Reality

The metaphor of the brick-and-mortar classroom will become less helpful as students grow closer to third-screen devices. Institutions have retrofitted classrooms to accommodate power outlets for computers and the lighting necessary for projectors. The rise of movable classroom furniture bespeaks of the demand for more nimble pedagogies. With mobile devices, teachers can take students on a field trip within the classroom.

Full-fledged virtual reality is for the most part beyond the veil. In the meantime, there are some rich digital environment renderings ready for classroom use. Panoramic cameras can capture the environment of holy sites for students to view through the third screen. In some instances, the images will be calibrated for immersive viewing—that is, the image changes in relation to the viewer's own movement. Students can explore with high-end headsets, cardboard rigs (e.g., Google Cardboard) or devices in hand.

I have had the most success with this activity when I have students explore a site for which they have a 2-D image. For example, in my New Testament class, I will show students a locus map of an archeology site and then have them find loci within the virtual landscape. Similarly, students in my Islam class may be familiar with common architectural features of a mosque or synagogue vis-à-vis a textbook picture. From there, I can send them on a scavenger hunt in one of the many 3-D examples online.

4. Information Production

Third-screen devices challenge not only how we think of study but also the type of work students can create. When educators remain flexible with their understanding of "work," then students can surprise us with well-thought-out productions.

Re-imag(in)ing Course Material

Contemporary Internet usage is highly referential. Students communicate with emoji (the battery of glyphs used in lieu of text) and Graphics Interchange Format (GIFs) from television, music videos and film. When conventional text is used, they often index comments with the use of hashtags, sometimes to the extent that a purposefully hyperspecific or whimsical hashtag can supplant the primary message.

During a lecture where I cover periods of history or narrative, I will sometimes translate the material into emoji or GIFs as a way to help students reimagine the content. In my New Testament survey, I had a Buddhist student from Thailand who entered the class with very limited knowledge of the Bible. When I asked someone to put into context a complicated multi-church dispute discussed in Paul's First Letter to the Corinthians, a student was able to do so with stunning command by approaching it as a message board with metacomments such as #TeamPaul and #TeamCephas. Lest one think she was being flippant, she outscored nearly all of the self-identified Christians in the class. She then texted the image to the students in the class, who incorporated it into their later review materials.

Third-Screen Interactivity as Genre

Third-screen interactivity may best be seen as a genre of student output that is every bit as legitimate as the worksheet or essay. Since students seek out mobile-friendly applications in and out of the classroom, we might reconsider how students present knowledge in these forms.

Have students create a mobile-friendly companion website to your course in lieu of a traditional essay assignment. The same skills they use to embed media and links in their social networks can be used on a number of website and blog platforms. If this seems daunting or excessive, establish a course hashtag on one or more designated social networks. Invite them to curate an ongoing thread with images, videos and links related to course content. Lastly, ask them to show you how to further course aims with the third screen. When students take ownership, they are preparing themselves to succeed.

Conclusion

Nobody knows your classroom better than you. Nobody thinks more about your students *as students* than you. Locate an area or two where you want to nurture student growth. Identify a relevant tactic that excites you and explore the possibilities. Use these tactics to plant seeds that will enliven the learning process in your context.

Third-screen teaching should not be an educational gimmick but an organic teaching solution. Whatever application you have students use, ultimately you are creating a community. Let the device remind all participants that personal communication is key to your mutual venture toward a learned future

Notes

1 "Star Trek," *IMDb*, accessed August 22, 2017, www.imdb.com/title/tt0060028/.
2 Kevin Anderton, "The Contest to Build the First Star Trek Tricorder Has a Winner [Infographic]," *Forbes*, last updated April 22, 2017, www.forbes.com/sites/ kevinanderton/2017/04/22/the-contest-to-build-the-first-startrek-tricorder-has-a-winner-infographic/.
3 Shelley Canright, *NASA: Do-It-Yourself Podcast: Rocket Evolution*, last updated July 13, 2009, www.nasa.gov/audience/foreducators/diypodcast/rocket-evolution-index-diy.html.
4 According to *The Routledge Dictionary of Modern American Slang and Unconventional English* (2009), the phrase "idiot tube" dates to 1968. For more on American government regulation of educational programming, see "Children's Educational Television," *Federal Communications Commission*, last updated October 25, 2016, www.fcc.gov/consumers/guides/childrens-educational-television.
5 Ted Friedman, *Electronic Dreams: Computers in American Culture* (New York: New York University Press, 2005), 116.
6 James Fields, "How Your Smartphone Is Turning You into a Zombie," *Tennessean*, last updated May 2, 2014, www.tennessean.com/story/money/tech/2014/05/01/james-fields-zombies-obsessed-smartphones/8582485/.
7 Ira Glass, "Status Update: Prologue," *This American Life*, WBEZ, first aired November 27, 2015, www.thisamericanlife.org/radio-archives/episode/573/status-update?act=0#play.

Third-Screen Teaching 15

8 Bill Davidow, "Exploiting the Neuroscience of Internet Addiction," *Atlantic*, last updated July 18, 2012, www.theatlantic.com/health/archive/2012/07/exploiting-the-neuroscience-of-internet-addiction/259820/.
9 Pam A. Mueller and Daniel M. Oppenheimer, "The Pen Is Mightier Than the Keyboard: Advantages of Longhand over Laptop Note Taking," *Psychological Science* 25, no. 6 (2014): 1159–1168; Ferris Jabr, "The Reading Brain in the Digital Age: The Science of Paper versus Screens," *Scientific American*, last updated April 11, 2013, www.scientificamerican.com/article/reading-paper-screens/.
10 Kelly J. Baker, *The Zombies Are Coming! The Realities of the Zombie* (Colorado Springs: Bondfire Books, 2013), Kindle edition, location 60–64.
11 Ibid., 74.
12 Jeff Brady, "Amish Community Not Anti-Technology, Just More Thoughtful," *All Things Considered*, NPR, last updated September 2, 2013, www.npr.org/sections/alltechconsidered/2013/09/02/217287028/amish-community-not-anti-technology-just-more-thoughtful. See also Donald B. Kraybill, *The Riddle of Amish Culture*, 2nd ed. (Baltimore: Johns Hopkins University Press, 2001).
13 Johan Huizinga, *Homo Ludens: A Study of the Play-Element* (Towbridge, UK: Redwood Burn, 1980 [1944]). For Huizinga, the notion of play within culture is the typifying aspect of *Homo sapiens* as "*Homo ludens*"—"the knowing human" as the human in sport or *re-creation*.
14 Amanda Lenhart, "Teens, Social Media & Technology Overview 2015," *Pew Research & Technology*, last updated April 9, 2015, www.pewinternet.org/2015/04/09/teens-social-media-technology-2015/.
15 Frank Newport, "The New Era of Communication among Americans," *Gallup*, last updated November 10, 2014, www.gallup.com/poll/179288/new-era-communication-americans.aspx.
16 Ira Glass, "Status Update: Finding the Self in Selfie," *This American Life*, WBEZ, first aired November 27, 2015, www.thisamericanlife.org/radio-archives/episode/573/status-update?act=1#play.
17 Bruce Lincoln, *Theorizing Myth: Narrative, Ideology, and Scholarship* (Chicago: University of Chicago Press, 1999), 208–9.
18 Marc Prensky, "Digital Natives, Digital Immigrants," www.marcprensky.com/writing/Prensky%20-%20Digital%20Natives,%20Digital%20Immigrants%20-%20Part1.pdf. Originally published in *On the Horizon* 9, no. 5 (2001).
19 Harold Pashler et al., "Learning Styles: Concepts and Evidence," *Psychological Science in the Public Interest* 9, no. 3 (2008): 106–8.
20 Jeff DeGraff, "Digital Natives vs. Digital Immigrants," *Huffington Post*, last updated September 7, 2014, www.huffingtonpost.com/jeff-degraff/digital-natives-vs-digita_b_5499606.html. Jeff DeGraff makes this point but qualifies that the "digital immigrants" that created many of our popular technologies did so without expecting the way "digital natives" would come to use them.
21 European Computer Driving License Foundation, "The Fallacy of the 'Digital Native': Why Young People Need to Develop Their Digital Skills," 2014, accessed September 27, 2017, http://ecdl.org/media/TheFallacyofthe'Digital Native'PositionPaper1.pdf.
22 Joshua Cuevas, "Is Learning Styles-based Instruction Effective? A Comprehensive Analysis of Recent Research on Learning Styles," *Theory and Research in Education* 13, no. 3 (2015): 308–333; Pashler et al., "Learning Styles," 112.
23 The best discussion of this age cohort and technology is Anna Garvey's "The Oregon Trail Generation: Life Before and After Mainstream Tech," *Social Media Week*, last updated April 21, 2015, https://socialmediaweek.org/blog/2015/04/oregon-trail-generation/.

24 Jim Collins, *Good to Great* (San Francisco: HarperBusiness, 2001), 92–103.
25 My students used standard text messaging. Stephanie McKellop (@McKellogs) had a similar teaching experience with Google Docs. Stephanie McKellop, Twitter post, December 20, 2016, https://twitter.com/McKellogs/status/811339472205910016.

Bibliography

Anderton, Kevin. "The Contest to Build the First Star Trek Tricorder Has a Winner [Infographic]." *Forbes*. Last updated April 22, 2017. www.forbes.com/sites/kevinanderton/2017/04/22/the-contest-to-build-the-first-startrek-tricorder-has-a-winner-infographic/.

Baker, Kelly J. *The Zombies Are Coming! The Realities of the Zombie*. Colorado Springs: Bondfire Books, 2013. Kindle edition.

Brady, Jeff. "Amish Community Not Anti-Technology, Just More Thoughtful." *All Things Considered*. NPR. Last updated September 2, 2013. www.npr.org/sections/alltechconsidered/2013/09/02/217287028/amish-community-not-anti-technology-just-more-thoughtful.

Canright, Shelley. *NASA: Do-It-Yourself Podcast: Rocket Evolution*. Last updated July 13, 2009. www.nasa.gov/audience/foreducators/diypodcast/rocket-evolution-index-diy.html.

Collins, Jim. *Good to Great*. San Francisco: Harper Business, 2001.

Cuevas, Joshua. "Is Learning Styles-Based Instruction Effective? A Comprehensive Analysis of Recent Research on Learning Styles." *Theory and Research in Education* 13, no. 3 (2015): 308–333.

Davidow, Bill. "Exploiting the Neuroscience of Internet Addiction." *The Atlantic*. Last updated July 18, 2012. www.theatlantic.com/health/archive/2012/07/exploiting-the-neuroscience-of-internet-addiction/259820/.

DeGraff, Jeff. "Digital Natives vs. Digital Immigrants." *Huffington Post*. Last updated September 7, 2014. www.huffingtonpost.com/jeff-degraff/digital-natives-vs-digita_b_5499606.html.

European Computer Driving License Foundation. "The Fallacy of the 'Digital Native': Why Young People Need to Develop Their Digital Skills." 2014. Accessed September 27, 2017. http://ecdl.org/media/TheFallacyofthe'DigitalNative'PositionPaper1.pdf.

Federal Communications Commission. "Children's Educational Television." Last updated October 25, 2016. www.fcc.gov/consumers/guides/childrens-educational-television.

Fields, James. "How Your Smartphone Is Turning You into a Zombie." *Tennessean*. Last updated May 2, 2014. www.tennessean.com/story/money/tech/2014/05/01/james-fields-zombies-obsessed-smartphones/8582485/.

Friedman, Ted. *Electronic Dreams: Computers in American Culture*. New York: New York University Press, 2005.

Garvey, Anna. "The Oregon Trail Generation: Life Before and After Mainstream Tech." *Social Media Week*. Last updated April 21, 2015. https://socialmediaweek.org/blog/2015/04/oregon-trail-generation/.

Glass, Ira. "Status Update: Finding the Self in Selfie." *This American Life*. WBEZ. First aired November 27, 2015. www.thisamericanlife.org/radio-archives/episode/573/status-update?act=1#play.

———. "Status Update: Prologue." *This American Life*. WBEZ. First aired November 27, 2015. www.thisamericanlife.org/radio-archives/episode/573/status-update?act=0#play.

Huizinga, Johan. *Homo Ludens: A Study of the Play-Element*. Towbridge, UK: Redwood Burn, 1980 [1944].

Jabr, Ferris. "The Reading Brain in the Digital Age: The Science of Paper versus Screens." *Scientific American*. Last updated April 11, 2013. www.scientificamerican.com/article/reading-paper-screens/.

Kraybill, Donald B. *The Riddle of Amish Culture*. 2nd ed. Baltimore: Johns Hopkins University Press, 2001.

Lenhart, Amanda. "Teens, Social Media & Technology Overview 2015." *Pew Research & Technology*. Last updated April 9, 2015. www.pewinternet.org/2015/04/09/teens-social-media-technology-2015/.

Lincoln, Bruce. *Theorizing Myth: Narrative, Ideology, and Scholarship*. Chicago: University of Chicago Press, 1999.

McKellop, Stephanie. Twitter post. December 20, 2016. https://twitter.com/McKellogs/ status/811339472205910016.

Mueller, Pam A., and Daniel M. Oppenheimer. "The Pen Is Mightier Than the Keyboard: Advantages of Longhand over Laptop Note Taking." *Psychological Science* 25, no. 6 (2014): 1159–1168.

Newport, Frank. "The New Era of Communication Among Americans." *Gallup*. Last updated November 10, 2014. www.gallup.com/poll/179288/new-era-communication-americans.aspx.

Pashler, Harold, Mark A. McDaniel, Doug Rohrer, and Robert A. Bjork. "Learning Styles: Concepts and Evidence." *Psychological Science in the Public Interest* 9, no. 3 (2008): 106–119.

Prensky, Marc. "Digital Natives, Digital Immigrants." www.marcprensky.com/writing/Prensky%20%-20Digital%20Natives,%20Digital%20Immigrants%20%20Part1.pdf. Originally published in *On the Horizon* 9, no. 5 (2001): 1–6.

"Star Trek." *IMDb*. Accessed August 22, 2017. www.imdb.com/title/tt0060028/.

2 Student-Created Podcasts as a Means of Knowledge Assessment

David Kneip

Student-Created Podcasts as a Means of Knowledge Assessment[1]

In the spring of 2014, I concluded my teaching semester by listening to one of my students talk for five minutes straight, at great personal depth, about a service opportunity in which she had engaged during that school year, also making connections with the attitude toward ministry that the Christian apostle Paul described in his letter called "2 Corinthians" that is preserved in the Bible. This experience may sound mundane for a religion course; however, the student in question is one who is rather shy, never spoke in class unless called upon, never came to my office hours to discuss course content, comes from a nonculturally dominant ethnicity and grew up in a remote, economically disadvantaged town of fewer than 300 people (according to the most recent census). In other words, from those bare descriptors alone, one would not be surprised by such a student simply blending into (or, sadly, drifting away from) a course in a four-year liberal arts college. The reason that I had this window into her mind was that she was not speaking to me in person; rather, she had recorded a podcast as part of a course assignment, and I had the privilege of listening to it.

Over the past decade, the digital genre of the "podcast" has experienced a significant boom. A podcast is a digital file used to disseminate information—usually audio, although sometimes video, and typically in the form of a monologue (e.g., lecture and commentary) or discussion (panel, conversation, etc.). As two educational practitioners who have used podcasts in their teaching have described them, podcasts are "assembled packages of audio (and increasingly video) content that can be accessed through computers and digital media players."[2] Many scholars have noted and described the wide range of uses for podcasts in universities since the early 2000s, but most of these uses involve "top-down" production such as professors podcasting their lectures for students who miss class or want a review or universities disseminating information to students in audio form rather than through brochures or e-mails.[3] Not surprisingly, as Alpay and Gulati show, results and opinions are somewhat mixed on the benefits of podcasts, especially when they are used to replace face-to-face lectures.[4] Nonetheless, because such "top-down" uses have been in place for over a decade, there is more extensive literature on that topic; far fewer studies, though, have focused on *student*-created podcasts and their uses in education.[5] The present chapter will describe a set of discoveries and experiences surrounding the use of student-created podcasts in a religion course in an American comprehensive university; here I will argue that podcasts are a valuable new tool that educators can use to assess student knowledge.

Digital Media and "Canned" Assignments

Years ago, while pinching pennies on a graduate student budget, I shared a hotel room with some colleagues at the US meetings of the Society of Biblical Literature and the American Academy of Religion. One evening in our hotel room, I noticed one of my roommates sitting hunched over at his computer, headphones on, listening intently to something. He seemed to be working quite intently, opening and closing this, and organizing that. When he took a break, I asked him what he was doing, and he told me he was listening to podcasts. I had not heard of them at that point, and so I inquired further. He gave me some sort of definition, explaining how interesting it was to be able to have interviews, discussions and lectures sent right to his computer and (optionally) to a mobile device for consumption whenever he wanted them. It sounded interesting, but I did not have any idea how I might use that information, and so we moved on in our conversation.

As the years went on, I heard and learned more about podcasts, but I did not yet engage in any consumption or creation of media of that genre. In 2009, however, my current institution, Abilene Christian University (ACU) in Abilene, Texas, hired me, and upon my arrival on campus, I was issued an iPod Touch for use in the classroom as part of a "Mobile Learning Initiative."[6] One of the unexpected benefits of having this device was that it was already tailor-made for downloading, storing and playing podcasts; having heard of podcasts before, I quickly came to enjoy listening to them on all sorts of topics.

At the same time, I was preparing to teach two sections of an interdisciplinary course that is required of all ACU students; the course is called Cornerstone and is intended to function as a foundation for our undergraduate education program. For that semester—the course's full campus rollout after having been piloted for a few semesters—the course developers crafted an assignment that required all students to create a podcast containing their reflections on their learning that semester. The students had also been issued iPhones or iPod Touches, and both of those devices had a preloaded app called "Voice Memos" that is perfect for creating rudimentary podcasts. Further, the students had access to a "how-to" video for assistance in creating the podcast. The course developers had worked with our on-campus Speaking Center (connected with our Communications Department) to develop an appropriate rubric, and the students had access to that same Speaking Center to help them prepare their podcasts. My understanding at the time was that the purpose of the assignment was for students to learn a new technology while also doing something different from a traditional paper assignment. I was not yet aware that this kind of assignment was similar to a pedagogical strategy called "Guided Discovery" in which students actually create course content (in this case, the fruits of personal reflection) by means of an instructor-designed activity that takes students through a series of steps to discover information.[7]

Not surprisingly, that first venture with podcasts met with mixed results. My e-mail records from that class indicate some technical problems (e.g., "I lost my audio—is there any way to recover it?" and "The file is too big to upload; can I e-mail it to you?"), but most students were able to complete the assignment with my help and that of the on-campus technology help desk. As a teacher, though, that first exposure to student-created podcasts opened the door to a wonderful tool for assessing my students' knowledge (in this case, a deeper awareness of their own thinking) and also getting to know the students on a deeper level.

What I discovered was that, from an educator's perspective, podcasts in their *content* are often quite like traditional papers—single-voice presentations of data, opinions, analysis and so forth—and instructors can employ various means to ensure that the words students speak are crafted just as closely. However, in their *form*, they are quite different in some important ways: while a podcast can be replayed just as a paper can be reread, podcasts are audio files in which the audience can listen to a presenter (typically the author) share content orally rather than the traditional consumption model of reading the words on a page. The experience is not unlike the difference between reading a Tennessee Williams play or Joss Whedon screenplay and seeing that same script live on stage or in a cinema: the textual *content* is the same, but the *experience* is different. Because of the similarities between papers and podcasts, the podcasts helped my students meet the course learning outcomes at a rate approximate to that of a paper. Further, because the classes were small (27 and 28 students in the two sections, respectively), I did not notice any difference in the amount of time it took me to grade the papers. In other words, the situation seemed like a seamless integration of new technology: no new burden on the teacher, with minimal disruption for students.

However, there was an unexpected benefit to the podcasts that was compelling enough to lead me to create my own podcast assignment for a religion course that I would teach the following spring. From a teaching perspective, the difference described earlier using a comparison between a screenplay and a movie turned out to be highly important, because it has nothing with aesthetics (although that may come into play) but rather with my students' *voices*. When my students recorded podcasts in that first fall of our Cornerstone class, I got to hear the living voices of *all* of my students—not just the ones who typically spoke up in class. Most educators, not least in religion courses, have experienced the common phenomenon of some students speaking up repeatedly and enthusiastically, while other students remain quiet or participate only occasionally and sometimes under duress. Of course, students are free to participate as they will, but teachers often want to hear from more of our students—or more *often* from many of them. When my students shared their self-reflections via podcast, I could hear their inflections, emotions that occasionally surfaced and pauses and pace of speaking that gave me insight into how they understand their own words and thinking. And I could hear those things from every single one of my students. As one scholar has written concerning podcasting in education, "There is magic in the human voice."[8]

Widening My Scope

At our university, all students take five courses in the Bible, Missions and Ministry Department; with an enrollment of almost 4,000 undergraduates and a typical graduation time frame of four to four-and-one-half years, our department teaches, on average, at least half of our student body (if not more) every single semester. Teaching that many students with our current faculty size means that, despite our best efforts and in light of the inevitable budget constraints that universities face, many of our religion classes are larger than we would like them to be. For a university that takes its religious heritage seriously, and for a department that views its teaching as fundamentally pastoral as well as intellectual, those class sizes can become a problem: we simply cannot get to know our students as well as we would like.

For each of my years at ACU but one, I have taught at least one section of our spring course for first-year students that focuses on the second half of the New Testament (the biblical books from Acts through Revelation). That course is a joy to teach, not least because we get to immerse students in the biblical text in newer and deeper ways than those to which they have been exposed before. However, as a survey-style class required of all first-year students, it is often larger and more content heavy than we might prefer, especially since we want students to have meaningful contact with the sacred scriptures of Christianity. I have taught sections of fewer than 30 students but also of more than 100. A common pedagogical coping mechanism for the large class size and the amount of material to be "covered" is to give objective tests as the primary or exclusive measure of knowledge acquisition, despite their limitations as appropriate means of such assessment.⁹ My colleagues and I often wish that we could assign papers and other kinds of projects to assess more knowledge and more kinds of knowledge, but class size almost always limits the possibilities here (and students typically do not prefer group work as a different strategy to manage this problem, especially when grades are involved). Without robust help from assistants or a reduced teaching load, it becomes nearly impossible to grade the kinds of assignments that we would like to give and that are repeatedly shown to increase the constructive learning of students.

Enter podcasts. In the spring semester after that first exposure to podcasts in the classroom, I taught two sections of this New Testament class: 1 general education section of 44 students and 1 honors section of 25 students. In an effort to go beyond objective testing, I had planned to assign papers to both of these sections. However, as I noted earlier, my positive experiences with podcasts in the fall—very few technical difficulties, a similar "rate of return" in terms of knowledge communication when compared with papers, a similar degree of rigor with regard to content and no noticeable difference in turnaround time for grading podcasts against that of grading papers—led me to assign them *instead of* papers in the spring. My hope was twofold: (1) that my assignments would help students have that meaningful contact with the Christian scriptures that we desire and (2) that the fact that they were podcasts would allow me to have meaningful contact with my students because of the opportunity to hear their voices.

For that semester of teaching my New Testament course, and for the three spring semesters that followed (a total of 8 sections and 369 students), I observed an implicit recommendation described in Ken Bain's *What the Best College Teachers Do*: to give repeated assessments of the same type so that students can show their growing competence with a given skill or a content base.¹⁰ My goal was to conceive of assignments that would approximate the kinds of things that individuals might be asked to speak about; my hypothesis was that most laypeople will rarely, if ever, be asked to *write* about religion, but they might be asked to *speak* about it in one context or another. As it happened, this hypothesis helped me "sell" the assignment to my students; while they might not question paper assignments, since they are so typical in higher education, they might wonder about the "need" for podcasts, and the real-life connection helped convince the students of their value.

Ultimately, I assigned three podcasts, due periodically throughout the semester, with content keyed to various landmarks in the semester.¹¹ Because one of the course goals is to teach students to look for the Christology apparent in various New Testament epistles so that they can see how the author's theology affects the ethical instructions the author gives, the first podcast invited the students to interview adult Christians whom they admired and then create a script that contains analysis of how the interviewees' own Christology leads to their ethics. Because a common phenomenon midway through a college religion course is some amount of disorientation regarding one's previously held beliefs, the second podcast asked students to choose a topic that has been considered in the first half of the semester, describe their prior understanding and then explain how the course material has challenged or deepened that prior understanding. Finally, because a course goal is to increase students' ability to contextualize the biblical texts into their contemporary world, the third podcast assignment required students to choose among a variety of prompts, all of which pushed them to connect the scriptural text with their own world (e.g., through service opportunities, ethical reflection).[12]

My assessment criteria were tied to the course goals and to the aims for the assignment. As the years progressed and I refined my primary criteria, these came to focus on how the students demonstrated understanding of the biblical text, connections with course materials (i.e., readings, discussions, etc.) and depth of understanding. Early on, I had emphasized more strongly the reflective component; to my dismay, I discovered that my students were much better at journal-style assignments, in which they were asked simply to share their opinions or experiences, than they were at more analytical tasks that asked them to interact with course material. As a result, I balanced the two emphases so that the podcasts functioned as reflective assignments that were also based in course content; in other words, they allowed for reflective work that simple objective testing struggles to measure, and they remained rooted in course content by going beyond a simple journaling assignment. However, podcasts are not simply about the content, just as papers are not, and so some assessment criteria were focused on students' *behavior* rather than their *understanding*. Examples here include whether they followed the directions for the assignment, whether they did appropriate preparation work with a script, whether they stayed on topic and so forth. However, as the years progressed, I realized that I had two separate classes of criteria; if I designed my rubrics such that content and behavior criteria were treated the same way, students could "behave well" with regard to the assignments' logistics while doing poorly on their content, resulting in a grade that did not accurately reflect their actual learning.

As it happens, my hopes were met and even exceeded. As before, students were able to complete the assignments with minimal technical difficulty and with approximately the same effort necessary for creating papers. Further, the content of the assignments allowed them the kind of meaningful contact with the sacred texts that I had intended and in a way that was connected with their own lives.[13] However, other benefits emerged that were either unexpected or outside of my primary focus.

At least two benefits accrued for the students. First, as originally intended by the Cornerstone assignment, my students' having three opportunities to create podcasts allowed them experience and increased their expertise with regard to this new form of digital media.[14] My experience was similar to that of Kemp et al., who reported a clear student sense of increased proficiency with the new technology after completing podcasting assignments.[15] We know that the ability to learn new skills, especially with regard to technology, is a key workplace skill in the twenty-first century, according to many employers;[16] as Armstrong, Tucker and Massad noted, podcasting allows students to gain experience and expertise doing just that.[17] Second, many educators have noticed that contemporary students often write like they speak rather than in a more formal academic register. As a result, it is not uncommon for students in classes outside of English, writing or composition departments to complain when writing papers; I suspect that part of this discomfort is that they know they are not good at formal writing, and they disdain "losing points" for their bad writing. However, because podcasts are typically performed in a more informal register, the students can speak in a more natural voice. To be sure, I am strongly in favor of students learning to write for academic audiences; however, in my prior experience teaching the course, I found that the burden of writing was impeding that meaningful contact with the Christian scriptures that I desired for my students. That was especially true with first-year students, many of whom may not have had a significant number of courses or depth of instruction in formal academic writing. By making *preparation* an explicit criterion for assessment and including examples of such on my grading rubric, I strongly encouraged my students to prepare a script, to rehearse and so forth; the results in my classes were that students were able to engage in the assignment, create podcasts with professional-quality scripts and avoid the anxiety that some of them experienced with a typical paper assignment.[18]

From the educator's perspective, I found multiple benefits as well. As I grew in my own competence in grading the podcasts, I learned that podcasts could actually be graded more quickly than papers, not merely at the same rate. The reason is the length of podcasts and their medium: I assigned podcasts with lengths of three to four minutes and five to seven minutes, which correspond to approximately two and three pages of double-spaced writing, respectively. Because I use rubrics for grading purposes, I found that I am able to accomplish a significant amount of grading while I am listening to the podcasts. As I determine which level a podcast will achieve on a given criterion, I can indicate that achievement in the appropriate way (whether the rubric is on paper or on-screen), and I can also write or type comments as I listen, even providing "in medias res" notes such as "We're halfway through, and you haven't said anything about the Bible yet." Should there be difficulties with the audio, I can pause, rewind, change the volume on whatever speakers I am using and so forth, and then I can continue grading. All in all, I found that I can grade a podcast of three to four minutes in (on average) seven minutes, and one of five to seven minutes in approximately ten minutes, without sacrificing meaningful comments and feedback for the students. Students noted the quality of the feedback in their conversations with me; one evaluation comment noted (with perhaps a bit of irony), "He actually provided feedback on the podcasts—that was wonderful!" Were I to grade papers of the same length, I would likely spend the same amount of time commenting on the content of the paper, but I would expect to spend more time critiquing the writing exhibited in the paper. With podcasts that last demand disappears, thus allowing me to move through the grading stack more quickly. That time efficiency is a significant gain for educators, who typically find that there is not enough time to do all that is required of them or that they desire, no matter the school level at which they teach. That gain only magnifies as the number of students grows—a change that typically results in more difficulty rather than success.[19]

From the perspective of religious education, however, the opportunity to hear my students' voices was perhaps the most satisfying benefit. Having had the experience of hearing my students' voices in the Cornerstone class, I was excited about the possibility of hearing them speak on religious topics. Sure enough, podcasts provided another even richer opportunity to accomplish this goal, because of the way that I set up the assignment. Because all of the podcast assignments had both reflective and analytical elements to them, I was allowed a window into the students' minds by listening to them talk. And as many educators know, getting students to talk about matters of religion can be quite challenging, especially in institutions (like mine) where they are required to do so by means of compulsory courses. The podcast achieves many benefits of an oral exam or conversation (face-to-face contact) without the stresses that often come for the student (having to perform "on the spot"); similarly, as already noted, it achieves many benefits of a paper (content communication) without the stresses associated therewith (the demands of formal academic writing).

Finally, on a personal/pastoral level, the podcasts were an excellent way to get to know my students and to connect with them, as I desired. One option I have not yet exercised with these assignments, but have used on other occasions, is creating my own simple podcasts for audio feedback on assignments of various kinds; this task can be accomplished in many ways, including Evernote, which requires e-mailing an audio file to students, or increasingly and much more simply with online learning management systems (such as Canvas, the learning management system that my university uses).[20] Far more often, my continuing the conversation has taken place face-to-face. On the first assignment, many students spoke about youth pastors, grandparents or other significant adult figures in their lives; their comments made it easy to initiate a conversation before or after a future class session with a simple comment such as, "Thank you for sharing about your grandmother; she sounds like an amazing woman!" Because the second assignment asked students to share texts on which their views had been challenged or deepened, I could do the same by saying, "What you said about Romans 9–11 was really interesting! Where do you think your views came from?" The third assignment allowed our conversation to focus on future plans as the semester came to a close: "I love your idea for living out Philippians 2 while you're on your summer internship! Let me know how it goes—I'd love to hear from you." As noted earlier, while our class sizes are sometimes large, our campus as a whole is not, and so students often expect or hope their religion professors will function as pastors, to some degree. These assignments provided conversational openings for me to fulfill that role.

Theological Reflections

The foregoing discussion may convince some educators to experiment with podcasts in their courses based on their pedagogical benefits alone. I would be thrilled if such were the case. However, as a confessing Christian myself, I cannot help but notice that there are connections between my experience teaching with podcasts and some theological convictions regarding the spoken word.

Among the other courses I teach at ACU are our classes in Christian worship. One of the fundamental features of Christian worship—and, in fact, in that of the other two monotheistic, Abrahamic faiths (Judaism and Islam)—is the importance of words, and spoken words at that. As Ruth Duck has written, "Worship is much more than words, and yet words bear much of the burden of interpreting the meaning of our actions, evoking our faith, and expressing our theology."[21] This claim should not surprise those of us who practice or teach the Abrahamic faiths, since all three of them claim that God has spoken to his people by a word.[22] Indeed, in the Christian tradition, believers speak of Jesus as the "Word of God" (influenced by biblical texts such as John 1:1ff.). In Christian worship, words may derive from various sources, among them ancient liturgies, historic confessions of faith, worldwide consensus texts, the words of scripture, local compositions and others, often in combination with one another. Regardless of their sources, though, the words Christians use in worship teach us of the power of the spoken word. As Duck has said, the reward of careful labor over the words of worship "is enlivened worship that nurtures Christian faith and discipleship in ourselves and those among whom we minister."[23]

In her compelling book *The Worshiping Body*, Kimberly Bracken Long began her chapter on "The Mouth: Voice and Speech" by noting the standard observation of the modern world as shifting from being "word-based" to "image-based"—along with some critiques of the view that that shift is benign.[24] Long then attempted to argue that "[s]peaking is at the core of what it means to be Christian" and that our speaking is a manifestation of our being made in the image of a God who speaks.[25] The reading and proclamation of the Bible is a key feature of worship in most of the branches of Christianity, and many Christians believe some version of the doctrine that Christ (again, the "Word" of God) is mysteriously made present in that reading and proclamation. This idea should certainly shape worship leading, but also the mundane, everyday speech that emerges from our mouths.[26] As both Jesus (as narrated in the Gospel of Matthew) and a writer who may have been his brother (in the epistle of James) remind us, our words can be deeply damaging and also wonderfully life-giving.[27] Jesus teaches, we learn in worship and we know from teaching that "speaking is not only about explaining, and hearing is not simply about understanding; they are also about apprehending, even experiencing, words."[28]

This last consideration is precisely what I experienced in listening to my students' podcasts. Although they may have thought that their speaking was merely "explaining" and that my hearing would be merely "understanding" (in the best-case scenario), much more was happening. I was being "caught" by their words and the thoughts that lay behind them—understanding more than just the words they said as I listened to their voices. I was invited into connection, into relationship—even if that relationship was something intended by the students to be shallow and perfunctory—just as Christians believe that we are invited into relationship with God even as God speaks to us today through a whole range of means.

Concluding Recommendations

Readers who are convinced by the foregoing presentation and rationale may yet wonder how one might get started and succeed with such a project. I conclude by offering some recommendations based on my own experience and research:

Choose Podcasts Assignments Wisely

I hope that this chapter has shown how podcasts can help students in reflective and analytical tasks. Lee, McLoughlin and Chan reported more broadly that podcasts are effective tools for helping students to conceptualize, whether they are teacher or student created.[29] In other words, podcasts are quite appropriate for tasks that demand the higher levels of thinking on Bloom's taxonomy of the cognitive domain (in its various forms), including application, synthesis and evaluation. However, if educators need to check student learning at the lower levels, I do not recommend podcasts, because they are simply unnecessary. Other forms of assessment are familiar to students and appropriate to that task so that introducing the variable of new technology becomes unnecessary. Further, educators should choose assignments that mirror actual (or imagined) real-life scenarios in which professionals may be asked to speak about their content. I mentioned earlier my choosing topics that mirror situations in which people might be asked to speak about matters of religion rather than write about them; Kemp et al. invited their science students to imagine giving a radio interview about geomorphology, as it is more likely that engineers may give an interview to a television station than to create written material for general consumption.[30]

Develop Prompts and Rubrics With a High Degree of Specificity

I have learned that highly specific prompts and rubrics are generally helpful in my teaching; that benefit is even stronger in this case because students sometimes wonder about the assignment as a whole, especially how to create a podcast. Unsurprisingly, less confusion about content helps reduce anxiety and concomitantly the number of questions about the technology.[31] One student commented in an evaluation that I needed to "explain the podcasts more"—a suggestion that I attempted to apply in future semesters with more specific prompts and better oral explanation.

Privilege Audio Over Video Podcasts

As more and more bandwidth has become available to individuals and institutions, more and more Internet usage has shifted toward bandwidth-heavy tasks (e.g., from text to image, from silence to audio, from image to video), as the usage patterns of YouTube and Netflix can attest. Consequently, both teachers and students might be attracted to the idea of creating video podcasts (perhaps as a more challenging task) rather than simple audio podcasts. Unfortunately, the challenges of creating video are numerous, such that I recommend avoiding this option. Video files are much larger than audio files, a difference that complicates matters for podcast creation and editing, as well as for file sharing. Further, video production creates opportunities—but also challenges—for matters that are not necessarily content related, such as lighting, costumes and others.[32] Finally, with the rising use of social media platforms (especially applications such as Snapchat), students have become quite comfortable seeing themselves in video such that it could be hard for them to switch to a more serious "register" in their performance.

Discover and Recommend User-Friendly Production Technological Tools

Because some students will be concerned about their competence in creating podcasts given their lack of background with that task (and despite whatever technological affinity and ability they may demonstrate with other tasks), it is best to find software that is simple to use. On the hardware side, the simplest recording option may be smartphones or other similar handheld or wearable devices; another simple solution (that can provide higher-quality audio) may be a microphone that can plug into a computer. On the software side, Evernote (many platforms) and the aforementioned Voice Memos app (iOS) are quite simple for producing voice-only podcasts. That goal can also be reached using Microsoft's program OneNote; as software designed for note-taking, it includes an option to record and insert audio tracks. As a result, teachers could assign students to type their scripts in OneNote, record them as audio, and then share them with the instructor. For more editing options, including the use of background music or multiple tracks, GarageBand is popular with Macintosh users but has a bit of a learning curve. Audacity has long been a program that is popular for creating podcasts; it is free, open-source and usable on both Macintosh and Windows platforms. Teachers report ease of use for their students, and many online tools are available to help both teachers and students learn the program.[33]

Create or Identify a Sample Podcast

Especially with new kinds of assignments, students often ask whether there are samples of prior work for them to view or listen to. Two ways instructors may address this concern are to either create or identify podcasts that match precisely or approximately the desired product. Identifying outside podcasts requires less technical work on the instructor's part, but it does necessitate explanations to students about which parts to imitate and which to ignore. On the other hand, creating one's own sample podcast requires more technical labor but less explanatory time. On that note, Bolden is right that creating a sample podcast is a wonderful way for educators to learn the technology themselves before teaching it to students, to recognize common pitfalls in creating podcasts and to prompt new thoughts on the part of students.[34]

*Consider Opportunities for Making Students'
Podcasts Available to Others*

Some teachers will want all students to have access to the other students' podcasts for this or that pedagogical reason. One useful tool, available at some universities, is iTunes U, which allows students to share their own podcasts and access those of their classmates.[35] Should a particular instructor's institution not participate in iTunes U, the institutional technology support office or team can likely help instructors find out what software would offer similar solutions and work best with the institution's system. Another option instructors may consider is to create or use their own podcast to broadcast student work. There are many instructional resources online that instructors may consult to begin a podcast. Instructors may then choose certain podcasts to publish or may simply make them all available, and students can then use their devices of choice to listen as they choose or are required. As with more traditional forms of student artifacts, there are many potential benefits for students' having access to their peers' work.

Start Small

I conclude with an adaptation of the advice given by Weyant and Gardner: I hope that educators who are convinced by this chapter feel no obligation to "go big" in their first implementation of a podcast assignment.[36] I was fortunate that my first experience was with a single assignment; I recommend that instructors find one or two activities that can be transformed into podcast assignments. That scope can make for an excellent pilot program. An alternative would be a single assignment that is repeated through a semester or year (as described earlier) so that students gain proficiency and educators limit variables that could complicate the learning process.

Notes

1 This chapter is the fruit of presentations made at the Faculty Fusion event at Abilene Christian University (Abilene, Texas) in August 2012 and at the annual meeting of the Society of Biblical Literature (SBL) in November 2013 in Baltimore, Maryland. I am grateful to the leaders of ACU's Adams Center for Teaching and Learning and the SBL program unit Academic Teaching and Biblical Studies for their sponsoring of the events in question, and to the many participants in the sessions for their helpful feedback and suggestions. I am further grateful to the editors of this volume for their invaluable assistance. Any errors or infelicities remain, of course, my own. Readers may correspond with me at david.kneip@acu.edu; I am quite content to share any assignment prompts or rubrics related to the class activities described in this chapter.
2 Benjamin Bolden and James Nahachewsky, "Podcast Creation as Transformative Music Engagement," *Music Education Research* 17, no. 1 (2015): 17–33, doi:10.1080/14613808.2014.969219.
3 Howard Harris and Sungmin Park, "Educational Usages of Podcasting," *British Journal of Educational Technology* 39, no. 3 (2008): 548–551, doi:10.1111/j.1467–8535.2007.00788.x. See also Richelle V. Adams's and Erik Blair's interesting and recent essay, "The Learner-Generated Podcast: Engaging Postgraduate Engineering Students in a Mathematics-Intensive Course," *Research in Post-Compulsory Education* 19, no. 2 (2014): 132–146, doi:10.1080/13596748.2014.897502.
4 Esat Alpay and Shelly Gulati, "Student-Led Podcasting for Engineering Education," *European Journal of Engineering Education* 35, no. 4 (August 2010): 415–427, doi:10.1080/03043797.2010.487557.

5 A recent review of literature on both kinds of podcasts can be found in Bolden and Nahachewsky, "Podcast Creation," 17–18.
6 "Evaluating a Campus-Wide Mobile Learning Initiative," *EDUCAUSE*, https://net.educause.edu/ir/library/pdf/LIVE115b.pdf. See also one of ACU's own publications on the topic at https://issuu.com/abilenechristian/docs/acu_ml_report_2010-11.
7 Cari L. Crumly, "Student-Centered Pedagogies and Tactics," in *Pedagogies for Student-Centered Learning: Online and On-Ground*, with contributions by Pamela Dietz and Sarah d'Angelo (Minneapolis: Fortress, 2014), 36.
8 Gardner Campbell, "There's Something in the Air: Podcasting in Education," *EDUCAUSE Review* (November/December 2005): 40.
9 In chapter 2 of Susan A. Ambrose, Michael W. Bridges, Michele DiPietro, Marsha C. Lovett, and Marie K. Norman, *How Learning Works: 7 Research-Based Principles for Smart Teaching* (San Francisco: Jossey-Bass, 2010), 40–65, the authors note the importance of deep and complex connections among the various discrete "units" of knowledge, if students want to progress from beginner-level understanding toward expertise. As they say, when students can more effectively *categorize* and *connect* their knowledge, they can enrich their learning. Unfortunately, because objective testing often encourages simply the memorization of those discrete units *apart* from context, it is only too easy for students to learn them and then forget them.
10 Ken Bain, *What the Best College Teachers Do* (Cambridge: Harvard University Press, 2004), 35–36.
11 As the reader will discover, I continued the path of assigning podcasts as individual tasks. For an interesting study of podcasts as a group assignment, see Lynne Powell and Fiona Robson, "Learner-Generated Podcasts: A Useful Approach to Assessment?" *Innovations in Education and Teaching International* 51, no. 3 (2014): 326–337, doi:10.1080/14703297.2013.796710.
12 To simplify the assignment by limiting the variables that students needed to consider, I instructed them to consider me the primary audience of the podcast. In other words, they did not need to attempt to conceive of a hypothetical audience. However, the work of Justine Kemp, Antony Mellor, Richard Kotter, and Jan W. Oosthoek, "Student-Produced Podcasts as an Assessment Tool: An Example from Geomorphology," *Journal of Geography in Higher Education* 36, no. 1 (2012): 117–130, doi:10.1080/03098265.2011.576754, has made me reconsider that position. As I will outline in the "Concluding Recommendations" section of this essay, I do think it is helpful for students to imagine a real-life situation in which they will need to be able to speak on the topic under consideration. Perhaps it is also useful for students to have to think of a hypothetical audience, at least in some assignments, since it might be useful pedagogically for students to reckon with a nonspecialist audience (i.e., *not* what the instructor represents).
13 These assignments connect admirably with the deep "learning principle" that Colleen Carmean and Jeremy Haefner call "contextual": the new knowledge "builds on the learner's existing knowledge" and "is integrated into the learner's world." "Mind over Matter: Transforming Course Management Systems into Effective Learning Environments," *EDUCAUSE Review* (November/December 2002): 29.
14 Happily, as Vivian Maria Vasquez notes in her article "Podcasting as Transformative Work," *Theory Into Practice* 54 (2015): 148, doi:10.1080/00405841.2015.1010848, basically all laptops sold on the current market already come equipped with all the hardware needed for students to make podcasts, thus overcoming a first potential hurdle automatically.

15 Kemp et al., "Student-Produced Podcasts," 123, 126.
16 See the summary of research on this topic conducted by the Association of American Colleges and Universities (AAC&U) entitled "It Takes More Than a Major: Employer Priorities for College Learning and Student Success: Overview and Key Findings," www.aacu.org/leap/presidentstrust/compact/2013SurveySummary. The AAC&U reports that the employers surveyed see "the capacity for continued new learning" as a crucial trait, and they affirm pedagogical practices that improve "application of skills."
17 Gary R. Armstrong, Joanne M. Tucker, and Victor J. Massad, "Achieving Learning Goals with Student-Created Podcasts," *Decision Sciences: Journal of Innovative Education* 7, no. 1 (2009): 149–54, doi:10.1111/j.1540-4609.2008.00209.x.
18 I have not conducted any research comparing the learning of my students who do complete the podcast assignments with some who do not (for example, if I taught two sections and used podcasts in only one of them). Perhaps not surprisingly, some students indicated on their student evaluations that the podcasts seemed unnecessary—that papers would have worked just as well. The research described and cited in Peter C. Brown, Henry L. Roediger III and Mark A. McDaniel, *Make It Stick: The Science of Successful Learning* (Cambridge: Belknap Press of Harvard University Press, 2014) would suggest that at least the assignments do increase the students' learning, but it may not matter for their content acquisition as to whether it issues in a paper or a podcast. See pages 220–223 for the authors' discussion of the importance of generation of knowledge and reflection on learning as productive strategies for lifelong learners. To this point, one of my students noted in a course evaluation that "the podcasts really helps [sic] me dig deep and truly understand what I had been learning."
19 In fact, taken together, this quicker grading and the use of clear criteria communicated by rubrics meet two of the assessment recommendations in L. Dee Fink's book *Creating Significant Learning Experiences: An Integrated Approach to Designing College Courses* (San Francisco: Jossey-Bass, 2003), 89–96.
20 For an interesting study on this topic, see Steve Cooper, "Delivering Student Feedback in Higher Education: The Role of Podcasting," *Journal of Music, Technology and Education* 1, nos. 2/3 (2008): 153–65, doi:10.1386/jmte.1.2.
21 Ruth Duck, *Worship for the Whole People of God: Vital Worship for the 21st Century* (Louisville: Westminster John Knox, 2013), 97.
22 To cite merely one example from each faith's text, see in the Hebrew Bible Exodus 19–20 (God's self-revelation on Mount Sinai), in the Christian New Testament the Synoptic narratives of Jesus's baptism and transfiguration (e.g., Mark 1 and 9) and in the Qur'an Sura 4:163–165.
23 Duck, *Worship*, 108.
24 Kimberly Bracken Long, *The Worshiping Body: The Art of Leading Worship* (Louisville: Westminster John Knox, 2009), 51–52.
25 Ibid., 52–53.
26 Ibid., 58–59.
27 Matthew 5:21–26, 43–44; James 3:1–12.
28 Long, *Worshiping Body*, 68.
29 Mark J. W. Lee, Catherine McLoughlin, and Anthony Chan, "Talk the Talk: Learner-Generated Podcasts as Catalysts for Knowledge Creation," *British Journal of Educational Technology* 39, no. 3 (2008): 517–518, doi:10.1111/j.1467-8535.2007.00746.x.
30 Kemp et al., "Student-Produced Podcasts," 119–121, 125–128.
31 A useful resource here is Shinjeng Lin, J. Christopher Zimmer and Velma Lee, "Podcasting Acceptance on Campus: The Differing Perspectives of

Teachers and Students," *Computers & Education* 68 (October 2013): 416–428, doi:10.1016/j.compedu.2013.06.003, which offers thought-provoking research results about ways educators might be more conscious of their own expectations and values, as well as those of students.

32 Gary R. Armstrong, Joanne M. Tucker, and Victor J. Massad, "Interviewing the Experts: Student Produced Podcast," *Journal of Information Technology Education: Innovations in Practice* 8 (2009): 82, http://jite.org/documents/Vol8/JITEv8IIP079-090Armstrong333.pdf. This page contains a brief section called "Podcast Basics" that is quite useful for interested parties.

33 See Powell and Robson, "Learner-Generated Podcasts," 332–333. In terms of tutorials, by the time this chapter is read, some of the links in Armstrong, Tucker and Massad, "Achieving Learning Goals," 152 may no longer function, but they may give readers ideas for their own online searching. The same is true for Annette Lamb and Larry Johnson's excellent suggestions and links in their article "Podcasting in the School Library, Part 2: Creating Powerful Podcasts with Your Students," *Teacher Librarian* 34, no. 4 (April 2007): 61–64; the setting in question is that of an elementary school, but as a result, the recommendations assume very little in terms of technological proficiency.

34 Benjamin Bolden, "Learner-Created Podcasts: Students' Stories with Music," *Music Educators Journal* 100, no. 1 (September 2013): 75–80, doi:10.1177/0027432113493757.

35 Myke Bartlett, "A Voice in the World: Podcasts and the Classroom," *Screen Education* 64 (Summer 2012): 70, http://theeducationshop.com.au/downloads/metro-and-screen-education-articles/screen-education-articles/a-voice-in-the-world-podcasts-and-the-classroom/, has suggested that there may be a certain cachet in students' seeing their names next to their favorite artists' in their iTunes library; students' actual reactions, of course, will vary.

36 Lee E. Weyant and Carolyn Gardner, "Wikis and Podcasts: An Application in Undergraduate Management Education," *Academy of Educational Leadership Journal* 15, no. 3 (2011): 139.

3 Who Do You Vote That I Am?

Using Student Response Systems in Religion Courses

Renate Hood

Introduction

Religious education faces challenges in addressing both the cognitive and affective domains in residential and online classrooms. Increasingly, institutions of higher education seek to meet expectations of student-centered learning while simultaneously paying attention to matters of religious formation and student retention. Using student response systems, also known as classroom response systems or audience response systems, is an effective means of boosting student motivation, augmenting classroom interaction and lowering the threshold for engaging religious, ethical and personal subject matter.

Using student response systems enables the formation of safe classroom environments, which is desirable in introductory religion classes, such as Bible survey courses, since a large portion of the student population often feels ill prepared to share its knowledge of or experience with the class content. Learning methods associated with the technology used by the teachers, rather than the technology itself, directly influences students' learning.[1] Hence student response technology that supports student learning methods in religion courses is the focus in this chapter.

Introducing Student Response Systems

Response activities provide effective opportunities for addressing religious subjects. Icebreakers facilitated by student response systems can lower subject-matter anxiety often associated with students' anticipated unfamiliarity with course content. Students appreciate the use of digital devices and anonymous or nonanonymous participation in polls and games.

Student response systems create positive classroom environments in which lectures and learning activities increase student motivation and course engagement.[2,3]

They are effective tools for extending and regaining students' attention in the twenty-first-century classroom.[4,5] They are effective both in large classrooms and in small-group teaching.[6] Not only are response activities helpful in the affective learning domain but also voting systems in particular lead to increased conceptual understanding.[7] This cognitive understanding is measured by checking students' comprehension of classroom learning activities by taking quick polls. Moreover, student response systems improve student learning by assisting instructors with the task of clarifying misconceptions about certain subjects based on instant student feedback.[8]

Student response systems likewise can aid students in retaining information from class sessions by reexposing students to the presented material through survey-style summative response quizzes at the end of class. Students typically find response systems appealing, thereby enhancing learning effectiveness.[9] In all, mobile response systems promote active learning,[10] increase student performance,[11] aid in collecting feedback and taking anonymous polls and serve as a useful tool for brainstorming in the classroom. In terms of classroom structure and course management, response systems are advantageous for keeping attendance and organizing tutorial sessions.

Audience response systems have been used for the last 40 years.[12] Of these years, student response systems have been used in education since 2003.[13] At this time, a variety of response systems are available that are fit for educational purposes. First, there are the traditional systems, often called "clickers" or "zappers," which are handheld devices that come in a variety of sizes. Known as personal or audience response systems, clickers operate with purchased software and student receivers, often depending on institutional support or student purchases. Online student response systems, or web-based response systems, are replacing these technologies at a fast pace since students can use them with any browser on various devices. Many students have computers or at least a mobile phone. Nearly all university students have cell phones (99.8 percent) and use texting as their main mode of written communication (97 percent).[14]

Most online student response systems are free. Device-agnostic response systems are both accessible and cost effective, and hence preferred by institutions, instructors and students over paid systems and devices. When comparing web-based response systems with traditional systems, the versatility of web-based approaches is apparent. Practical limitations of clickers include not only the cost of clickers but also the reality that polling can take place only during lectures since the connection of the device takes place live.

Current examples of web-based response systems include systems that are used both synchronously and asynchronously. There are a variety of web-based systems currently available, some synchronous and some asynchronous. Here are a few examples: Poll Everywhere makes use of multiple choice polling and open survey polling. Additionally, Poll Everywhere uses word clouds and is easily accessible from a smartphone, computer or other devices that have access to a browser. Kahoot is popular with students because of its colorful display. Instructors can prepare real-time quizzes or polls in multiple-choice format that students can take individually or in teams. Kahoot is used for quick student preparedness inventories and discussion starters. Socrative, another student response system, allows for polling on the fly and maintenance of classroom flow. Instructors like the structure that Socrative provides for post-polling follow-up. Quizlet, on the other hand, is more content focused and is often used as a review aid or exam preparation tool.

Quizizz has steadily gained popularity as a student response system since it provides a group-wide, individually paced polling or learning opportunity that is visual to the entire group. Some students appreciate the "cool factor," since it has avatars and meme options. AnswerGarden is yet another growing web-based response method that enables the fielding of questions from the entire group and the gathering of group feedback. GoSoapBox offers students the ability to indicate subject-matter confusion anonymously by allowing the instructor to turn off names. Pear Deck, a web-based platform that requires a membership, enables live sessions. Students can connect with the instructors' presentation on their own devices, allowing interaction during lectures. Instructors can upload previously developed PowerPoint presentations and insert response activities such as multiple-choice questions, interactive drawings and draggable pins and images. Additional web-based response sites and methods include Let's Go Vote, VotApedia, SMS Poll, Survnvote, Text the Mob and TurningPoint ResponseWare. With so many options available, the pedagogical applications are numerous.

Practical Issues When Implementing Student Response Systems

Awareness of practical matters when implementing the careful use of technological teaching tools such as student response systems is essential. Student feedback indicates not only successes but also drawbacks when these teaching aids are employed. Instructors' levels of confidence in the use of such technology is important. Students have observed that different teachers have divergent comfort levels in the use of student response systems, and, hence, effectiveness may vary.[15] Instructors may use varied amounts of preparation time and set up student response systems and time distribution on synchronous questions in different ways, some more suitable to their learning objectives than others. Most students, for instance, deem 30 seconds too long to answer a question, so preparation and structured lining up of the questions and answers is important.[16]

A relaxed feel is most desired by students, with polls and questions implemented as a natural part of the classroom flow. When multiple-choice questions are used, students deem it of utmost importance to have the instructor explain all alternatives, both why the correct answer is the right one and why the incorrect answers are not valid.[17] Furthermore, the inclusion of the answer "I don't know" is strongly preferred by students, as it provides a pedagogical alternative to guessing.[18]

Benefits of Using Student Response Systems

Student interaction entails behavioral, emotional and cognitive engagement. Technology can facilitate a conducive environment for engaged learning. Clicker-based response systems can enable polling only during a classroom session. Web-based polling, on the other hand, facilitates pre-class polling and equips the instructor with data to adapt the planned student learning assessments and lecture accordingly. Student response systems, in fact, are useful at various stages of the learning experience: prior to starting the lecture, about 30 minutes into the lecture and at the end of the lecture.[19] Using a student response system at the beginning of class ensures that topics from the previous class are related to key topics in the current lecture by way of review questions. Using a student response system halfway through the classroom flow aids in keeping the students' attention and ensuring the students' comprehension. Polling at the end of class time enables reflection on the presented subject matter and highlighting of key elements of the lecture.

Using Student Response Systems When Teaching Religion

In many institutions, introductory religion courses are a required part of a core curriculum. Varied student populations form the makeup of these course classrooms—some students are familiar with the course content and others have an affinity for the course content, while yet other students are unaccustomed to or even uncomfortable with or indifferent to the course content. Furthermore, subject-matter anxiety is a reality in these settings. Response activities provide opportunities for engaging students by addressing both the cognitive and affective domains in a manner that lowers possible course subject-matter apprehension.

Icebreakers can introduce a welcoming course environment and increase classroom cohesion. Specifically, icebreaker polls in the form of forced-choice surveys with movie titles or vacation destinations can facilitate an inviting atmosphere for course participation. Kahoot is uniquely suited for such polls. Other options for icebreaker activities include asking similar questions by way of a word-cloud student response system facilitated by systems such as Poll Everywhere. Word associations can form low-threshold emotional engagement in religious subject matters in the classroom. The instructor can start the word cloud, for example, by typing "God" on a blank screen. As students provide their one-word or short-phrase submissions, the student response system builds a word cloud that is visible to the entire class on the screen. Because of the anonymous nature of the submissions, students are free to express themselves. Students value anonymity in answering questions.[20, 21] The open atmosphere this anonymity sets determines the tone for the remainder of the course and develops the contours of a learning community.

In some circumstances, students may think a certain spiritual vocabulary or set of religious presuppositions is required to succeed in a religion course. However, when certain unbound associated words appear on the screen in a word cloud, the instructor can seize the opportunity to invite the students to speak their minds in class and in assignments, and assure them of freedom of opinion in religious and confessional matters. Classroom mechanics are shaped and improved when students have a visual idea of the classroom makeup. Initial polling at the beginning of the course in terms of familiarity with the subject matter provides grounding to the course dynamics and in-class participation. In a general education course called Engaging the New Testament, one such poll gathered through the web-based student response system Poll Everywhere uses the following polling responses when asking students how they feel about their preparation for the course:

- I grew up with Sunday School—this will be a breeze.
- I'm nervous but am quite familiar.
- I'm from a Christian family, but the Bible is a bit vague.
- Goodness, I have hardly ever read the Bible.
- Seriously, what is a Bible? Ha!

Poll results typically display a broad spectrum, which allows for an opportunity to lighten the classroom atmosphere. The instructor can use these responses to tell all students that the course will be taught from an academic perspective. This reinforces the premise that prior familiarity with course material is not required. The other answers, too, are used in the classroom to create an atmosphere of acceptance and understanding.

An open atmosphere likewise is encouraged when an open-ended poll facilitated by a student response system is used. Poll Everywhere and AnswerGarden are conducive for such open-ended surveys. Questions such as "What did Jesus look like?" provoke interesting perspectives: from funny comments to clichés and ethnocentric misnomers. The instructor can engage the answers gathered in the survey in a constructive manner and coach the class in this particular example toward a discussion of Jesus as an ancient Middle Eastern man.

At some point during a lecture, a poll facilitated by a student response system can introduce a new topic for discussion. One such discussion in a religion class may concern the identity of the historical Jesus. Kahoot is helpful as a conversation starter since it presents four answers with the option of a video or a picture to accompany the question. The question potentially asked is, "Who is the historical Jesus?" The four possible answers represent four main perspectives. Another option is to have three of the four answers represent main perspectives with an alternative "I don't know" answer. Either way, after the students take the poll, the answers form the class talking points and can evolve into lengthy discussions.[22] Each one of the potential answers is reviewed by the instructor in class, including attention given to "I don't know."

Religious and ethical subjects are sensitive or deemed a private matter in the eyes of some students. Hence, in the case of general education courses, response activities, in particular, those incorporated into the classroom presentation, provide effective means for broaching religious subject matters with diverse student populations. Student response system polling platforms such as Socrative or Kahoot, or a fully integrated method such as Pear Deck, are helpful in taking inventory of students' religious leanings through options and then using the voting outcome to divide students into groups according to their indicated preferences for further student-oriented, group-learning exercises.

Polls can engage students in lectures by posing questions from the material in real time. In a Bible course, for example, the instructor may discuss a question posed by Jesus in Mark 8:29, "Who do you say that I am?"[23] In the text of the New Testament in which Mark is located, the question is answered in various ways in the narrative. A real-time poll engages students by asking them the same question, "Who do you say [vote] that I am?" Poll Everywhere or Kahoot would allow for various answers. An open survey approach, such as is possible with Poll Everywhere, enables students to formulate their answers and post them on the screen. The lecture can continue with the real-time participation by students as a bridge to the next part of the classroom learning experience.

General education religion course instructors often struggle with lack of student motivation. Greater course autonomy can increase student motivation with regard to intrinsic goal orientation, task value and self-efficacy.[24] Students often appreciate the use of student response systems as part of educational technology.[25] Student response systems are useful in gathering feedback regarding course structure; suggestions by students about course components to keep, adjust or add; and input concerning dispersion of the course grade components, all contributing to course autonomy. High rates of feedback are achieved when student input and surveys are an intentional part of the social environment of the classroom.[26]

Not only are response tools valuable aids in encouraging motivation but also they are effective tools for increased student attention spans. Periodically checking in with students to gauge comprehension with an interactive poll maintains students' engagement and regains students' attention. Pear Deck enables such a periodic check-in throughout the lecture. Quizizz likewise is conducive for this task since it is self-paced and allows students to pair up. A Quizizz quiz game allows for real-time viewing, which increases student involvement.

When discussing religious subjects, a firm knowledge base is essential. Hence introductory religion courses are typically information heavy. Many students who are unfamiliar with religion are concerned about their academic success in such courses. Proper understanding of course content is important. Ensuring student comprehension of course material leads to greater conceptual understanding and informed religious and ethical discussions. Kahoot, Pear Deck and Quizizz are helpful response systems that provide instant feedback and clarify misconceptions about subject matter. Quizizz furthermore has a "homework" option that can keep a quiz open for one or two weeks. At any point within this window of time, an instructor can discuss the progress in a classroom setting. This approach can reinforce key concepts and assist in students retaining information from class sessions.

AnswerGarden enhances learning effectiveness and openness and is particularly helpful in advanced religion classes because it allows instructors to ask a question and the group to provide answers. Most universities have a learning management system such as Canvas, Blackboard or Moodle that includes some form of a discussion board. However, the benefit of AnswerGarden is the element of anonymity. An example of a question asked prior to an advanced religion class is, "Why does suffering exist?" or, "Why does God allow suffering?" Answers gathered provide a guide for small-group or large-group discussions, or can frame the direction of the classroom lecture.

Midcourse surveys provide helpful feedback for the instructor and aid in the planning of the second half of the course. These surveys are helpful not only in residential classes but also in hybrid or fully online courses as well.[27] Poll questions can include questions regarding specific course design such as course assignments or comprehending course content. Survey questions aimed at students' openness to discuss various religious views or differing theological stances empower them and provide valuable information.

For those students who are hesitant about taking religion courses, student response system tutorial sessions are effective methods for student success. Moreover, student presentations, which are part of both introductory religion courses and advanced religion courses, are greatly enhanced by students using student response systems. Guest-speaker-facilitated religion classes or presentations benefit from the use of response activities as a framework for introducing subject matter and speakers. As student response systems continue to develop and expand, so will their ability to enhance meaningful learning environments for religious studies.

Conclusion

Student response systems are among the many helpful technology tools that enhance learning in religion courses. They have proven their effectiveness over the past four decades. Now a regular tool in the twenty-first-century classroom, religion instructors are encouraged to embrace this technology. Students respond positively to implementation of the use of web-based technology, as it facilitates student-centered learning. Student response systems favorably affect student motivation, enhance student interaction and lower students' apprehension concerning religious studies matters.

Notes

1. Richard E. Clark, "Reconsidering Research on Learning from Media," *Review of Educational Research* 52 (1983): 453.
2. Stuart Draper and Michael I. Brown, "Increasing Interactivity in Lectures Using an Electronic Voting System," *Journal of Computer Assisted Learning* 20 (2004): 94.
3. George Masikunas, Andreas Panayiotidis, and Linda Burke, "The Use of Electronic Voting Systems in Lectures Within Business and Marketing: A Case Study of Their Impact on Student Learning," *Research in Learning Technology* 15 (2007): 20.
4. Gerald Bergtrom, "Clicker Sets as Learning Objects," *Interdisciplinary Journal of Knowledge and Learning Objects* 2 (2006): 106.
5. Jane E. Caldwell, "Clickers in the Large Classroom: Current Research and Best-Practice Tips," *Life Sciences Education* 6 (2007): 15.
6. Harin Sellahewa, "Using an Online Student Response System in Small Group System: A Pilot Study," *ITALICS: Innovations in Teaching & Learning in Information & Computer Sciences* 10 (2011): 5.
7. Catherine H. Crouch and Eric Mazur, "Peer Instruction: Ten Years of Experience and Results," *American Journal of Physics* 69 (2001): 978.
8. Madal Lal Gupta, "Interactive Teaching and Learning by Using Student Response Systems," *The International Journal of Learning* 17 (2010): 372, 383.
9. Abram Walton, Scott Homan, Linda Naimi, and Cynthia Tomovic, "Student Perceptions of a Wireless Audience Response System," *Interactive Technology and Smart Education* 5 (2008): 214.
10. James T. Boyle and David J. Nicol, "Using Classroom Communication Systems to Support Interaction and Discussion in Large Class Settings," *Association for Learning Technology Journal* 3 (2003): 57.
11. Sumangala P. Rao and Stephen E. DiCarlo, "Peer Instruction Improves Performance on Quizzes," *Advances in Physiology Education* 24 (2000): 55.
12. Selcuk Karaman, "Effects of Audience Response Systems on Student Achievement and Long-Term Retention," *Social Behaviour and Personality* 39 (2011): 1431–1440. Cited in Pete Bridge and Mary-Anne Carmichael, "Audience Response Systems Can Facilitate Communal Course Feedback," *Focus on Health Professional Education: A Multi-Disciplinary Journal* 16 (2015): 74.
13. Robin H. Kay and Ann LeSage, "Examining the Benefits and Challenges of Using Audience Response Systems: A Review of the Literature," *Computers and Education* 53 (2009): 827.

14 M. Hanley, "Feature Phone Versus Smartphone Usage and Advertising Acceptance Among College Students: A Six-Year Analysis," (Unpublished manuscript 2010). Cited in Herb Shon and Laurie Smith, "A Review of Poll Everywhere Audience Response System," *Journal of Technology in Human Service* 29 (2011): 237.
15 Kjetil L. Nielsen, Gabrielle Hansen, and John B. Stav, "Teaching with Student Response Systems (SRS): Teacher-Centric Aspects That Can Negatively Affect Students' Experience of Using SRS," *Research in Learning Technology* 21 (2013): 4.
16 Ibid., 6.
17 Ibid., 9.
18 Ibid.
19 Sellahewa, "Online Student Response Survey," 3.
20 Gupta, "Interactive Teaching and Learning," 380.
21 Bridge and Carmichael, "Audience Response Systems," 82.
22 Bridge and Carmichael, "Audience Response Systems," 80.
23 English Standard Version.
24 Teresa Garcia and Paul R. Pintrich, "The Effects of Autonomy on Motivation and Performance in the College Classroom," *Contemporary Educational Psychology* 21 (1994): 477.
25 Bridge and Carmichael, "Audience Response Systems," 82.
26 Ibid.
27 Keith Farwell, "Keeping an Online Class Interesting and Interactive," *Distance Learning* 10 (2013): 31.

Bibliography

Bergtrom, Gerald. "Clicker Sets as Learning Objects." *Interdisciplinary Journal of Knowledge and Learning Objects* 2 (2006): 105–110.
Boyle, James T., and David J. Nicol. "Using Classroom Communication Systems to Support Interaction and Discussion in Large Class Settings." *Association for Learning Technology Journal* 3 (2003): 43–57.
Bridge, Pete, and Mary-Ann Carmichael. "Audience Response Systems Can Facilitate Communal Course Feedback." *Focus on Health Professional Education: A Multi-Disciplinary Journal* 16, no. 3 (2015): 73–85.
Caldwell, Jane E. "Clickers in the Large Classroom: Current Research and Best-Practice Tips." *Life Sciences Education* 6, no. 1 (2007): 9–20.
Clark, Richard E. "Reconsidering Research on Learning from Media." *Review of Educational Research* 52 (1983): 445–459.
Crouch, Catherine H., and Eric Mazur. "Peer Instruction: Ten Years of Experience and Results." *American Journal of Physics* 69 (2001): 970–978.
Draper, Stuart, and Michael I. Brown. "Increasing Interactivity in Lectures Using an Electronic Voting System." *Journal of Computer Assisted Learning* 20 (2004): 81–94.
Farwell, Keith. "Keeping an Online Class Interesting and Interactive." *Distance Learning* 10 (2013): 27–32.
Garcia, Teresa, and Paul R. Pintrich. "The Effects of Autonomy on Motivation and Performance in the College Classroom." *Contemporary Educational Psychology* 21 (1994): 477–486.
Gupta, Madal Lal. "Interactive Teaching and Learning by Using Student Response Systems." *The International Journal of Learning* 17 (2010): 371–384.

Hanley, M. "Feature Phone Versus Smartphone Usage and Advertising Acceptance Among College Students: A Six-Year Analysis." Unpublished manuscript, 2010. Cited in Herb Shon and Laurie Smith. "A Review of Poll Everywhere Audience Response System." *Journal of Technology in Human Service* 29 (2011): 237.

Karaman, Selcuk. "Effects of Audience Response Systems on Student Achievement and Long-Term Retention." *Social Behaviour and Personality* 39 (2011): 1431–1440. Cited in Bridge and Carmichael. "Audience Response Systems Can Facilitate Communal Course Feedback." *Focus on Health Professional Education: A Multi-Disciplinary Journal* 16, no. 3 (2015): 73–85.

Kay, Robin H., and Ann LeSage. "Examining the Benefits and Challenges of Using Audience Response Systems: A Review of the Literature." *Computers and Education* 53 (2009): 819–827.

Masikunas, George, Andreas Panayiotidis, and Linda Burke. "The Use of Electronic Voting Systems in Lectures Within Business and Marketing: A Case Study of Their Impact on Student Learning." *Research in Learning Technology* 15 (2007): 3–20.

Nielsen, Kjetil L., Gabrielle Hansen, and John B. Stav. "Teaching with Student Response Systems (SRS): Teacher-Centric Aspects That Can Negatively Affect Students' Experience of Using SRS." *Research in Learning Technology* 21 (2013): 1–13.

Rao, Sumangala P., and Stephen E. DiCarlo. "Peer Instruction Improves Performance on Quizzes." *Advances in Physiology Education* 24 (2000): 51–55.

Sellahewa, Harin. "Using an Online Student Response System in Small Group Teaching: A Pilot Study." *ITALICS: Innovations in Teaching & Learning in Information & Computer Sciences* 10 (2011): 1–5.

Walton, Abram, Scott Homan, Linda Naimi, and Cynthia Tomovic. "Student Perceptions of a Wireless Audience Response System." *Interactive Technology and Smart Education* 5 (2008): 214–229.

4 Teaching Religion With Clickers

Kristy L. Slominski

Student response systems such as clickers can be used to address various challenges of teaching religious studies. These multiple-choice remotes or mobile apps, which allow users to select an answer and see a real-time chart of the aggregate responses, encourage students to take stances on complex religious issues and to acknowledge the range of perspectives within the classroom. Students using clickers are less likely to conform to the answers of their peers compared to hand raising, thus maximizing the presence of diversity on the topic of religion.[1] Moreover, response systems provide an opportunity to integrate students' assumptions and perspectives about religion without putting individuals on the spot for their beliefs. Within the secular settings of public colleges and universities, where religious studies professors might be cautious about students sharing their own religious beliefs, this controlled form of input is especially useful. Clickers transform deeply personal viewpoints into indirect data, providing distance to aid critical analysis and a level of anonymity that protects students from having to identify themselves visibly with subject matter that is academically scrutinized in the classroom.

While clickers easily translate into a variety of educational settings, this chapter focuses on teaching religious studies within state-funded institutions of higher education. It is informed by my experiences using iClicker remotes to teach introductory courses on American religions at the University of California, Santa Barbara, and courses on religious diversity and world religions at Georgia State University.[2] I initially began using clickers to record and manage attendance, participation and quiz scores within classes that ranged from 90 to 200 undergraduates. Although clickers are often associated with large classes, many of their uses and advantages can be adapted for smaller settings.[3] I have increasingly come to appreciate their benefits for gathering feedback, soliciting opinions, prompting discussion and highlighting diverse viewpoints regarding religion.

Benefits of Clickers in the Classroom

Although a growing variety of mobile apps are available with similar functions, clicker remotes are particularly advantageous for instructors who do not permit cell phones within their classrooms. The main reason for banning cell phones is to avoid the distractions that texting and other noneducational phone functions pose to the users and those around them. According to one study, 90 percent of students reported that they notice when other students check their phones, which pulls attention away from class material.[4] When professors are distracted by students' cell phone habits, it disrupts the learning environment for everyone. Several studies indicate that cell phone usage in class negatively affects academic performance, and substantial research confirms that "students cannot multitask nearly as effectively as they think they can."[5] Clicker remotes can also bypass the challenges of inconsistent wireless service and cell phone plan limitations that students sometimes face with mobile apps. For classes that require participation as part of the grade, clicker remotes are a reliable data gathering option. Remote prices range between $20 and $55 depending on the brand. At the universities where I have taught, many students needed iClicker remotes for other classes and therefore already had the product or could borrow it from someone not using it that semester. They also had the option of selling them back to the campus bookstore at the end of the semester, making costs comparable to the subscriptions required of some mobile apps. Whether remotes or mobile devices are used, most of the examples described next can be adapted for a variety of student response systems.

The general benefits of student response systems are widely cited, although little work has been done on their implementation for the teaching of religion.[6] As Derek Bruff has summarized, most studies agree that clicker implementation "often increases student attendance, participation, and enjoyment of classes and provides students and instructors with useful feedback on student learning."[7] Clickers fit the preferences of Millennial students for instantaneous feedback, personalization and opportunities to share opinions using technology. As John Immerwahr has emphasized, members of today's "thumb generation" integrate technology into most aspects of their lives and are often very positive about sharing opinions through technologically mediated means.[8] Students who are generally not outspoken in class tend to like clickers more than those who are comfortable raising their hands, since verbal participation is not a problem for the latter group.[9] Another study indicates that a student's level of enjoyment of clickers does not necessarily correlate to his or her performance in the course. While students with lower technology proficiency had a less favorable view of clickers than those with high proficiency, the former had stronger levels of engagement and better grades than the latter.[10]

Clickers allow each student to contribute and engage materials regularly in class. They let users provide anonymous feedback on the course, comprehension, progress and interests while also supplying incentives to come prepared, opportunities to take stances and to learn about the opinions and assumptions of peers and chances to test their understanding of readings and lectures. Student-generated data can be used to inspire discussions and to make lectures more relevant to student experiences. Prior to introducing a topic, clicker questions pique students' interest and alert them to critical issues, while those asked after a lesson assess their grasp of key points and provide a chance for them to further process the material. Clicker questions alter the traditional lecture format, resetting students' attention.[11] They also save paper, time otherwise spent hand grading and much of the guesswork regarding students' interests and command of the material.

To maximize the benefits of clickers, especially for increasing attendance and engagement, researchers recommend making them a part of the course grade. Most clickers coordinate with classroom management systems such as Blackboard to make uploading and managing grades simple. I generally assign clicker scores 10 to 20 percent of the final course grade to create a low-pressure incentive to attend class, to read before class, to study for quizzes and to stay actively engaged in our sessions. Students earn up to six points in each class period through three quiz questions and three opinion or feedback questions. Students therefore earn 50 percent participation for the day by just clicking and full credit for answering all quiz questions correctly. Since the iClicker system lets instructors manually assign and adjust points after class, on some days, I offer just one opinion question worth three participation points. At the end of the semester, I drop the three lowest clicker scores for each student, which includes the zero points received for days absent. The software's flexibility, automatic grading and compatibility with classroom management systems make managing attendance, participation and quiz scores significantly easier for my large courses.

While the benefits outweigh the costs for my own teaching style and some of my teaching contexts, it is important to acknowledge limitations of this technology. Teachers might find it difficult to adjust to clicker software or hardware, and some clicker settings might not sync with university systems. Some will find that the process of waiting for clicker responses (typically about 45 seconds depending on the question's complexity) creates awkward interruptions in the flow of class, although this helped me to become more comfortable with silences and to improve my transitions between activities. Professors can also talk during the polling time to offer additional factors to consider as students finalize their selections. Most instructors integrate clicker questions within PowerPoint or other presentation software, providing an additional hurdle for those who prefer to teach without computers.

Furthermore, it is difficult to develop effective multiple-choice questions that encourage critical thinking and do not feel redundant. Fortunately, many resources exist to assist instructors with this challenge.[12] One risk is that topics become oversimplified when reduced to multiple-choice formats. However, assessing students through electronically graded quizzes is sometimes necessary within large classes that do not have teaching assistants and for non-tenure-track educators who have heavy teaching loads and minimal institutional support. Pairing clicker questions with discussions or writing tasks helps to prevent students from believing that all issues boil down to A, B, C, D or E. A study by Stephanie Cole and Gregory Kosc has affirmed the importance of discussions based on clicker questions, since these "offer students an opportunity to instruct one another, and to start working with the material while still in class."[13] Another study encourages professors to turn the multiple-choice format into an advantage by using it to explore the limitations of survey methods.[14] Since religious studies uses sociological surveys, this is a way for students to engage with one of our discipline's methods. One student, for example, told me that although he enjoyed seeing the diversity of religious opinions, sometimes the choices were worded in ways that did not match his views. This realization provided a teaching moment to highlight the pros and cons of survey methods, and the need to analyze how questions and answer choices are phrased.

Clicker Questions for Religious Studies

At the beginning of a course, I use clickers *to get to know my students*. For example, I ask them how many prior religious studies courses they have taken to determine the class's degree of knowledge about the discipline. Showing the results assures those who select zero courses that they are not alone and that I know that not everyone has religious studies experience. Clickers also assess their primary goal for the course, with options such as "to learn about my own religion," "to learn about a variety of religions," "to learn about history and culture," "to complete a university requirement" or "other." Choosing an answer requires them to reflect on what they want to get out of the course, which, hopefully, reminds them that there is something at stake and that I am committed to helping them achieve their goals. It allows me to understand their motivations better while also providing them information about the discipline as I walk through how the course could contribute to each of the goals. I introduce strategies to maximize their potential success in each area, emphasizing the need for them to be actively engaged in their own learning. For those who indicate that their main goal is to learn about their own religion, I elaborate on the differences between learning a religion within a faith-based setting and learning about it within a secular university from the interdisciplinary academic perspective of religious studies. By encouraging students to reflect on their own views and then translating their beliefs into analyzable data, clickers can help to mediate the gap between some students' goals of developing their own faith and my objective of teaching about religious diversity from a nonconfessional standpoint.

Throughout the course, I use clickers *to familiarize and engage students with the core concerns of religious studies*. In order to introduce the discipline's ongoing debates about the definition of religion and to guide students in critical thinking, I present a variety of scenarios and ask whether or not they constitute "religion."[15] For example, is practicing yoga every morning a religious practice? Is sending out Christmas cards? Is the idea that "good things happen to good people" a religious belief? For the various scenarios, students use their remotes to select yes, no or it depends. This requires them to think about their own definition of religion (as well as those introduced in class) and how "religion" might apply—or not—to the situation. I then have students turn to a partner and explain the reasons for their choice. This is followed by a large-group discussion of reasons why the example should or should not be considered religious, including unknown factors that could affect the assessment. As we contemplate why someone might choose "it depends," students often raise the issue of religious identification (Do the people consider themselves to be religious? Do they connect these practices or beliefs to a particular religious system?) or the degree to which the practices integrate religious teachings (Does the yoga practitioner know anything about Hinduism? Do the Christmas cards include Christian references?). Pairing clicker questions with discussions provides opportunities to consider the complexity of religion, to review working definitions of religion for the course and to acknowledge alternative definitions held by academics and religious people. As a follow-up, you can alter a scenario slightly to see whether certain details affect their answers, thus pushing students to confront various assumptions and biases. For example, I might describe the yoga practitioner as an immigrant from India or a white college student, exploring whether and why social location and race may affect views about the behavior.

As part of the process of getting to know the discipline, I inquire about the methods of religious studies scholars. In one exercise, students take a stance on the best way to measure religion: either through membership in religious institutions, attendance at worship services, self-identification, strength of beliefs or degree of practice. The choices introduce them to examples of survey approaches, and the responses reveal which aspects students privilege as the core markers of religion. It opens discussion about methodological challenges, the advantages and disadvantages of each way of quantifying religion and distinctions between theological and religious studies approaches. Challenging students to defend their initial perspective sharpens critical thinking, argumentation and communication skills. By showing the clicker graph—which often reveals a range of selections—students see that their ways of viewing religion are not the only ways and that each choice has limitations for understanding the complexity of religion.

To encourage students to think about the relationship between academics and society, I integrate questions about the roles and responsibilities of religious studies scholars. This type of question encourages students at research universities to consider the potential effects and applications of research. For example, I might say that the government is suspicious about a new religious movement and is seeking advice about how to regulate the group. Should religious studies scholars get involved? After students answer, I inquire about possible reasons that someone might select yes, no or it depends. Related questions examine whether academic experts have a responsibility to testify in court, to speak to the press or to publish their findings in formats and styles accessible to nonacademic audiences. These discussions emphasize connections between the way religion is studied and the effect of this knowledge on the treatment of religious people.

During quizzes, I use clickers *to assess understanding of the assigned reading and course concepts*. I also add easy recall questions to test how many students completed the reading. As Cole and Kosc have pointed out, having students first consult their textbooks or one another on questions that the majority of students answered incorrectly is often more effective than simply telling them the correct answer.[16] In addition to providing incentives and reminders to read before lectures—which helps students to better contextualize that day's lecture and discussions—quizzes allow students to check their understanding of the material, to learn which concepts I consider important enough to assess and to familiarize themselves with my way of phrasing questions in preparation for exams. In my experience, many students appreciate low-stakes clicker quizzes because they can see and discuss the answers immediately, and it motivates them to do the reading before class. At the same time, the instant feedback allows me to address significant misunderstandings promptly. For introductory religious studies courses, quickly correcting misconceptions—especially those that might fuel religious intolerance—has the potential to affect how students discuss religion and interact with religious people outside of the classroom.

Another way to check comprehension and to stimulate active engagement with course material is to ask comparative questions such as, "How many differences can you name between Protestantism and Catholicism? (a) zero, (b) one to three, (c) four to six, (d) seven to nine, or (e) more than ten." This type of question invokes students' competitive nature and causes some of them to acknowledge that they *should* be able to name more differences at this point in the semester. After logging their answers, I then have them turn to a partner and list the differences, which we later compile as a group. It requires that they first consider their own knowledge of the topic, then add to that information by listening to peers and, finally, hear a review as I summarize the conversations. This means that students are exposed to three versions of the information compared to the one account they would have received in a lecture alone. Since discussions are based on student-generated ideas, the resulting lists are often more creative than my original lecture notes.

Before exams, clickers allow students to shape the review session by *asking them which religions and concepts to review*. Often, the terms and themes that receive the most votes are not the ones I assume need review. The anonymity of clickers lets students be honest about the concepts that confuse them, since some people are embarrassed to raise questions if they think others already understand. Numerous students in my courses have indicated that the review questions were their favorite type of clicker questions because they resulted in very useful review sessions. This is in line with research findings that students perceived one of the most beneficial functions of clickers to be their assistance with exam preparation.[17]

There are numerous ways in which clickers can enable students to shape a course, from choosing between learning activities to deciding which topic to cover next. I sometimes offer a choice between the case studies that the class will learn since myriad examples could be used to teach the basic features of each religion. To underscore this point and to encourage students to continue learning on their own, I share optional resources about the case studies that did not "win" the clicker survey. Clicker classrooms have the potential to become more democratic about the use of class time and the direction of the course, creating a more student-centered learning environment through lessons personalized to the needs and interests of the group. Such variation in my teaching from class to class—especially when I teach multiple sections of the same course in one semester—also helps me to avoid monotony.

After exams, I use clickers *to determine which resources and study strategies were effective*. I may ask students to identify which of the following was most helpful for exam preparation: making vocabulary cards, filling out the comparison chart, completing the review crossword, rereading texts and notes or meeting in a study group. This prompts a discussion of how to improve study habits for the next exam and reminds students that other methods exist if their previous ones failed them. Such questions also reveal which resources I should continue to offer or encourage. As a way to assess student reception of the course material, I ask them of which topic or religion they have learned the most. For example, after the first unit of my world religions course, I ask whether they learned more new information about indigenous traditions, Hinduism or Buddhism. Their selections, along with discussion, indicate where the greatest knowledge growth occurs and why this might be. Determining which aspects students deem most educational helps me to adapt those effective strategies into other parts of the course.

I employ clickers in a variety of ways in relation to *in-class and take-home assignments*. When classroom activities include multiple steps, students use their remotes to tell me when they have progressed from step

A to step B and so forth. Consulting the clicker chart, therefore, tells the groups whether or not they need to speed up. If it shows that some are about to finish early, it prompts me to give further instructions on how to use the extra time, thus reducing downtime in the classroom. When introducing an activity or assignment, a clicker question—or several— checks whether students fully comprehend the task. For new writing projects, clickers can measure knowledge of library research and source gathering processes. At various points before paper or project deadlines, I often ask, "How far along are you?" and list the various stages of the project as the options. This question reviews the steps involved and tells them whether they are ahead of or behind their classmates. Students can be extremely influenced by their peers, so this tactic provides another level of encouragement beyond deadline reminders from the professor.

To further assist with assignments, I use clickers *to teach and assess reading and writing skills*. This is important given the large number of nonmajors and nonhumanities students in lower-division religious studies courses. For close readings, I present a passage and pose a series of questions about it, such as, "Who is the audience of this passage?" or, "Which course concept does this exemplify?" I also ask them to identify the best paraphrase of the passage. Using this mini-exercise, we discuss why the wrong answers are incorrect and how to improve paraphrasing within their papers. A similar strategy can be done with citations by having them select which citation represents the format requested for their assignment. Another approach is to post writing samples and have students grade them based on specific criteria, requiring them to evaluate various writing techniques and to articulate what makes them effective or ineffective. This exercise could be used as practice for peer reviewing. Seeing how peers would grade the same paper can create more consistency across the peer-reviewing process and perhaps provide a reality check for what an A+ paper in a religious studies course looks like.

As we dig deeper into the topics of the course and the parameters of religious studies, I integrate more clicker questions that ask students *to take stances on controversial issues*. I appreciate this function the most because clickers can be used to scaffold and otherwise structure important discussions. Using their remotes, students record their positions on a broad debate and then brainstorm possible factors that might influence people to select each option. Phrasing the discussion broadly allows students to acknowledge and discuss the complicated factors freely without needing to defend their own answers. Next, I introduce specific details of a related case, followed by a reevaluation using the original clicker question to see whether the concrete case study changed their positions. This serves to reinforce the complexity and historically situated nature of many debates, to show that it is okay to revise conclusions in the presence of new information and to provide visual evidence of the variety of opinions present within the classroom. While often there is some shift in reactions after discussing specific cases, I am careful to remind students that the public university is a place of diverse opinions. The goal is to encourage students to develop thoughtful, evidence-based stances and respectful strategies of discussion rather than enforce any one particular viewpoint.

For example, I often ask students to weigh in on legal cases concerning religious freedom, challenging them to recognize the intricacy of these situations. On the topic of Native American religion, I introduce the following: a mountain within a national park is considered both a sacred site and the best place for rock climbing. Would you (a) allow both groups to use the site, (b) ban rock climbing, (c) ban religious rituals, (d) designate separate areas for climbing and rituals or (e) designate separate times for climbing and ritual. After they answer and discuss the choices, I then introduce the actual case to which I am alluding: the controversy involving rock climbers on Devil's Tower in Wyoming, a site considered sacred to a number of indigenous tribes, including the Lakota. This case is particularly useful for introducing First Amendment issues. Here, claims to religious freedom are in tension with the "separation of church and state" since the site is designated as public land within a national park. It is also valuable for discussing the history of governmental policies and military actions against Native Americans, Native American religious views of the land, various rulings on what constitutes "religion" within America and the fact that decisions regarding the treatment of religion are complex and ongoing. The National Park Services' resolution in this case aligned most closely with the option of designating separate times for climbing and ritual, since they instituted a voluntary ban on climbing in the month of June, when a number of sacred rituals occur. However, I emphasize how none of the choices would have made everyone involved happy, so there is no "perfect" answer in this complicated reality. Prefacing this case with a clicker question meant that the students were already thinking about what *they* might do, were listening for factors that could change their stance and, hopefully, had more of a stake in learning about the background and outcome of the situation. As one study of clickers argued, asking students to take a stand increases their "emotional investment" in an issue.[18] I found this to be true for my class; students were able to envision different perspectives while engaging their emotions productively. One student explained during office hours that being encouraged to take a stance on various cases gave her a chance to reflect on her own religious beliefs, which was one of her goals for the course.

Clickers let students connect their personal experiences and viewpoints to the course material without encouraging confessional debates. As a religious studies professor at a state university, I discourage students from sharing their own religious beliefs during in-class discussions. This extends to the types of questions that they ask, and I spend time teaching them how to translate faith-based curiosities into critically framed academic questions that can be answered using the tools of religious studies. There are many reasons for my cautiousness surrounding students' religious commitments, from the desire to keep students from proselytizing to my concerns about blurring the lines between faith-based and secular studies of religion. At the same time, however, I cannot completely overlook this important facet of students' lives, especially because it affects how some of them engage (or resist) the course material. In ongoing debates about how to teach world religion courses and whether professors of religion should engage with students' beliefs, many have concluded, "Ignoring students' personal interests in religion is counterproductive for effective learning."[19] Clickers provide a more controlled way of acknowledging and soliciting students' opinions about religious situations. Asking a clicker question creates the space for students to think through any personal relevance that the topic has for them and then share their perspectives in a limited way. The answer chart enables us to build a discussion around the compiled data, which can be analyzed without putting any one student on the spot for his or her viewpoint. For each choice, I ask them to brainstorm some reasons why their peers might have made that selection. This requires them to consider other perspectives without feeling the need to explain or defend their own answers (although I am sure that many students share their own rationales as they explain why someone else might select a certain answer). Compiling student views in this way transforms personal stances into indirect data, allowing students to transition from being the subjects of inquiry to the critical investigators.

While some questions can be adapted for use without clickers, and some feedback could be gathered through hand raising, clickers offer a visual, formal way to acknowledge students' answers and perspectives, and a private means of communicating with their peers and with me. Anonymity is important for sensitive topics relating to religion so that students do not feel the need to self-censor if they think that their instructor or peers would find their stance unpopular. When I post the graph of responses and keep the poll open during opinion questions, students also see if someone switches answers during discussion, emphasizing the message that hearing multiple perspectives can change attitudes about religion.

Perhaps more than the transformation of students, clickers can inspire the "transformation of teachers." As one study argued, the effective use of clickers can "help instructors move from teacher-focused approaches to more learner-focused approaches in teaching."[20] The questions discussed earlier highlight how, in many ways, clickers *helped me to teach about religion*. I have become a more creative teacher as I strive to find useful and varied ways of incorporating clickers and structuring multiple-choice questions. I am better at "listening" to student responses, integrating diverse viewpoints and adapting my class plans based on the surprises and feedback. Most importantly for religious studies, clickers enable me to balance the need to acknowledge the views and experiences that students bring into the classroom, including religious commitments, with my objective of teaching students how to analyze religion from secular academic perspectives.

Notes

1 Jeffrey R. Stowell, Terrah Oldham, and Dan Bennett, "Using Student Response Systems ('Clickers') to Combat Conformity and Shyness," *Teaching of Psychology* 37, no. 2 (April 2010): 135.
2 The iClicker remotes that I assigned run on the iClicker Classic software, which uses an instructor base and does not require an Internet connection. See www.iclicker.com/. Another widely used remote system is Turning Technologies: www.turningtechnologies.com/.
3 Hannah Sevian and William E. Robinson, "Clickers Promote Learning in All Kinds of Classes- Small and Large, Graduate and Undergraduate, Lecture and Lab," *Journal of College Science Teaching* 40, no. 3 (January 2011): 14–18.
4 Michael J. Berry and Aubrey Westfall, "Dial D for Distraction: The Making and Breaking of Cell Phone Policies in the College Classroom," *College Teaching* 63, no. 2 (2015): 65.
5 Jeffrey H. Kuznekoff and Scott Titsworth, "The Impact of Mobile Phone Usage on Student Learning," *Communication Education* 62, no. 3 (2013): 233–252. Quotation from Douglas K. Duncan, Angel R. Hoekstra and Bethany R. Wilcox, "Digital Devices, Distraction, and Student Performance: Does In-Class Cell Phone Use Reduce Learning?" *Astronomy Education Review* 11, no. 1 (2012): 1.
6 The primary teaching journal for scholars of religion, *Teaching Theology and Religion*, does not contain articles that exclusively address student response systems as of June 2017. Only one article mentions clickers, but the discussion is limited to one paragraph. Amy DeRogatis et al., "Teaching Very Large Classes," *Teaching Theology and Religion* 17, no. 4 (2014): 357.
7 Derek Bruff, *Teaching with Classroom Response Systems: Creating Active Learning Environments* (San Francisco: Jossey-Bass, 2009), 5.
8 John Immerwahr, "Engaging the 'Thumb Generation' with Clickers," *Teaching Philosophy* 32, no. 3 (2009): 233–245.
9 Stephanie Cole and Gregory Kosc, "Quit Surfing and Start Clicking: One Professor's Effort to Combat the Problems of Teaching the U.S. Survey in a Large Lecture Hall," *History Teacher* 43, no. 3 (2010): 407.
10 Jennifer A. Zapf and Adolfo J. Garcia, "The Influence of Tech-Savvyness and Clicker Use on Student Learning," *International Journal for the Scholarship of Teaching and Learning* 5, no. 1 (2011): 1.
11 Diane M. Bunce, Elizabeth A. Flens, and Kelly Y. Neiles, "How Long Can Students Pay Attention in Class? A Study of Student Attention Decline Using Clickers," *Journal of Chemical Education* 87, no. 12 (December 2010): 1438–1443.
12 Roberta Sullivan, "Principles for Constructing Good Clicker Questions: Going Beyond Rote Learning and Stimulating Active Engagement with Course Content," *Journal of Educational Technology Systems* 37, no. 3 (March 2009): 335–347.
13 Cole and Kosc, "Quit Surfing," 403.

14 Stephanie Mollborn and Angel Hoekstra, "'A Meeting of Minds': Using Clickers for Critical Thinking and Discussion in Large Sociology Classes," *Teaching Sociology* 38, no. 1 (2010): 25.
15 In this approach, I was influenced by Catherine L. Albanese's Introduction to American Religion course at the University of California, Santa Barbara. Although she did not use clickers, her questions about whether scenarios constituted "religion" always prompted a handful of students to debate the issue and raise important questions about the boundaries of religious life.
16 Cole and Kosc, "Quit Surfing," 403.
17 Marc Patry, "Clickers in Large Classes: From Student Perceptions Towards an Understanding of Best Practices," *International Journal for the Scholarship of Teaching and Learning* 3, no. 2 (2009): 9.
18 Immerwahr, "Engaging," 236.
19 Brian H. Smith, "Teaching the Devout Student: Faith and Scholarship in the Classroom," *Teaching Theology and Religion* 16, no. 2 (April 2013): 133. See also Carolyn M. Jones Medine, Todd Penner, and Marjorie Lehman, "Forum: Teaching With, Against, and To Faith," *Teaching Theology & Religion* 18, no. 4 (October 2015): 363–386.
20 Yifat Ben-David Kolikant, Denise Drane, and Susanna Calkins, "'Clickers' as Catalysts for Transformation of Teachers," *College Teaching* 58, no. 4 (2010): 127.

Bibliography

Berry, Michael J., and Aubrey Westfall. "Dial D for Distraction: The Making and Breaking of Cell Phone Policies in the College Classroom." *College Teaching* 63, no. 2 (2015): 62-71.

Bruff, Derek. *Teaching with Classroom Response Systems: Creating Active Learning Environments*. San Francisco: Jossey-Bass, 2009.

Bunce, Diane M., Elizabeth A. Flens, and Kelly Y. Neiles. "How Long Can Students Pay Attention in Class? A Study of Student Attention Decline Using Clickers." *Journal of Chemical Education* 87, no. 12 (December 2010): 1438–1443.

Cole, Stephanie, and Gregory Kosc. "Quit Surfing and Start Clicking: One Professor's Effort to Combat the Problems of Teaching the U.S. Survey in a Large Lecture Hall." *History Teacher* 43, no. 3 (2010): 397–410.

DeRogatis, Amy, Kenneth Honerkamp, Justin McDaniel, Carolyn Medine, Vivian-Lee Nyitray, and Thomas Pearson. "Teaching Very Large Classes." *Teaching Theology and Religion* 17, no. 4 (2014): 352–368.

Duncan, Douglas K., Angel R. Hoekstra, and Bethany R. Wilcox. "Digital Devices, Distraction, and Student Performance: Does In-Class Cell Phone Use Reduce Learning?" *Astronomy Education Review* 11, no. 1 (2012): 1–4.

Immerwahr, John. "Engaging the 'Thumb Generation' with Clickers." *Teaching Philosophy* 32, no. 3 (2009): 233–245.

Jones Medine, Carolyn M., Todd Penner, and Marjorie Lehman. "Forum: Teaching With, Against, and To Faith." *Teaching Theology & Religion* 18, no. 4 (October 2015): 363–386.

Kolikant, Yifat Ben-David, Denise Drane, and Susanna Calkins. "'Clickers' as Catalysts for Transformation of Teachers." *College Teaching* 58, no. 4 (2010): 127–135.

Kuznekoff, Jeffrey H., and Scott Titsworth. "The Impact of Mobile Phone Usage on Student Learning." *Communication Education* 62, no. 3 (2013): 233–252.

Mollborn, Stephanie, and Angel Hoekstra. "'A Meeting of Minds': Using Clickers for Critical Thinking and Discussion in Large Sociology Classes." *Teaching Sociology* 38, no. 1 (2010): 18–27.
Patry, Marc. "Clickers in Large Classes: From Student Perceptions Towards an Understanding of Best Practices." *International Journal for the Scholarship of Teaching and Learning* 3, no. 2 (2009): 1–11.
Sevian, Hannah, and William E. Robinson. "Clickers Promote Learning in All Kinds of Classes- Small and Large, Graduate and Undergraduate, Lecture and Lab." *Journal of College Science Teaching* 40, no. 3 (January 2011): 14–18.
Smith, Brian H. "Teaching the Devout Student: Faith and Scholarship in the Classroom." *Teaching Theology and Religion* 16, no. 2 (April 2013): 132–149.
Stowell, Jeffrey R., Terrah Oldham, and Dan Bennett. "Using Student Response Systems ('Clickers') to Combat Conformity and Shyness." *Teaching of Psychology* 37, no. 2 (April 2010): 135–140.
Sullivan, Roberta. "Principles for Constructing Good Clicker Questions: Going Beyond Rote Learning and Stimulating Active Engagement with Course Content." *Journal of Educational Technology Systems* 37, no. 3 (March 2009): 335–347.
Zapf, Jennifer A., and Adolfo J. Garcia. "The Influence of Tech-Savvyness and Clicker Use on Student Learning." *International Journal for the Scholarship of Teaching and Learning* 5, no. 1 (2011): 1–11.

5 "Seeing" the Sacred Landscape

A Digital Geographies Approach to Contextualizing Ancient Sites in Religious Education

Kyle M. Oliver

Introduction: The Case for Context

When my wife, now an Episcopal priest, returned from the Holy Land in the final year of her M.Div. studies, she brought with her a renewed and deepened excitement for the scripture and history of our faith. This formation phenomenon had become familiar to me as a student and then staff member at a seminary that encouraged intercultural immersion experiences, especially in sites important to the development of the Anglican/Episcopal tradition. Those who have been on a trip like this, or spoken with someone who has, will know the kind of enthusiasm I mean. For example, my wife and others on the Palestine of Jesus Pilgrimage testified to a better understanding of the role that *walking* played in Jesus's ministry.

To include such trips in seminary curricula is part of a broader strategy that Foster et al. call in their landmark study of clergy education "pedagogies of contextualization."[1] This approach acknowledges the "dynamic character of the content and agency of contexts"—both those where the trainees will serve and those that helped form the traditions for which these students will serve as stewards and guides.[2] Of course, learners need not literally travel in order to explore the context of scripture and religious practice. For example, in a recent "Race Matters" blog post for the Wabash Center for Teaching and Learning in Theology and Religion, Wil Gafney provides a detailed description of the activities that support her introductory Hebrew Bible course's objective to introduce "the West Asian, East African and ancient Near Eastern contexts of the Hebrew Bible" to students who rarely understand even the "basic regional geography"—let alone, for example, the "white cultural constructions that have been imported onto and into the text."[3] These activities include exploring linguistic connections to other Afro-Asiatic languages, conducting detailed map work and studying the problematic "visual representations of Egyptians, Israelites and other ancient peoples as Europeans" in widely used popular, educational and devotional resources.[4] Her discussion underscores the importance of sophisticated contextual understanding, not only for the purpose of treating the scriptures with integrity but also for decentering whiteness in contemporary church and classroom.

Although I have chosen the two concrete examples earlier from my own primary setting, Christian seminary education, I hope it is clear that the importance of context extends to all areas of religious education and religious studies. Even the earliest effort I could find to establish learning standards in American religious education presented as a model Bible curriculum that devoted two of its five themes to substantially contextual questions rather than to content as such.[5] A century later, we live in an era of pervasive religious illiteracy and increasing exposure to religious diversity.[6] Against this backdrop, it becomes even more urgent for us to teach and learn about difference generously and knowledgeably[7]—toward what Mary Hess calls a "community of communities" understanding of faith identity.[8] That cannot happen in an environment where believers and nonbelievers ignore the historical, sociocultural and geophysical contexts that nurtured and continue to nurture their own faiths (if any) and the faiths of their neighbors.

This chapter focuses on a very particular pedagogy of contextualization common to religious education classrooms of many faiths, learning contexts and grade levels: teaching about important religious sites. In particular, our goal is to help students encounter these sites. Pilgrimages and immersions are the pedagogy of contextualization *par excellence*, as my wife and her travel companions can attest. Consider their experience as it relates to the contextual learning activities in Gafney's Biblical Studies course. Certainly, the pilgrims experienced or re-experienced the linguistic distance between their native English (or other Indo-European tongue) and the Afro-Asiatic Hebrew and Arabic (both modern and ancient) that surrounded them while in the Holy Land. The students also embodied (by foot and by bus ride) a great deal of "map work"—hence the comments about appreciating how far Jesus and his disciples walked. Finally, the pilgrims met not "visual representations" of Middle Easterners but actual people living in the region, most of them nonwhite.

Of course, a physical visit has plenty of pedagogical limitations besides being prohibitively expensive and otherwise inappropriate for a significant majority of religious education contexts. Perhaps a virtual visit offers some of the best of both worlds. Such an experience is now easily and inexpensively available through new media technologies such as searchable religious photo, sound and video archives; interactive and annotatable mapping software; and even virtual reality tours. Learners can see the sites, their surroundings and the people making religious meaning in these landscapes. They can take in something of the language, the visual and sonic culture and the ritual spaces. And they can do so in an increasingly high-fidelity manner that privileges first-person perspectives and even simulated embodiment.

Critical Tool: New Digital Geographies

Although this is a practical volume, I believe a small amount of theory is necessary for asking sound pedagogical questions about this endeavor. It is with this need in mind that I introduce the new digital geographies. Literacy scholar and educational anthropologist Lalitha Vasudevan defines digital geographies as "emerging landscapes that are being produced through the confluence of new communicative practices and available media and technologies."[9] She gives the example of photo-sharing application Flickr, engagement with which constructs a (hybrid) digital geography that connects the physical spaces where users take the photographs, the tools and environments (both physical and digital) in which users edit them and the online platform where they upload, explore and comment on their own and others' creations.[10] Moreover, Vasudevan notes that mobile devices with Internet access contribute to the fluidity with which learners can move among, communicate in and make connections between physical spaces and online spaces.[11] In a related piece, she and Kevin Leander further expand this multimodal understanding of hybrid spatiality while discussing the "cycling" behavior of a teenager playing an online video game and switching rapidly between the overhead map view of a planet and the virtually embodied view of the player's avatar moving through the landscape.[12] In this final sense, any visitor navigating a physical religious site with help from a smartphone mapping application is having a digital geographies experience.

I find this theoretical lens useful for a discussion of religious educational site-seeing because it extends rather than substitutes for our pre-Internet experience of place, and because it allows us to ground our thinking in everyday experiences of hybrid spatiality. Indeed, nearly all of us directly experience digital geographies as we engage common, integrated social practices.[13] For example, I was recently quite mesmerized by Facebook posts from a colleague in congregational ministry, whose trip to the Holy Land served as the opportunity to create a digital geography connecting the physical sites she visited to the hybrid community she convenes among Facebook friends—many of them members of the congregation she and I serve together. Here are a few representative examples of her photo annotations (see also Figure 5.1):

1. Followed the pilgrim path in Jerusalem, in Gethsemane, with its ancient olive trees and the Church of the Holy Sepulcher. Crowds and more crowds like the Passion story.

60 Kyle M. Oliver

2. The place of the Incarnation at Bethlehem. Where the wall divides the traditional "shepherd's fields," and people's hearts. Lord, have mercy.
3. A day in the desert: Masada, Qumran, Jericho. Hot dry air and the extremity of devotion, zeal, and ongoing desperation.
4. Our last day. One more splash in the Mediterranean at Jaffa, and a final prayer at Emmaus. Now to figure out how to share this all with others![14]

Figure 5.1 Informal Religious Education Through a Digital Geography Connecting Bethlehem and a Congregational Minister's Facebook Followers[15]

To my reading, her contemplative tone and accessible brevity reflect a range of implicit design considerations in constructing this hybrid educational space. She knows her followers are unlikely to read lengthy captions in the course of their casual encounters with her content in the midst of everyday life. She understands that the visual mode is likely more effective than the text mode in communicating both a general "sense of place" and the spiritual impact of the sites she is visiting. Finally, she chooses in her role as a faith leader visiting one religiously diverse setting (Israel/Palestine) and serving another (New York City's Upper West Side) to use a prayerful rather than an analytical tone and, where possible, to highlight the shared anguish of religious conflict.

Both Vasudevan's definition of digital geographies and my ministry colleague's example of informal instruction within them foreground for us some central opportunities and challenges facing educators who wish to use new media to help their students explore religious sites. In my view, these include the following interrelated principles:

1. New media tools and spaces provide finite, selective and socially constructed representations of the sites we want our students to encounter. A great many sociocultural, geopolitical, technical and temporal considerations determine our students' access to ancient sites via new digital geographies.[16] While there is no "neutral" way to visit a site, including in person,[17] both ideology and happenstance shape *mediated* experiences still more significantly. As Gafney's discussion of representation exemplifies,[18] this selectivity and shaping is not limited to *new media* representations of ancient religious cultures and locations. Nevertheless, when a mediated experience promises to be immersive, to simulate the experience of being "really there," it may be harder for students (and teachers) to identify, critically, how the people who designed and implemented the hybrid experience shaped it even in unintentional ways.

For example, Christian vlogger/educator Matthew Moretz created a two-part YouTube series[19] re-enacting and explaining a Stations of the Cross devotional experience as part of his *Father Matthew Presents* series. These videos are a useful (and free) teaching resources created by a gifted amateur media maker. One obvious way Moretz's perspective frames the immersion experience is through the very decision to present a tour of Jerusalem as a Stations of the Cross activity. There's nothing wrong with this choice, but it shapes the literal path Moretz takes through the city as well as the commentary he presents at stops along the way. A Jewish or Muslim guide would have a different story to tell—a different route with different stops and verbal annotations.

It's also worth noting how complex some of these design decisions can become for resource creators and how that complexity trickles down to the user experience. In these videos, the title music that plays over the opening credits comes from a European and likely Christian classical tradition. This choice, on first listen, seemed to me to undercut the value of the video for providing a culturally authentic immersion in contemporary Jerusalem. Even the Christian experience of Jerusalem is likely to "sound" quite different from this opening sequence more often than not. However, viewers of these videos later learn that this music was actually recorded during an encounter that happened on the tour, when Moretz visits a church and stops to listen to a rehearsing brass ensemble. Given this additional information, is the editorial choice of music "authentic" or "representative"? Well, yes and no, which is exactly why Jerusalem is such a fascinating, vibrant and tortured place. The more important point from a pedagogical perspective is that I had watched this video several times before even thinking to ask this question. That should be a cautionary tale for educators wishing to use media artifacts for contextual study. Again, there is no neutral or perfectly representative experience.

2. **New media tools and spaces are sites of active meaning making and spontaneous social exchange.** Just as the "medium" of an in-person pilgrimage inevitably shapes the message in ways a trip guide cannot fully control, connecting our students to authentic digital geographies affords the opportunity for experiences that may both support and counteract the learning goals we put in place. Moreover, in the process of engagement, our students may create artifacts (e.g., comments and annotations) that become part of the environment others will experience.[20]

Across the two Stations of the Cross videos on *Father Matthew Presents*, there are 13 comments from users, including 2 from Moretz himself. In one sense, these represent spoken exchanges while "taking the tour," such as a participant may overhear from a fellow group member on-site. In another sense, they are more like a signed guest book or even "digital graffiti," for they are now semipermanently associated with Moretz's original artifact and may be noticed and studied by subsequent viewers. One of these comments is worth citing verbatim:

> Father, I live in India. I have just returned from a Jerusalem visit, last fortnight. Had done the Via Dolorosa Stages with a guide. Father, your video is simply brilliant! I wish I had seen this before I went there. Though I am a Hindu, yet having a Christian Missionary schooling background, I had come to love the Lord (Jesus) since childhood. The Holy Sepulchre Church (stations) were "electrifying"—one could feel His Presence. . . . as I am doing now, watching your video. Thanx again.[21]

There's a lot happening here. Commenter sanjoy sen explicitly acknowledges the potential value of a digitally mediated experience of the site before an in-person visit. He also complicates possible preconceived notions about how a non-Christian can experience this devotionally curated tour. Most intriguingly, he raises questions about multiple religious belonging generally and Hindu understandings of the person and role of Jesus of Nazareth in particular. It's not difficult to imagine religious educators who would be excited to engage this comment with their students and others who might choose to try to steer them clear of it.

3. **New media tools and spaces require receptive, expressive and navigational literacies to ensure students' full participation.** To see, hear, move and interact when visiting a site via digital geographies may require technical and social skills[22] our students have not fully developed. Thus while our choice to engage in this particular pedagogy of contextualization has the added benefit of helping students develop digital literacy practices, it may also require supplemental instruction and support in order to realize these literacies. For example, if I wish to use Google Earth's compelling virtual reality app to facilitate a student tour of a city important to the history of religions, I need first to acquaint that student with the somewhat complex controls for navigating movement—including how to toggle on or off the "comfort mode" feature that helps users avoid motion sickness. Just as in an on-site visit, no student wants to feel left behind, much less experience physical discomfort. The difference is that when moving through digital geographies, we cannot necessarily assume students already possess the skills they need in order to keep up and to care for themselves along the way.

Pedagogical Tools: New Media Resources for Digital Contextual Study

Having derived three guiding principles from digital geographies theory, we are now in a position to survey and evaluate a variety of new media tools for experiencing ancient sites in the context of religious education. What follows does not aspire to be a comprehensive list or a rigorous typology. My selections are motivated by a desire to introduce resources that readers might not have encountered or might not have considered to be useful in their place-based pedagogies of contextualization. In the spirit of participation and co-creativity that is at the heart of the approach I have been outlining, interested readers can access (and request to contribute to) a curated collection via this chapter's companion Pinterest board.[23]

Resources for Immersion: Virtual Reality

Virtual reality (VR) has come a long way since the days of huge helmets and suits, low resolution and excruciating loading and lag times. That being said, the high-end consumer systems are still quite expensive— probably not worth the cost for religious educators given the small amount of relevant content that is currently available. For teachers, then, the most significant development in VR technology has been the release of Google Cardboard, a low-cost ($10–$20) device that turns any iOS or Android smartphone into a passable headset for viewing VR content. All this basic system "knows" is how I am moving my head, and yet the effect it achieves is quite remarkable.

If you want to give your students an understanding not only of what a site looks like but also of its scale and its architectural or topographical construction and layout, VR resources are an exciting tool. They can capture something of the grandeur of a site such as the Blue Mosque in Istanbul or the Swaminarayan Akshardham in New Delhi. They also provide some individual freedom to explore interesting details, especially when the resource connects multiple 360-degree viewing points that users can travel between. On the whole, the third of our principles from the previous section is an especially significant consideration for our use of VR resources in the classroom; *navigating* VR spaces is not always intuitive, and learners may bring some anxiety to the experience. Teachers wishing to use VR tools to curate immersion experiences in sacred landscapes would do well to prepare themselves and their students very thoroughly, and choose destinations that are worth the extra effort to see in this remarkable way.

Google Expeditions[24] is the currently available tool that most effectively brings together relevant content, accessible technology and strong pedagogical affordances. The operative metaphor for using this software is that of a multistop field trip. Google has created hundreds of tours in partnership with museums, educational publishers, research labs, nongovernmental organizations and others.[25] Tours of potential interest to religious educators include Holy Places of Jerusalem, Grand Mosque of Abu Dhabi, Gothic Treasures in England, Angkor Wat and a number of religion-oriented multisite tours such as Places of Faith around the World, Aztec and Mayan Ruins and Gods and Goddesses.

After downloading tour content, preferably to a tablet, the guide can then recruit explorers to connect to the tour. Explorers only need a Google Cardboard headset and a phone-sized mobile device with the app and a connection to whatever Wi-Fi network the guide is connected to. Each tour is divided into a series of "scenes," the equivalent of a stop where the guide provides narration while participants look around (see Figure 5.2). When the guide initiates a scene, that particular 360-degree photograph is displayed on explorers' headsets. The designers of this high-quality resource have created a digital geography that is easy for

"Seeing" the Sacred Landscape 65

Figure 5.2 Screenshot of the First Scene of the Swaminarayan Akshardham Tour on Google Expeditions (Guide View on iPad)

explorers and guides to navigate. It focuses the social exchange and meaning making on in-person connections between participating learners and it presents attractive—albeit both finite and also somewhat sterile[26]— views of "must-see" destinations. For now, it offers the next-best thing to visiting in person if our educational goal is a sort of embodied, visual understanding of a site.

For adventurous educators and students, there are several ways to replicate some of the affordances of Google Expeditions in a more do-it-yourself manner. **Sites in 3D**[27] is the closest experience I know of to Google Expeditions. Along with its accompanying iOS and Android apps called Sites in VR, this website is another 360-degree photograph resource. Included in the database are dozens of both well- and lesser-known (primarily) Muslim sites, including many famous mosques. All of the sites can be visited via desktop computer or by pairing the mobile apps with the impressive array of supported VR headsets. For teaching Islamic sites visually, Sites in 3D has much better coverage than any other resource I know.

For an even less filtered experience, educators might consider sending students off to explore a site using **Google Earth** (on the desktop or paired with a high-end VR system such as the HTC Vive) and/or **Google**

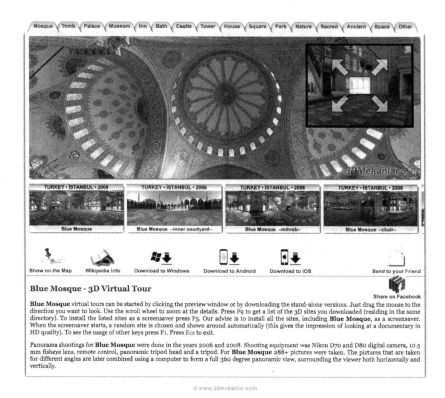

Figure 5.3 Screenshot of the Blue Mosque Featured Tour on Sites in 3-D (Full-Screen View on Desktop)

Maps/Google Street View (on the desktop or with Google Cardboard). With these tools, one can cycle between an overhead map view and a virtually embodied street view, navigating the landscape in either modality just like the gamer in Leander and Vasudevan's chapter. This full functionality is mostly available in cities, with a significant additional bias toward the developed world. Still, almost any site that is of interest to tourists will at least include user-published, 360-degree photos. For example, even though Cambodia is outside the full-featured coverage area of Google Earth, virtual visitors will still find dozens of photos, including many 360-degree views created by both Google and visitors (see Figure 5.4). Some of these viewpoints are connected for self-guided navigation. An interesting application of Google Earth for the purposes of geographical contextual exploration is **Google Lit Trips**.[28] This educational project uses Google Earth's annotation features to create guided tours of the sites corresponding to important works of literature. Some of the tours in this collection may be of interest to religious educators (e.g., *The Diary of a Young Girl*; see Figure 5.5).

"Seeing" the Sacred Landscape 67

Figure 5.4 Screenshot of 360-Degree Photo of Angkor Wat[29] (Browser View on Desktop)

Figure 5.5 Screenshot of Google Lit Trip for *The Diary of a Young Girl* (Full-Screen View on Desktop)

Resources for Immersion: Audio, Video, Conventional Photography

Of course, 360-degree photos are not the only way to immerse oneself in the sights and sounds of a religious destination using online media collections. Especially for those who may feel overwhelmed, or even occasionally physically uncomfortable, using VR tools, the more familiar fare of audio, video and still photography can still be extremely valuable. Here the creative and curatorial perspectives of contributors to these collections make our first and second digital geographies principles important to bear in mind, as we saw in the example of Moretz's video-based Stations of the Cross. We should encourage our students to ask why certain photos, videos and sound files were posted, and what creators may have chosen, intentionally or unintentionally, to leave out. Perhaps even more importantly, we should encourage our students to be thoughtful and respectful participants in the discourse afforded by comment boards, discussion forums and other social features common on these platforms.

Sacred Destinations[30] is my favorite static media collection for studying religious sites. I used it extensively when preparing for my own seminary immersion trip to Rome. It's a thorough and self-described "encyclopedic" and "ecumenical" site full of location descriptions and a lot of both original and Creative Commons–licensed photography. The creator of the site has an M.Phil. in religious history from Oxford, so while she claims not to be "an academic expert on sacred places or art,"[31] she is nevertheless a credible and curious co-explorer. The coverage of the site is global but skews heavily toward European destinations.

Folkways is "the nonprofit record label of the Smithsonian Institution" and offers both a powerful search engine for its extensive catalog and generous track previews on its website.[32] Using the genre (sacred) and region filters on a recent visit, I was soon listening to a wedding song of the Burgi tribe in Ethiopia and "Alligator Song" by a group of Aboriginal singers from the remote Cape York Peninsula in Northeast Australia. Once I had found these tracks, I discovered each was available via YouTube, courtesy of the Smithsonian, and the complete Folkways collection seems to be included as part of the Smithsonian Global Sound for Libraries collection from Alexander Street/ProQuest. While this means of exploring sacred sounds is indexed only as finely as a country search rather than by city or site, it is nevertheless an impressive collection for meaningful cultural immersion across a wide geographic range.

Some museums offer excellent online access to their collections, which can be rich sources of media relevant to important sites. For example, the website for the Metropolitan Museum of Art's recently closed exhibit **Jerusalem, 1000–1400: Every People Under Heaven**[33] is a multifaith media treasure trove. It includes annotated images of 45 of the exhibit's objects, a gallery breakdown of the exhibit as it existed at the museum, an excellent "Voices of Jerusalem" first-person video series (also available as a YouTube playlist) and the full exhibit audio guide available as a SoundCloud playlist.

Of course, I would not have known about this exhibit were I not a member of the Met. This observation raises an issue that new media content creators refer to as the "discoverability" problem. There is so much content online about a given religious site. Some of it is excellent, but most of it is useless or worse. Finding the signal amid the noise is the educator's constant struggle, again a matter of navigational literacy in digital geographies. When a specialist collection like the ones I've mentioned earlier is unavailable or unknown, I recommend narrowing the search for resources by type of media. For video, YouTube is an obvious place to look; for photography, Flickr; and for music and speech, SoundCloud.[34] Even cursory searches will turn up some stunning media, especially if one is willing to make occasional use of Google Translate. My recent finds include a beautiful collection of religion-related photos by Indian photographer Natesh Ramasamy and an extensive playlist of liturgical chant from Coptic Christians in Jerusalem.[35] An added advantage of wandering the world's religious sites through the digital geographies of user-created media is the chance to interact, as did the remarkable commenters on Moretz's video, as we discussed earlier.

Resources for Expression and Synthesis: Place-Based Annotation and Curation Tools

Of course, "taking in" religious sites through immersion is just one way to study their historical, sociocultural and geophysical contexts via digital geographies. Vasudevan's definition of this concept and these latter, increasingly social, examples should make clear that sensory experiences are just one learning modality of the many available to us. Another relevant opportunity afforded by these new media spaces is for students to engage with them creatively: to bring something new into the digital world, thus extending the digital geography. What I find particularly valuable is the possibility of using place-based annotation tools and other curation software to help *students* become knowledgeable guides to the sites they study. From a media literacy education perspective, such a strategy corresponds to the practice of helping students become not only critical consumers of online media texts but also creators of them as well. From a religious education perspective, media creation of this kind can help students demonstrate integration of newfound contextual knowledge of religious sites with other subject-matter content from a course.

Let me close with two examples of the kind of creative work I have in mind. Both build on digital immersion experiences to enrich and extend the creators' experience of relevant religious sites and associated digital geographies. The first is an assignment[36] conceived by my colleague Shamika Goddard and contributed to a resource site for incorporating digital literacy instruction across the theological education curriculum.[37] Rather than write a traditional summative paper for her church history course, Goddard wanted to create a piece of media that would help her connect her history learning to the geography of the Reformation. She used Google Earth's annotation tools along with screen recording software to create a video that in most respects resembles an automatically advancing Google Lit Trip. Her work, and this comparison, is a testament to the fact that motivated students can create learning artifacts of the same kind and quality as instructors and even resource designers if their immersive learning experience is personally meaningful (see Figure 5.6).

The second example (Figure 5.7) is a pair of lower-tech artifacts from my own seminary experience. When I used Sacred Destinations to prepare for my Rome immersion course, I found myself frustrated with my inability to keep track of where each of the sites of our upcoming study were located. I created, and shared with my classmates, a Google Maps artifact simply pinpointing each site in the city. Upon revisiting my map more than six years later, I realized that if I were using it to study Roman sites today (either in person or from home), I would have included much more in my site annotations than a simple link to the relevant page on Sacred Destinations. Had I taken the class last semester, I might have shared some of my course reflections in site reviews, geotagged my Flickr photos of the trip and used my devices to access the official websites and unofficial ephemera that connect our physical sites of study to their associated digital geographies.

I have created a new learning artifact to make this speculation more concrete. It's a curated Flickr gallery of photos that illustrate some of the connected architectural and philosophical points that I wrote about in a final essay when I took the original course. The photographers I cited

Figure 5.6 Screenshot of "Mapping the Reformation—From Luther to Junker Jörg"[38]

"Seeing" the Sacred Landscape   71

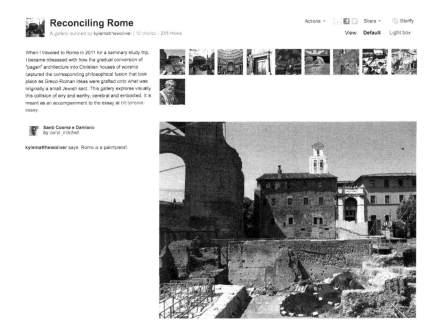

Figure 5.7 Screenshot of Reconciling Rome Gallery on Flickr (Full-Screen View on Desktop)[40]

will receive notification that their images have been included in a new gallery, and they may see my annotations and even the link to the essay. But of course, the main point is that constructing the artifact helped *me* learn. Both this activity and reviewing my original map reconnected me with and deepened the contextual knowledge of early Christianity that I developed in my studies and that has lain mostly dormant in the intervening years.[39] As an educator, what's appealing to me about these examples is that 2-D map annotation and photo gallery curation are simple technical tasks that nevertheless make visible a student's analytical and synthetic thinking. Not everyone will want to learn the skills necessary to create an artifact similar to Goddard's video. But the bar is much lower for these latter tasks—it's not unreasonable to expect *any* religious education student to engage their contextual learning through these kinds of creative means.

Whether an instructor fully embraces this "new culture of learning"[41] to the extent that it shapes not only in-class activities but also assignments and assessments as Goddard and I have envisioned, I hope I have made the case that digital geographies should have some place in *any* study of important sites in the religious education classroom. On a purely human level, these destinations are too beautiful and too resonant for us not to help our students see them. And on the pedagogical level, these landscapes embody powerful contextual knowledge that can make the difference in how our students understand world religions—their own and others'. The world is too divided and too violent a place not to do everything we can to create learning experiences that engender empathy and a desire for deep and humane understanding. In other words, to *show* my students Jerusalem is to heed the Psalmist's plea to pray for its peace.

Notes

1 Charles R. Foster et al., *Educating Clergy: Teaching Practices and Pastoral Imagination* (San Francisco: Jossey-Bass, 2005), 127–155.
2 Ibid., 127.
3 Wil Gafney, "Race Matters: Biblical Representations in the Seminary Classroom," *Wabash Center Blogs: Race Matters in the Classroom*, August 27, 2015, http://wabashcenter.typepad.com/antiracism_pedagogy/2015/08/race-matters-in-the-classroom.html.
4 Ibid.
5 Robert L. Kelly, "Suggestions for Standardization and Supervision," *Religious Education* 13, no. 5 (1918): 358.
6 See Stephen Prothero, *Religious Literacy: What Every American Needs to Know And Doesn't* (New York: HarperCollins e-books, 2009).
7 Mary E. Hess, "Playing Our Way into Complex Adaptive Action in Religious Education" (presentation, Religious Education Association Annual Meeting, Pittsburgh, November 4–6, 2016, www.religiouseducation.net/papers/rea2016-hess.pdf), 1.
8 See Mary E. Hess, "Designing Curricular Approaches for Interfaith Competency," in *Teaching for a Multifaith World*, ed. Eleasar S. Fernandez (Eugene, OR: Pickwick, 2017), 34–55.
9 Lalitha Vasudevan, "Education Remix: New Media, Literacies, and the Emerging Digital Geographies," *Digital Culture & Education* 2, no. 1 (2010): 62.
10 Ibid.
11 Ibid., 65.
12 Kevin M. Leander and Lalitha Vasudevan, "Multimodality and Mobile Culture," in *The Routledge Handbook of Multimodal Analysis*, ed. Carey Jewitt (New York: Routledge, 2009), 134–136.
13 Hess, *Engaging Technology*, 2. See also Elizabeth Drescher, *Tweet If You ♥ Jesus* (New York: Church Publishing, 2011), especially 34–54.
14 Katharine Flexer, Facebook photo posts from Israel/Palestine visible to Flexer's friends, May 13–17, 2017.
15 Ibid. Shared by permission of the photographer.
16 Matthew Zook et al., "New Digital Geographies: Information, Communication, and Place," in *Geography and Technology*, eds. Stanley D. Brunn, Susan L. Cutter, and J. W. Harrington Jr. (New York: Springer, 2004), 155–156.
17 Vasudevan, "Education Remix," 66.
18 Gafney, "Race Matters."

19 Matthew Moretz, *Father Matthew Presents the Stations of the Cross (Part One)*, YouTube video, 8:03, May 11, 2010, www.youtube.com/watch?v=j_ ol1VWqC7M; Matthew Moretz, *Father Matthew Presents the Stations of the Cross (Part Two)*, YouTube video, 8:27, May 24, 2010, www.youtube.com/watch?v=4px48zXLxsg.
20 Vasudevan, "Education Remix," 68.
21 sanjoy sen, n.d., comment on Moretz, *Stations (Part Two)*.
22 Vasudevan, "Education Remix," 63.
23 Kyle Matthew Oliver, *Seeing the Sacred Landscape*, Pinterest board, July 31, 2017, www.pinterest.com/kyleoliver/seeing-the-sacred-landscape/.
24 Google for Education, *Google Expeditions*, website and mobile app, accessed July 31, 2017, https://edu.google.com/expeditions/.
25 Ibid.
26 For example, there are more birds than people depicted in the tour I took of Swaminarayan Akshardham. This "after hours" feel made it possible to focus on the architectural highlights, but it also undercut the sense of being immersed in a lively site of contemporary Hindu worship.
27 Ercan Gigi, *Sites in 3D[/VR]*, website and mobile apps, accessed August 1, 2017, www.3dmekanlar.com/sites.html.
28 Jerome Burg, *Google Lit Trips*, website and downloadable Google Earth-compatible media, accessed August 2, 2017, www.googlelittrips.org/.
29 Kaur Aare Saar, *Angkor Wat*, user-contributed Google Street View 360-degree photo, https://goo.gl/maps/jS83hqstm1M2.
30 Holly Hayes, *Sacred Destinations*, website with images, text and embedded maps, accessed August 2, 2017, www.sacred-destinations.com/.
31 Ibid.
32 Huib Schippers et al., *Smithsonian Folkways Recordings*, website with audio clips, accessed August 2, 2017, http://folkways.si.edu/.
33 The Met, *Jerusalem 1000–1400: Every People Under Heaven*, website with multimedia resources, accessed August 2, 2017, www.metmuseum.org/exhibitions/listings/2016/jerusalem.
34 Say a prayer that SoundCloud survives its recent financial woes. It really is a gem.
35 Links available on the Pinterest board.
36 Shamika Goddard, *Mapping the Reformation*, web page with YouTube videos and documents, accessed August 2, 2017, http://digitalliteracytoolkit.org/faculty/portfolio-item/mapping-reformation/.
37 Kyle Matthew Oliver et al., *Digital Literacy Toolkit for Theological Educators*, website with downloadable resources, accessed August 2, 2017, http://digitalliteracytoolkit.org/faculty/. For background see Kyle Matthew Oliver et al., "Digital Media for Ministry Asset Mapping: An Exploratory Study in Theological Education" (presentation, Religious Education Association Annual Meeting, Pittsburgh, PA, November 4–6, 2016, https://religiouseducation.net/papers/rea2016-oliver1.pdf).
38 Goddard, *Mapping the Reformation*.
39 For those who are interested, I have made the artifacts available at http://bit.ly/rome-map, http://bit.ly/rome-gallery and http://bit.ly/rome-essay.
40 Kyle Matthew Oliver, *Reconciling Rome*, Flickr photo gallery, accessed August 3, 2017, www.flickr.com/photos/kyleoliver/galleries/72157684461650451/. The large photo pictured is by daryl_mitchell, published under a Creative Commons Attribution-ShareAlike license (see https://creativecommons.org/licenses/by-sa/2.0/).
41 See Mary E. Hess, "A New Culture of Learning: Digital Storytelling and Faith Formation," *Dialog: A Journal of Theology* 53, no. 1 (2014), 15.

Bibliography

Burg, Jerome. *Google Lit Trips*. Website and downloadable Google Earth-compatible media. Accessed August 2, 2017. www.googlelittrips.org/.

Drescher, Elizabeth. *Tweet If You ♥ Jesus: Practicing Church in the Digital Reformation*. New York: Church Publishing, 2011.

Foster, Charles R., Lisa Dahill, Larry Golemon, and Barbara Wang Tolentino. *Educating Clergy: Teaching Practices and Pastoral Imagination*. San Francisco: Jossey-Bass, 2005.

Gafney, Wil. "Race Matters: Biblical Representations in the Seminary Classroom." *Wabash Center Blogs: Race Matters in the Classroom*. August 27, 2015. http://wabashcenter.typepad.com/antiracism_pedagogy/2015/08/race-matters-in-the-classroom.html.

Gigi, Ercan. *Sites in 3D[/VR]*. Website [and mobile app]. Accessed August 1, 2017. www.3dmekanlar.com/sites.html.

Google for Education. *Google Expeditions*. Website and mobile app. Accessed July 31, 2017. https://edu.google.com/expeditions/.

Hayes, Holly. *Sacred Destinations*. Website with images, text, and embedded maps. Accessed August 2, 2017. www.sacred-destinations.com/.

Hess, Mary E. "Designing Curricular Approaches for Interfaith Competency." In *Teaching for a Multifaith World*, edited by Eleasar S. Fernandez, 34–55. Eugene, OR: Pickwick, 2017.

———. *Engaging Technology in Theological Education: All That We Can't Leave Behind*. Lanham, MD: Rowman & Littlefield, 2005.

———. "A New Culture of Learning: Digital Storytelling and Faith Formation." *Dialog: A Journal of Theology* 53, no. 1 (2014): 12–22.

———. "Playing Our Way into Complex Adaptive Action in Religious Education." Presentation at the Religious Education Association Annual Meeting, Pittsburgh, November 4–6, 2016. www.religiouseducation.net/papers/rea2016-hess.pdf.

Kelly, Robert L. "Suggestions for Standardization and Supervision." *Religious Education* 13, no. 5 (1918): 356–363.

Leander, Kevin M., and Lalitha Vasudevan. "Multimodality and Mobile Culture." In *The Routledge Handbook of Multimodal Analysis*, edited by Carey Jewitt, 127–139. New York: Routledge, 2009.

The Met. *Jerusalem 1000–1400: Every People Under Heaven*. Website with multimedia resources. Accessed August 2, 2017. www.metmuseum.org/exhibitions/listings/2016/jerusalem.

Moretz, Matthew. *Father Matthew Presents the Stations of the Cross (Part One)*. YouTube video, 8:03. May 11, 2010. www.youtube.com/watch?v=j_ol1VWqC7M.

———. *Father Matthew Presents the Stations of the Cross (Part Two)*. YouTube video, 8:27. May 24, 2010. www.youtube.com/watch?v=4px48zXLxsg.

Oliver, Kyle Matthew. *Reconciling Rome*. Flickr photo gallery. Accessed August 3, 2017. www.flickr.com/photos/kyleoliver/galleries/72157684461650451/.

———. *Seeing the Sacred Landscape*. Pinterest board. Accessed July 31, 2017. www.pinterest.com/kyleoliver/seeing-the-sacred-landscape/.

Oliver, Kyle Matthew, Elisabeth M. Kimball, Stacy Williams-Duncan, and Isabella Blanchard. "Digital Media for Ministry Asset Mapping: An Exploratory

Study in Theological Education." Presentation at the Religious Education Association Annual Meeting, Pittsburgh, PA, November 4–6, 2016. https://religiouseducation.net/papers/rea2016-oliver1.pdf.

Oliver, Kyle Matthew, Stacy Williams-Duncan, Elisabeth M. Kimball, and Sarah Stonesifer. *Digital Literacy Toolkit for Theological Educators*. Website with downloadable resources. Accessed August 2, 2017. http://digitalliteracytoolkit.org/faculty/.

Prothero, Stephen. *Religious Literacy: What Every American Needs to Know–And Doesn't*. New York: HarperCollins e-books, 2009.

Schippers, Huib, et al. *Smithsonian Folkways Recordings*. Website with audio clips. Accessed August 2, 2017. http://folkways.si.edu/.

Vasudevan, Lalitha. "Education Remix: New Media, Literacies, and the Emerging Digital Geographies." *Digital Culture & Education* 2, no. 1 (2010): 62–82.

Zook, Matthew, Martin Dodge, Yuko Aoyama, and Anthony Townsend. "New Digital Geographies: Information, Communication, and Place." In *Geography and Technology*, edited by Stanley D. Brunn, Susan L. Cutter, and J. W. Harrington Jr., 155–176. New York: Springer, 2004.

Part II
Leveraging Technology in and out of the Classroom

6 "If You'll Tweet Along With Me"

Effectively Using Social Media in Religious Education

Rob O'Lynn

Learn This First: *All Social Media Is Relational*

By nature, I am a communicator, a preacher to be specific. As such, my life centers on sending and receiving messages. One way I do this is through social media. Since social media is a form of communication, we will begin with a summation of the theory of media as espoused by Marshall McLuhan. Whether we realize it or not, all communicators have been influenced by McLuhan's theory, encapsulated in the maxim "the medium is the message."[1] As McLuhan writes, "The 'message' of any medium or technology is the change of scale or pace or pattern that it introduces into human affairs."[2] To McLuhan, the way a message is communicated is potentially of more value than the message itself because the medium is what gives the message its context *and* content. Therefore, knowing *how* we communicate is as essential, if not more so, than *what* we communicate. If you do not believe this, just think back to the last misunderstanding you had over an e-mail or text message.

McLuhan believed that miscommunication often occurred not only because the content was mishandled but also because an ineffective system of delivery was used. Meaning can be derived from any medium logically and rationally if the sender has properly packaged his or her content and delivered it in an effective way.[3] Thus McLuhan crafted his concepts of "hot" and "cold" media to challenge communicators to be more intentional in how they communicate meaning. For McLuhan, *hot media* is media that "extends one single sense in 'high definition,'" meaning the receiver achieves a "state of being well filled with data" with low participation.[4] He says "low participation" because the receiver needs to work little in order to arrive at a meaning. McLuhan uses an example of a photograph for *hot media* because a photograph contains a significant amount of data. It captures a moment of time in its immediate context and can be logically understood with only the smallest amount of detail. In terms of social media, an example of *hot media* would be a post on Instagram. Regardless of what has been posted, the image has both content and context, and, therefore, has meaning.

Cool media, then, is exactly the opposite; it extends one sense (or multiple senses) in "low definition" and requires "high participation" in order to achieve meaning.[5] In short, it takes a lot of work on the part of the receiver to ascertain meaning. McLuhan uses a phone call as an example because when a person is speaking on the phone only the ear is engaged and only at an inferior level. Emotion in the voice, facial expressions and even posture are missing, and these factors normally communicate a great deal. In terms of social media, an example would be a "thin" tweet (this will be discussed in more detail next). After reading a few words from a friend in a newsfeed, we wonder what the friend means. There is simply not enough data available to understand the message fully, and thus we engage more intently than is necessary because we misinterpret the wispy comment or we scroll on rather than engage in a potentially needed conversation. It is important, then, that as we continue to integrate social media into the teaching practice, we focus on integrating "hot" approaches to media rather than "cold" approaches.

Digital Citizens and Tribal Leaders

When it comes to engaging social media in higher education, including religious education, there is a similar concept: *digital citizenship*. According to the Digital Citizenship website, *digital citizenship* is "a concept which helps teachers, technology leaders and parents to understand what students/children/technology users should know to use technology appropriately."[6] Digital citizenship consists of "the norms of appropriate, responsible technological use."[7] Inherent in this concept are two intertwined ideas: the idea of what defines a digital citizen and the idea of how a digital citizen functions. Understanding how these concepts operate interdependently will help us establish a concept of not only "digital citizenship" but also of pedagogical effectiveness in regards to social media and higher religious education.

As both creators and users operating simultaneously, the web is in a constant state of evolutionary development. There are, however, some basic concepts that are generally agreed upon, including the following levels of citizenship:

- "Digital natives" are people who use technology fluidly. They embrace new applications and operate with a sense of responsibility and stewardship. Although their ability to work fluidly is often confused with being antisocial, they demonstrate how technology can be effectively integrated into people's lives. Digital natives believe that social media is *relational* (it connects people and ideas).
- "Digital immigrants" are people who use technology although not fluidly. They have accepted that we live in a wired world, but the use of technology does not come easy for them. They are willing to learn

and do make valuable contributions to the technology world. Digital immigrants believe that social media is *functional* (it allows people to work smarter).

- "Digital aliens" are people who do not use technology unless it is absolutely necessary (i.e., e-mail for work, text messaging with only select people). Opinions range from isolationist (if we ignore Facebook it will go away) to apocalyptic (didn't we learn anything from Huxley and Orwell?). Digital aliens believe that social media is *divisive* (it isolates and segregates people).[8]

A person does not have to remain in the second or third levels of digital citizenship. It is possible to move out of the *alien* category to the *immigrant* or *native* category, although it will require some "reprogramming." However, it should be understood that this first concept—*digital citizenship*—is mostly functional and focuses more on the user's understanding and use of the actual technology rather than how he or she behaves in the digital world.

The second concept—how a digital citizen functions—is more operational and practical. Most media scholars refer to this as "netiquette."[9] There are, however, three aspects of functioning that we can address here. First, social media users seek to be *relational*. Despite refrigerator magnets that say selfies are a good way to let everyone know that you are alone, we post pictures of ourselves working out, getting ready for a function or even preparing to work on an essay about using social media in higher education to share with our digital communities. We hope to make a connection and engage with another person. Second, social media users seek to be *generous*. Michael Hyatt solidified this aspect as one of the defining components of digital citizenship through the formulation of his "platform" concept. Responsible social media users recognize that they have something to share and are willing to share it.[10] When I attend a conference, I often live-tweet so that those not in attendance can benefit from what I am learning. Also, when I read, I often share quotes both to encourage conversation about what I am reading and to introduce that book or article to my larger audience. Third, social media users seek to be *influential*. As one of the professors in my doctoral program reminded us, we are seeking to expand our influence, not our image. We have the potential for drawing an audience from every corner of the globe through social media and, therefore, must use our powers for doing good.

This leads me to one final idea before moving on to briefly discussing the conceptual framework for this chapter—the idea of *tribal leadership*. Seth Godin achieved a significant amount of popularity a few years ago by talking about this concept in his book *Tribes*.[11] Dave Logan and his associates at the University of Southern California, however, conceptualized the idea after spending ten years studying an emerging approach to leadership that they would later coin as "tribal leadership."[12]

When my son was playing youth soccer, I noticed that one team stayed together each season. This group of kids always played for the same coach. Eventually, they even had warm-up suits. So being the curious soul that I am, I asked some of the parents why they kept their kids with the same coach. Their answer was at the heart of *tribal leadership*: he had created a culture of fun and excellence that honored and supported the talent level of the kids on the team. The team's ethic was, "Have fun, work hard and be respectful." Did they always win? No. However, this volunteer YMCA soccer coach had successfully created a tribe that others wanted to be part of. This coach was relational, generous and influential, and, as a result, he built a tribe. His effort was small, yet it was effective, and it teaches us some basic principles about education.

In terms of social media, *tribal leadership* relates to our followers. As of this writing, I have about 750 followers on Twitter. While some of these are "bot accounts" (accounts that simply purchase "follows" in hopes that those followed will follow back and boost the bot account's numbers), many of my followers are students at the university where I teach, religious leaders and professional educators. Based on my experience, these persons have followed me because they like what I have to say in terms of teaching, ministry, spiritual formation or social media usage, and they enjoy the conversations we engage in regarding these topics.

Practical Applications

For the remainder of this chapter, we will look at several social media applications that can be used in higher religious education. Each section will include a brief introduction to the application, some considerations to keep in mind when using the application and an example or two that how the application can be used in teaching.[13]

Facebook

At the time of this writing, Facebook is the third most accessed website among users in both the United States and the world. Originally launched in February 2004, the purpose of Facebook is to provide networking between users. The original purpose was to connect college students at Harvard University and Stanford University with one another (think an early version of LinkedIn). However, it quickly expanded to the global village to the point that it is the most widely used social networking site in the world (and even had a movie made about its inception). Nearly two billion users are connected to Facebook, and the number grows each day. And although the function of Facebook is evolving from a place to upload posts about what you are eating for lunch and to play games like Farm Story or Candy Crush to a source of news, weather and sports (not to mention event invites) that now rivals Google, the purpose of Facebook is still very much about connecting people to one another.

Facebook does have a few restrictions in terms of length of posts, the size of a photo or GIF that can be uploaded, yet it offers several useful features. One of the more popular applications in Facebook is the group application, which allows a user to establish a closed group where only invited users can join and participate. The theater where my daughter and I perform uses groups for each show to communicate important information such as rehearsal details, costume ideas and even videos of dance numbers.

The group application also works well with students. You can set up closed groups easily, invite students to join (obviously, they must be Facebook users prior to being invited) and establish a semester-long discussion among the students. For example, assign each student to facilitate a conversation topic each week through the closed group. The student must search for a suitable article and post it in the closed group so the other students can reply to it. It works similarly to a discussion forum in your learning management system, but will have a more informal feel because of the social media context.

Twitter

Twitter has become so ingrained in Western culture that "tweeting" has become synonymous with posting updates. News programs often run tweets 24 hours a day, and many entertainment outlets will often connect celebrities with fans through "Twitter takeovers" where fans can ask questions and get actual responses from the celebrities. According to Alexa.com, Twitter holds a consistent eighth place on its popular usage scale both in the United States and in the world. The original purpose of Twitter was to be a resource exchange where news and research could be posted and disseminated quickly. Launched in 2006, it has morphed into a true social media outlet where the exchange of ideas prompts conversation almost instantly. Its popularity and influence has grown exponentially, both positively and negatively among its 319 million users, as users continue to wrestle with what it means to be "relational," "generous" and "influential."

When it comes to engaging users with Twitter, knowing how to tweet is key. There are three basic kinds of tweets: "thick," "thin" and "throwaway." "Thick" tweets contain some form of discussion prompt (i.e., "read this" or "ICYMI" (in case you missed it) or a question) and a link to a website. This, then, segues to the actual media under consideration. This is what I have found most popular among my students, as they will tweet me articles or videos and engage in a conversation with me about the material (no links or open-ended questions to prompt discussion). "Thin" tweets contain some form of content, although that content is locked within the tweet. Examples of "thin" tweets are quotes from books we are reading or from speeches we are listening to (aka, "live-tweeting") or those philosophical musings that are ubiquitous with Twitter. "Throwaway" tweets are posts such as status updates (such as when I post something silly my daughter says, when I comment about a movie that I enjoyed or when I air a frustration I have with my former cable provider) and serve to remind us that even the most enlightened user is, after all, human.

In addition to the actual process of tweeting, there are two other avenues for engaging students through this social media application. The first avenue is the Twitter poll. Polls are easy to construct and will show up on any news feed that follows you. Using a hashtag, such as a course number (i.e., CMP 404 or BNT 235) will alert Twitter's internal algorithm to push it to users who are also using that same hashtag. Recently, I used a Twitter poll in a sermon to gauge my congregation's understanding of the doctrinal topic we discussed that morning. A similar approach could be used in a systematic theology, ethics or evangelism course. The second avenue is the thread, what David Congdon (@dwcongdon) calls #TwitterSeminary. The thread idea works by the author constructing a discussion in about 40 tweets and posting the tweets in numerical order in a fairly quick fashion. This allows other users to read along as the posts come and respond as appropriate. An instructor could assign this in place of a research paper, which compels a student to communicate fully the argument for a particular position in no more than 650 words (the average tweet is 16 *words*). The advantage is that any topic can be discussed in a thread. The challenge is articulating well in such a limited capacity.

Instagram

Originally devised as a photo and video-sharing app for Apple, Instagram was launched in 2010 and mainlined for other platforms in 2012. Although "selfies" were already popular before the advent of Instagram, this server turned any iPhone or Android user into a professional photographer overnight. With its collection of filters and editing lenses, Instagram has almost single-handedly made traditional cameras obsolete. According to Alexa.com, it is the fourteenth most popular website in the United States and the eighteenth most popular website in the world. Through a combination of geotags (location markers) and hashtags, users can search for similar posts with just a word or two. Additionally, users can upload one-minute videos to Instagram with a level of quality that is significantly better than either Facebook or Twitter. Although it is solely a mobile site when it comes to posting "grams," Instagram does have a searchable desktop site.

One of my favorite exercises using Instagram is to have students track their reading for online courses. For example, in a course on spiritual formation, I ask students to take photos of their course reading (both from the Bible and from textbooks) and post the picture with the course hashtag and comments about what they are connecting to or struggling with in the reading. I assign points based on the frequency and quality of their posts. This same assignment can also be used to track attendance in that so many posts equal so many attendance points or simply being present for the course for that week.

Snapchat

The running joke in the tech world is that the applications that we have previously discussed have become generational. To be honest, there is some truth to this. Each year, I teach at a youth conference hosted by my university, and when I ask participants what applications they use, I find fewer and fewer hands going up for Facebook and Twitter, and more and more hands going up for Instagram and Snapchat. Launched initially in 2011 as Picaboo and only for iPhone users, Snapchat has become *the* younger Millennial social media application, allowing users to share person-to-person videos or photos called "snaps." Although Snapchat's temporary and self-deleting nature has given rise to concerns of encouraging frivolous and illicit behavior, most studies indicate that users' posts have embraced a simple, fun and fairly clean (as long as you consider poop emojis clean) protocol for the app. In some ways, it is Facebook all over again, just aimed at a much younger (and, granted, more impressionable) clientele. According to Alexa.com, Snapchat does not yet rank in the top 50 United States websites on Alexa.com. However, over 165 million global users are using Snapchat on a daily basis, and it is a pretty good guess that some of them are our students.

Two of the immediate issues with using Snapchat in the educational context are the need for direct connections and the temporary nature of the "snap." Followers can see a "snap" only when it is directly sent to them, unless the user adds it to his or her "story," which all followers have access to. Additionally, these posts are temporary and can generally only be replayed once unless the follower takes a screen shot of it. In short, my son referred to Snapchat as "private Instagram." Despite these limitations to the application, Snapchat can be used in the higher-education context. In my evangelism course, I ask my students to craft a two-minute testimony to share with the class for feedback. Rather than sharing it in person, students can "snap" an abbreviated version of their testimony for their followers. Additionally, as part of the Integration of Faith and Learning initiative at my university, I ask new faculty to create thirty-second videos explaining how they practice integrating faith and learning. Similar short-lived assignments can be constructed and shared through Snapchat given that the concerns mentioned earlier are addressed in advance.

Wikipedia

Most people do not consider Wikipedia a social media site because it is a free online encyclopedia. However, because its content is user driven and open-source, it is very much a form of social media. Launched in 2001, the initial purpose of Wikipedia (then called Nupedia) was to provide free information to online users. Content was supposed to be written by experts and submitted for a formal review process. However, Wikipedia quickly embraced a free and open policy that allows any user to write about any subject, regardless of whether that content is accurate. An oft-cited example to the downside of this open policy is known as the "Seigenthaler incident," where an anonymous editor altered information about journalist John Seigenthaler to insinuate that he had been involved in the assassination of President Kennedy.[14] Despite its flaws, Wikipedia attempts to portray accurate and relevant information, and has evolved as the Internet has evolved, currently ranking seventh in the United States and fifth globally on Alexa.com.

An example of how to use Wikipedia in the classroom is a fun little game that one of my colleagues uses to show how we are all connected through technology. The point of the game is to see how fast one can get to the entry for God by using Wikipedia. With a subject like "Iran," it is actually as fast as three clicks: (1) type "Iran" in the search bar, (2) click on "Christianity" under Iran's recognized religions and (3) click on "God" under theology. Another more interactive example includes having students build a wiki page. In a course on the Pentateuch, I required students to join work groups and construct a wiki page on one of the first five books in the Hebrew Bible. Students were required to choose a content section, such as author, date, themes or bibliography; draft a wiki page with help from their group; and then present the page in class. Another example is to have students verify the content and citations on a featured article on Wikipedia. It is common for the phrase "citation needed" to appear in a Wikipedia article. Find some of those and challenge the students to determine the original reference through online research.

Pinterest/Evernote

Although Pinterest was not initially designed to be a social media site, it has certainly become one, thus confirming the *social* side of social media ("all social media is relational"). The purpose behind Pinterest, initially, was to provide users a way of cataloging ideas and interests in order to encourage them to actively pursue those interests. The app provides users a personalized way of storing ideas that is based completely on their interest. My wife's Pinterest account, for example, has several categories, such as various travel plans, home décor ideas, special meals and recipes and artwork that has inspired her to paint her own pictures. Officially launched as an iOS-compatible-only application in 2011, Pinterest has quickly grown in popularity, at least in the United States, as it is twenty-second on Alexa.com.

There are many options for using Pinterest in the classroom. Students in a course on religious history could create an art board where they "pin" pieces of art that reflect the perspectives of a particular religion. Whether it be icons, tapestries, portraits or sculptures, these images could be cataloged for discussion, helping students see how engagement with faith is demonstrated through visual art. Another example comes from a course on evangelism. In class, I use a book that includes several recipe ideas in which the ingredients or the dish itself communicate basic tenants of the Christian tradition. In a world religions class, students could use Pinterest to create a recipe group page for sharing "faith-based" recipes in which the ingredients or the dish itself represents something related to that religion. Ideas include recipes for a traditional Passover meal, a dish for celebrating the end of Ramadan or a comparison of traditional American and Chinese New Year meals.

In many ways, Pinterest and Evernote are quite similar in that neither site was initially designed to be a social media site. Both sites were designed to be cloud-based storage platforms. Evernote is basically a digital note-taking app, a word-based version of Pinterest, although one can store pictures in Evernote. Although not nearly as popular as many of the other sites discussed here (it is currently around 350 on Alexa.com's popularity scale, and its popularity has dropped since it became a pay site), it is a site worth mentioning. Initially launched in 2008, it has become as ubiquitous as a Post-It note. There are certain notes that I make publicly accessible, primarily resource lists. A creative example might be to start a resource list on essential writings for a particular faith tradition. Start the list and share it as an open-source document, meaning those with Evernote can access and edit the file. Over the course of the semester, see how many resources the students add to the list and then provide the complete list at the end of the course.

YouTube/Vimeo

Posting videos has, in many ways, become a profession for many Millennials and young Gen Xers by way of selling ad space on a YouTube channel. Originally launched by three PayPal employees in 2005, YouTube is now the second most popular website *in the world* behind Google, according to Alexa.com. Today, it is *the* social media site. Users can post videos, comment on videos, create playlists or channels, and even broadcast through YouTube's ever-growing list of options. Videos can range from between just a few seconds to 600 hours. Mainstream and cable networks now rebroadcast their programming on YouTube, and some independent film companies use YouTube to distribute their programs freely to the general public. There is also a subscription version called YouTube Red, which offers ad-free programming.

The possibilities for using YouTube in the classroom are limited only by the user's imagination. In many of my preaching courses, students are required to preach before a live congregation. When I was a college and seminary student, I would take a cassette recorder with me to the church, record the sermon and then return the tape to my professor for evaluation. Today, I ask my students to film themselves preaching their sermons and upload them to either YouTube or Vimeo (I prefer Vimeo, which I will discuss next), and then share the link through either Twitter or Facebook. In one of my advanced preaching courses, I ask the students to create a media project, either a filmed testimony, a recreated Bible story or an original film that can be used as a video illustration for a sermon. Again, the video is uploaded and shared via a link on a social media site. Although my students almost always push back at the assignment, it has become a class favorite because it gets them involved in a type of creative production that is becoming more and more common in American worship services.

As I mentioned earlier, I prefer Vimeo over YouTube. Although it was actually founded sooner than YouTube (2004), it has lagged behind YouTube in popularity (it currently sits just near the bottom of Alexa.com's top-100 sites in the United States). However, it has four qualities that make it worth investigating. First, Vimeo offers higher video quality (it has been offering HD quality for nearly a decade), whereas YouTube's quality varies according to the videos that are uploaded. Second, it is ad free at all times. Third, and perhaps most importantly, the user maintains the copyright of the material. When a user uploads content to YouTube, the user gives the copyright to YouTube, which means YouTube can use it for its purposes without the user's permission. Finally, videos upload to Vimeo much faster than they do to YouTube. I would encourage teachers thinking of using a video site to consider these pros and cons when crafting assignments.

Tumblr

Blogging has been a staple component of the Internet almost since the advent of the Internet. With the publishing world becoming more and more saturated, writers seeking to get their content out quickly turned to early websites such as Blogger and now to sites such as WordPress as an outlet. And while the history and application of blogging is too great to discuss in this chapter, we will take just a moment to discuss one site that combines the social aspect of Facebook and Instagram with the verbiage of Blogger: Tumblr. Originally founded in 2007, Tumblr promotes itself as a "microblogging" site and currently ranks seventeenth in the United States and just in the top-50 globally on Alexa.com. Tumblr allows the user to post visual blogs, primarily through images that are meant to create ongoing stories (think still-frame films or animated comic book frames). Unlike Blogger or WordPress, examples of traditional text-driven blogs, Tumblr offers content that is more visual and seeks to generate "likes" for the material produced rather than comments for interaction.

Most professional education programs are moving more and more to portfolios, and Tumblr offers a great way to construct a visual portfolio with its evolving storytelling feature. This can be a helpful application for a fieldwork or field education course. Every semester, I supervise students working in congregational or parachurch organizations. They are expected to work alongside the resident ministry staff as a temporary but full-time ministry staff member. At the midpoint and endpoint of their fieldwork, students are required to write an extensive evaluation of their experience that includes examples of activities that demonstrate competency toward our department's five standards for professional development. Through Tumblr, students can post photos chronicling their various experiences, demonstrating how they have engaged their ministry context. Additionally, in this fieldwork course, I require weekly process notes where the students comment on their weekly activities. This could also be replaced with a weekly microblog on Tumblr, where photos are uploaded to demonstrate activity.[15]

Google+

Google is more than a search engine; it is a cultural icon. It would be safe to say that almost everyone knows what Google is. After all, it is the most used website in the world, according to Alexa.com. And since its launch in 1998, it has become much more than just a search engine. Whether using Gmail, YouTube (yes, it is owned by Google), Google Scholar, Google Maps, Google Books or any of a host of applications, a user can log into Google one time and complete countless tasks all within one seamless application.

While most people would not consider Google a form of social media, it certainly meets the relational criteria of all social media. The purpose of Google is to bring people together. I offer a couple of quick examples of using Google in the classroom as this chapter closes. First, assign a group presentation on a set of concepts that are central to the core content of the course. Have the students craft the presentation using Google Slides, and ask them to share the presentation with you. Second, as a version of the Evernote assignment mentioned earlier, construct a resource list in Google Docs. Last year, in my course on congregational administration, I required the students to build annotated bibliographies around several core subjects. The students worked in pairs through Google Docs and shared their doc with me prior to the presentation day. There are two immediate benefits here: (1) you can work with the students on crafting the presentation and (2) you can see who actually contributes to the group. Even if these presentations are not shared with the larger public, they fit the category of social media because they bring students together through media avenues.

Conclusion

In this chapter, we have discussed the value and meaning of social media and how to incorporate various avenues of social media into the higher religious education classroom. It is hoped that these examples will encourage the reader to experiment with the ones provided and seek out other ways of connecting students through social media. Social media is here to stay, as outlets such as Pew Research continue to detail.[16] Regardless of how you engage students, remember that *all social media is relational*![17]

Notes

1 Marshall McLuhan, *Understanding Media: The Extensions of Man*, 2nd ed. (Cambridge, MA: MIT Press, 1994), 7.
2 Ibid., 8.
3 Ibid., 16–20.
4 Ibid., 22.
5 Ibid., 23.
6 Mike Ribble, "Welcome to the Digital Citizenship Website," accessed May 29, 2017, www.digitalcitizenship.net/Home_Page.php.
7 Ibid.
8 Rob O'Lynn, "Social Media and Preaching: A Primer," accessed May 29, 2017, www.workingpreacher.org/craft.aspx?m=4377&post=3267.
9 For more on the topic of "netiquette," I would refer the reader to the Digital Citizenship (www.digitalcitizenship.net) or Commonsense Media (www.commonsensemedia.org) websites for more on this topic.
10 Michael Hyatt, *Platform: Get Noticed in a Noisy World* (Nashville: Thomas Nelson, 2012), 129.
11 Seth Godin, *Tribes: We Need You to Lead Us* (New York: Portfolio/Penguin, 2008).
12 Dave Logan, John King, and Halee Fischer-Wright, *Tribal Leadership: Leveraging Natural Groups to Build a Thriving Organization* (New York: Harper Business, 2008). This book was released in January 2008, while Godin's book *Tribe* was released in October 2008.
13 All of the rankings reported in this section are according to tracking provided by Alexa.com, accessed May 29, 2017, www.alexa.com/topsites.
14 Katherine Q. Seelye, "Snared in the Web of a Wikipedia Liar," *The New York Times*, December 4, 2005, accessed July 3, 2017, www.nytimes.com/2005/12/04/weekinreview/snared-in-the-web-of-a-wikipedia-liar.html.

15 For more on a digital portfolio through Tumblr, see Aaron J. Moore, "Communicating Experiential Learning Through an Online Portfolio in Tumblr," in *The Plugged-In Professor: Tips and Techniques for Teaching with Social Media*, eds. Sharmila P. Ferris and Hilary A. Wilder, Chandos Social Media Series (Oxford: Chandos Press, 2013), 201–210.
16 Pew Research Center, "Social Media Fact Sheet," January 12, 2017, accessed July 4, 2017, www.pewinternet.org/fact-sheet/social-media.
17 As the discussion continues about how to use social media in teaching, never forget the resource that is right in front of you—your institutional learning management system. Many of the applications discussed in this chapter, such as group discussions and Wiki articles, are likely available as plug-ins through a course shell.

7 Social Media in Higher-Ed Religion Studies

Brooke Lester

One instructor wages a war of inches against the distractions by which social media allures her students from the sanctuary of the classroom, while another burbles enthusiastically about the Twitter thread erupting around that day's lecture. To one instructor, it is self-evident that real community takes shape only where bodies are physically present with each other, while another instructor testifies that her adolescent isolation ended with discovery of a "dot-sci" newsgroup about evolution in 1993. Educators yet on the near side of this experience gap will naturally have questions concerning social media's affordances and dangers for learning and formation.

Formation, Community and Social Media in Religion and Theology

Formation is always an aspect of education alongside learning. If "learning" involves the development of knowledge, skills and enduring understandings,[1] then "formation" involves the development of such attitudes, values, behaviors and sense of purpose as are purported to characterize a community that the learner is to understand as representing the subject matter, discipline or field at hand. Participating in a community's educational processes, the learner is transformed toward embodiment of that community's worldview and norms.

Even prior to such considerations of a learner's formation in relation to a community, learning itself is already irreducibly transformative and social. Put another way, "learning" is not a bare acquisition of knowledge and skills that waits for "formation" to come along and effect real change in the learner. A biblical studies student may acquire knowledge of the content and likely historical settings of Proverbs and Ecclesiastes, but once she earns the *enduring understanding* that the Bible comprises disparate theological perspectives, she is already transformed—even before being *formed* into the ways that any community might reckon with this insight.[2] While a "banking," "mechanistic" or "cognitive" model of learning sees knowledge as something acquired by the learner from an expert,[3] a constructionist (or constructivist) approach, whereby learners forge knowledge by synthesizing prior understandings with new discoveries, already presumes the transformation of the learner in the process of generating knowledge.[4] Further, constructionism argues that such knowledge making "happens especially felicitously" where the learning happens socially and toward the building of publicly shared artifacts.[5] The construction of knowledge is already itself a process of transformation dependent on community.

Community can denote geographic proximity, but in educational terms, it more often denotes a shared topic of interest (a community of interest or of inquiry),[6] or in the sense of "communion," it entails a "profound meeting or encounter"[7] with other persons or with a transcendent reality. Instructors of religion and theology frequently describe their efforts to facilitate the development of communities of inquiry and of profound encounter. While the concept of "community" can be so idealized as to seem ineffable, one may helpfully break it down to such more measurable constituent parts as acceptance, reciprocity and trustworthiness. Here "acceptance" denotes openness to others, curiosity and welcome. "Reciprocity" refers to a sense of confidence that as I give to the group, the group will give also to me, albeit "over the long haul" rather than through immediate quid pro quo. "Trustworthiness" means confidence that the community's people and institutions will "act in a consistent, honest, and appropriate way."[8]

The value of social media for higher religious and theological education, then, will depend on how these various media provide opportunity for learners to thrive in transformative communities that promote acceptance, reciprocity and trustworthiness.

What Are Social Media?

Social media can be understood as those online media that involve user-generated content, are organized around service-specific user profiles and facilitate the development of social networks larger than any one service.[9] Additionally, social media are *social*, presupposing interactivity rather than mere unidirectional broadcasting. The broadcasting model of Internet content-generation is often referred to as *Web 1.0* and the interactive model of social media as *Web 2.0*.

Social media involve user-generated content, rather than owner-generated content. *New York Times* columns are generated by the *New York Times* and its paid writers. Social media content is generated by users who are not owners of the service nor its employees or contractors; indeed, users likely pay to assume the role of content creator, whether directly through fees or indirectly by agreeing to be served advertisements or surrender valuable personal data. It is sometimes estimated that 90 percent of Internet users only consume content, with 9 percent of users interacting with content (as via comments) and only 1 percent creating content.[10] Social media provide learners the opportunity to become, through the social and artifact-building aspects of the learning process, among those few who decide what the Internet will be.

Social media are organized around service-specific user profiles. To blog using WordPress.com, one needs a WordPress.com account and a user profile, or "bio." To upload videos to YouTube, one requires a YouTube account, providing a user-specific "channel" on which to post one's content. A user may have half-a-dozen (or more), service-specific user profiles and enjoy the corresponding freedom to align these profiles into one recognizable persona or keep each distinct. As learners undergo transformation in education, use of social media prompts them to negotiate and declare such identities as they choose.[11]

Social media facilitate the development of social networks that are larger than any one service. Not all users will avail themselves of the possibility; many of Facebook's billion-plus subscribers may never use any other social media. Yet a Facebook post may call attention to comments on a WordPress blog post. A Twitter user may include in his or her tweet a link to a Facebook status update. YouTube videos editorialize concerning discourse happening on Twitter. Though services may enforce certain kinds of closed borders, social media on the whole tends toward openness, posing challenges to educators and institutions accustomed to thinking of class-related interactions as nestled safely behind brick-and-mortar walls or the password-protected confines of a learning management system (LMS).

Social media are social. Users who expect to be able to expound uninterrupted from some unassailable platform are like Web 1.0 historical dinosaurs ponderously dotting the Web 2.0 landscape. The environment is designed for interaction, whether via hyperlinks, comments sections or @mentions ("at-mentions") and other forms of user notification. This willing surrender of total control over public discourse may trouble institutions, threatening carefully planned and centrally controlled "branding" in unpredictable ways: "What if our learners say things on social media that embarrass us? What if we receive criticism in our public social media conversations?" Educational institutions must determine how the value of social media use justifies these unfamiliar risks.[12]

What Are the Services, and What Can We Do With Them?

Tools come and go, and for this reason, it is preferable to focus on principles and practices more than on particular tools or services.[13] That said, we can only envision principles and practices with regard to existing tools. So it makes sense to briefly describe currently available services. Things change rapidly, but information here is accurate up to August 2017.

Blogging is a form of short-to-long-form writing; 250–1,000 words is typical, but any length is possible. A comment section normally permits readers to react and respond, though this feature can be disabled. As the name (short for "web log") implies, posts are usually arranged by date, with most recent entries ordered at the top.

Microblogging is a form of very short writing: Twitter permits 140 characters (not words!), and most GNU Social and Mastodon communities permit 500–1,000 characters. In 2011, Facebook increased its limit from 500 to over 63,000 characters. Relationships on microblogging platforms may be symmetrical, as on Facebook (you and I must be "friends" with one another), or asymmetrical, as on Twitter (you may "follow" me, seeing what I tweet, even if I do not "follow" you). Such asymmetry of "following" provides users very high ability to manage their "feeds," or what they see. This is true to such a degree that what Twitter "is" is quite different for different users, so that one may speak of inhabiting "celebrity Twitter," "academic Twitter," "Black Twitter," "weird Twitter" and others.

Video sharing allows users to host audio-video content on services such as YouTube or Vimeo on a "channel" corresponding to the user's account. Each video has a unique web address, or URL, that may be shared so that others may view the video. Twitch is a live-streaming video service.

Photo sharing, as with, for example, Flickr or Instagram, functions largely like video sharing. Snapchat facilitates a different kind of photo sharing: short videos are shared much as one sends a text message, and then they are quickly made inaccessible to the recipient. Pinterest allows the sharing of collections of "found" images discovered on the Internet, not user-generated images.

Social bookmarking allows users to collect Internet bookmarks to their user profile and share collections of bookmarks with others. Bookmarks are "tagged" for convenient searching (user-created tags might include, for example, "Buddhism," "politics" or "Bible"). Delicious and Diigo are two popular social-bookmarking services.

Other forms of social media include social gaming (as afforded through real-time chat tools such as Discord), discussion forums (as, for example, with "Google Groups") and even product-review platforms as provided, for example, by Amazon.

Asynchrony, Openness and Anonymity

Learners and educators overwhelmed by the possibilities and the rapidity of change in social media might find it helpful to think about these services in terms of synchrony and asynchrony ("Are we there at the same time?"), openness and closedness ("How private or public is it?") and anonymity and onymity ("How identifiable are the people involved?").

Interactions on social media may be synchronous or asynchronous, but tend toward asynchrony. In a synchronous Twitter chat, participants use the service as a real-time "chat" platform, writing and responding to one another on some topic for, say, an hour on a given weekday evening.[14] Far more typically, Twitter (as also Facebook) is used for asynchronous exchanges in which one replies to another user's tweet perhaps long after he or she published it. Also asynchronous are comments to blog posts and online videos, and engagement with socially posted photographs and other art, as on Flickr. While instructors may relish the immediacy of real-time classroom discussion, asynchrony has its virtues. Learners often value the greater time to reflect, the ability to contribute "out of the spotlight" and the inability for a few extroverted or self-important participants to dominate the conversation.

YouTube videos may be public (visible to all and included in search results), unlisted (visible to anyone with its web address or "URL" but not included in the results of web searches) or private (visible to only a specified list of users). Blogs are typically visible to all but may be private to the author or to specified subscribers. Tweets on Twitter are visible to all by default, including people who do not themselves have Twitter accounts, whereas even public Facebook status updates are visible only to people who are currently logged in to a Facebook account. Both Twitter and Facebook allow direct messages between users, which are "private" within the bounds of the platform's terms of service.

"On the Internet, nobody knows you're a dog," goes a joke first published in 1993.[15] Educators and learners show reasonable concern that anonymity (and pseudonymity) on the Internet can provide a refuge for abusive behavior such as trolling (disrupting or derailing discourse for sport) or hate speech. At the same time, pseudonymity also protects persons who may suffer retribution "IRL" (in real life) for their Internet speech. Google and Facebook have both attempted to enforce "real name" policies for user accounts, though Google eventually relaxed its policy in the face of criticism.[16] Facebook continues to require users to use names that they could support with "an ID or document from [their] ID list."[17] Google's policy covers its blogging and video-hosting platforms (Blogger and YouTube), while other blogging and video-hosting services (such as WordPress and Vimeo, respectively) typically simply permit pseudonymity.

Given, then, these tools with their respective constraints and affordances, to what kinds of use may they be put in higher-ed religion and theology?

Social Media in Traditional and "Connected" Courses

Any instructional model can incorporate the use of social media. Course designs vary in terms of how strongly they emphasize the kind of peer-to-peer interaction for which social media suggest themselves. A face-to-face class may or may not incorporate use of a LMS such as Blackboard, Moodle, or Canvas; a traditional fully online or blended course is likely to depend on such a system. Insofar as the LMS attempts to extend or replicate the face-to-face classroom—closed, controlled and temporary—the face-to-face and online/blended classes are alike in that they may choose or not to take up the additional affordances of social media use for learning. Some learners and instructors will crave the security of the closed LMS, while others chafe at the artificiality of, say, the blogging or wiki features of the LMS, as well as the need for yet another log-in, preferring course-related interactions to happen "where they already are" on social media networks. Distinct from traditional face-to-face and online/blended learning environments, however, the "connected course" represents a remarkable evolution that is so dependent on social media for its structures that it merits attention in its own right.

Traditional Face-to-Face and Online/Blended Courses

For many, the traditional face-to-face class has little to do with social media. Perhaps an intrepid instructor here or there uses a Facebook group or a blog to keep learners up to date on course-related "housekeeping," but by and large, the learning goes on as in days before Web 2.0, or even before the web itself. Other instructors do use social media in face-to-face learning, both within the classroom itself and between sessions.

In the classroom, learners might be invited to take notes collaboratively on a shared Google Doc. During a "fishbowl" discussion, wherein learners rotate in and out of an "inner circle" of conversationists from an "outer circle" of listeners, the listening outer circle might be encouraged to sustain a "backchannel" of comments and questions on Twitter using an agreed-upon hashtag.[18] Students inclined to browse Facebook during class might be recruited to publish provocative or inquiring Facebook status updates on the topic at hand, reporting back to the class on any engagement. Instructors favoring a "flipped classroom," wherein learners accomplish reading and viewing (information "consumption") outside of class in order to spend more in-class time participating in meaning-making activities, might especially welcome the possibilities of social media for enhancing face-to-face activity.

Outside the shared block of synchronous brick-and-mortar time, instructors might ask learners to contribute to a unique Twitter hashtag—for example, offering each other real-time reactions in progress to an assigned book. Also between class sessions, learners might engage one another on a (private or public) Facebook Group or Google discussion forum. The use of social media "around" the face-to-face class can help learners engage the course material and one another periodically throughout the week, preventing the dread phenomenon whereby the subject matter is forgotten until a night-before cram session (if even then!).

For the online/blended class, all of the "between-sessions" activities described earlier for the face-to-face class are also, of course, available. Further, the online instructor likely already has practice transposing her favorite classroom activities into an online mode, probably using an LMS. For example, a debate between two teams may be organized such that learners inhabit two separate discussion forums for internal strategizing and upload statements and responses to one another into a shared LMS drop box. For this instructor, it will be an easily made imaginative leap to reorganize the debate using Google Plus "circles" and shared Google Docs or via Facebook Groups and Messenger. Student presentations find a natural home on YouTube, Vimeo or Twitch. If one likes learners to facilitate discussions, a Twitter chat is an excellent venue. Learners doing research might be encouraged to "crowdsource" their inquiries on social media—just as their professors do.[19] Whether it is think-pair-share activities, games or collaborative writing, either synchronous or asynchronous, once students are familiar with a handful of services, the imagination finds few barriers to novel solutions.

Connected Courses and Networked Learning

Whereas face-to-face and traditional online/blended courses may use social media to extend or spice up their basic frameworks, "connected courses" depend on social media for their very being. A website serves as a kind of hub or home base, and learner activities and interactions take place on blogs, Twitter, Google Groups, YouTube—or anywhere that the designers (or learners) decide.

In 2008, George Siemens and Stephen Downes organized an online course called "Connectivism and Connected Knowledge," or CCK08. Enrolling a cohort of tuition-paying students in the conventional way, the course was also open to an effectively unlimited number of outside participants. As its name suggests, the course sought to model "connectivism," an approach to learning building on constructivism to posit that, in the digital era, learners build knowledge on shared networks. Here and in its successor courses, including CCK09 and CCK11, the instructors developed a model wherein learners were provided the scaffolding on which to develop the networked communications on which the knowledge of the course would be built.[20] Dave Cormier, in conversation with Bryan Alexander, coined the term *MOOC* for the experiment, though the term would only capture the larger public imagination as applied to the rather different large-scale courses later offered by MIT and Harvard, and hosted on commercial platforms such as Coursera and Udacity.[21] Since that time, several "open courses" or "connected courses" have run, usually (but not always) with a subject matter related to education or learning. In these courses, an openly available website serves as a "hub" on which a program of activities can be published (or developed in real time by participants), blog posts indexed and social media conversations and artifacts aggregated. Learners participate in such courses by blogging on their own blogs, conversing via Twitter, curating and sharing collections of web bookmarks, sharing photographs via Flickr, doing digital storytelling on YouTube—the social media sky is the limit. As Cormier would eventually propose,[22] "The community is the curriculum."[23] The network building associated with such a course is virtually unlimited in scope: through the use of organizing hashtags and RSS[24] feeds, all that activity happening "out there" can be aggregated back at the "hub" for easy navigation by all participants.

A connected course poses challenges of organization and assessment. At the same time, its promises are unique to its unusual structure.[25] The learning community is easily comingled with interested outsiders with diverse backgrounds and perspectives. Project- or problem-based learning comes naturally where meaning-making activities are situated outside of any closed physical or virtual "classroom." Finally, the basic structure is almost infinitely malleable, a proven framework with easily replaced parts. Don't like Google? Have learners do their collaborative writing on Etherpad, TitanPad or some other alternative to Google Docs. Wary of Twitter during the throes of an ugly election cycle? Look into GNU Social or Mastodon for smaller-scale microblogging with more specialized communities. Haven't heard of any of these and don't have any idea where to begin looking? Ask around—on social media.

Community Revisited

Having offered this brief and incomplete survey of use cases, we see that social media provide educators a complex set of constraints and affordances out of which instructors may, once well-enough informed, craft learning experiences suited to their own particular goals and contexts. These experiences may be, depending on design choices, relatively private or public and largely synchronous or asynchronous, and allow learners to choose degrees of onymity. Available social media tools provide means by which a course designer can develop possibilities for learners to participate in community-building norms of acceptance, reciprocity and trustworthiness.

Still, given the extent to which social media are almost irreducibly *public*, questions of learner safety go beyond those usually encountered in traditional course design. Whatever practices an educator habitually takes concerning face-to-face or online codes of conduct for an enrolled body of learners, her usual arsenal of enforcement strategies will hold few terrors for the larger public with whom her learners interact on Twitter or in the comments sections of blog posts or YouTube videos.

Further, one will observe how large, for-profit corporations that are accountable to shareholders rather than to their users, who do not pay directly for their services, dominate the social media space. In what ways can platforms be considered trustworthy, as for their own veiled purposes they make sudden and unpredictable changes in user experience, feature availability and codes of conduct?

Besides becoming competent with designing learning experiences that, in themselves, foment community, educators find themselves having to become prepared to guide learners knowledgeably concerning a broader array of competencies around self-disclosure, identity and harassment in the worlds of social media.

Social Media and Public Learning

Using social media for education means escorting learners out of the relatively closed environs of the face-to-face classroom or the LMS and into the relatively open environs of the social web. The term *relative* in each instance is important. Classroom covenants notwithstanding, there are few barriers to a learner sharing the words of a classmate with outsiders (another student, a school administrator, a clergy official, a reporter). The social web affords possibilities for more or less private (or at least one-on-one) conversation, though these possibilities can be abstruse. Sound, up-to-date understandings of privacy and identity in social media can promote thriving and prevent needless suffering for educators and learners alike.

Of course, long before the invention of social media, educators and learners have been navigating issues around self-disclosure, identity and harassment. Women, scholars of color, LGBTQ scholars and disabled or neurodivergent scholars sometimes describe themselves as effectively having had to "present" (so far as possible) as straight, cisgender, white, able-bodied, neurotypical men in order to succeed in traditional academic spaces. More recently, learners are apt to insist that these academic spaces change in order to allow all participants to thrive while presenting themselves in the ways that they choose. Face-to-face and online educators, with their institutions, develop strategies for ensuring that learners have equal access not only to the learning space but also to the shared power to shape its discourse, its aesthetic and its norms.[26] Educators and learners engage in disputes about "free speech" and "safe spaces" in higher-education classrooms, raising questions about where speech becomes incitement, whether free speech for some entails curtailed opportunities for speech for others, and whether educational institutions are obliged to provide venues for speakers representing all perspectives. Just as online educators find themselves adapting these insights in progress from the physical to the virtual classroom, educators embracing social media seek to adapt the principles and practices of diversity-embracing community building to an ever-changing environment over which participants have only incomplete control.[27]

Self-Disclosure, Identity and Harassment

Although warnings about excessive self-disclosure to the Internet are easily found and understandably made, experience shows that a degree of self-disclosure is a natural element of appropriately professional social media practice.[28] Early participants in the academic "blogosphere" commonly—and often through the protective strategy of pseudonymity—discussed institutional matters in the context of rank, gender and home lives. Networked scholars today, when not seeking research-related help or sharing nascent ideas and projects, will take time to exchange memes, commiserate as parents, trade recipes and otherwise present publicly as "whole people." Learners, invited or required to participate in social media in class work, will either already have habits of greater or lesser self-disclosure on their own accounts or, if new users, will soon be socialized into the habits of self-disclosure characterizing the social media spaces they are asked to inhabit. Positively, these practices of self-disclosure create possibilities for personal learning networks that promote learning and persist beyond the last days of any given class. At the same time, experience shows that not all persons enjoy equal opportunity to "be themselves" on the Internet in relative peace. Hindrances include not only individual bad actors on social media but also specific features and systems of moderation on any given social media platform.

Traditionally marginalized populations, especially when expressing opinions, are apt to experience harassment of varying kinds on social media, especially on Twitter, where posts are public by default and easily shared. A veritable glossary of terms describes the categories of harassment that are typical: mansplaining, dog-piling, sea lions, targeted harassment including death threats and rape threats, doxxing.[29] Existing tools for coping with harassment, for the most part, lay the burden on the harassed user and are available only after the damage has already occurred. What is more, platform features that seem innocuous to better-protected users may in fact lend themselves to abuse. For example, Twitter users can search all other users' bios and tweets for strings of text. This can help well-meaning users find like-minded others ("theology," "parenting," "seminary," "football"). Malicious users, however, use this search feature to find targets ("trans," "intersectionality," "feminist"). Similarly, Twitter allows "quote tweets," whereby a user can effectively incorporate a screenshot of another user's tweet into a new tweet of his or her own. In practice, this can lend itself to such malicious practices as "calling out" (spreading the original tweet for shaming purposes) or taking a tweet out of the context of a "thread" of multiple tweets of which it is a part. The relatively new social media platform Mastodon has, so far, avoided coding into its design these search features or anything analogous to Twitter's "quote tweets" in large part because its original user community consisted largely of participants describing bad experiences on Twitter. Clarity about Mastodon calls for an understanding of the differences between centralized platforms and decentralized "federated" platforms such as GNU Social and Mastodon.

Centralized and Decentralized Platforms for Social Media

When Twitter changed the way that users are mentioned in tweets in the fall of 2016, users raised concerns that the new approach hindered strategies by which populations at particular risk of harassment protect themselves.[30] In August 2017, Facebook announced a commitment to remove "violent threats and posts celebrating hate crimes," appearing to reverse a previous tendency to err on the side of political free speech,[31] and Google simultaneously refused to provide hosting to the white supremacist site The Daily Stormer.[32] Users can feel by turns betrayed or elated by such changes, but will consistently feel all but powerless to affect them, as these social media behemoths make their decisions against an economic model of gathering user data, selling it to information brokers and serving it back to users as advertisements for the benefit of shareholders. The centralized, for-profit, totalizing character of the major social media services can seem almost a law of nature.

If Alexa wants to interact with Brenda's Twitter account, Alexa will need a Twitter account. If Jin wants to make a comment to Terrance's Facebook status update, then Jin will need to do this from a Facebook account of his own. For most users, this situation seems so natural as to be all but inevitable; how *else* would such interactions happen? Yet at the same time, users take for granted the ability to exchange e-mails from distinct platforms, say between a Gmail account (provided by Google) and an iCloud account (provided by Apple). This is because e-mail providers agree to a *decentralized* ecosystem wherein different platforms share standards making interactivity possible. Just so, in contrast to Twitter's centralized platform, there exists a "federation" of distinct microblogging services, all with their own codes of conduct and user agreements, across which account holders may freely follow one another and interact in a "fediverse" comprising as many such "mini Twitters" as anyone wishes to create. This fediverse began with communities built on the GNU Social software platform during 2010–2013 and exploded into renewed life in 2016–2017 with the technologically compatible but distinct Mastodon communities.[33]

Late in 2016, Twitter was reeling from Gamergate, a social media movement of targeted harassment of certain women game developers,[34] as well as a US election cycle in which accounts identifying with white supremacy or Nazism were frequently judged by Twitter not to violate their respective terms of service. In this context, the newly arrived Mastodon stood out for explicitly forbidding content promoting National-Socialist ideology (the site is hosted in Germany where such content is illegal), racism, sexism and xenophobia. The earliest population (in the fall of 2016) was distinctly politically leftist, largely LGBTQ (and particularly transgender), often "furry"[35] and enthusiastic for indie game development.[36] Mastodon permits users far more granular control over privacy than does Twitter and allows users to place potentially upsetting content behind "content warnings," meaning that readers first see the content warning (e.g., "US politics" or "cartoon gore") and can choose to uncover the content or not. As users came to disagree about codes of conduct or areas of interest, new communities (called "instances") using the Mastodon software were developed, usually federating with existing instances. In such an arrangement, Albert (a member of, say, the instance Mastodon.Social) can follow, and be followed by, Bianca (a member of a different instance, say Witches.Town), although their instances are distinct in flavor and may have contradictory codes of conduct. Users who desired even fewer limitations on speech than enforced by Twitter also developed several instances, and today online tools exist to help new users find instances that suit their personal needs regarding freedom of speech, use of content warnings, antiharassment policies, topics of community interest and other axes. The original community, Mastodon.Social, numbers over 81,000 users, and total users of Mastodon instances exceeds 600,000 as of August 2017.

Conclusion

Social media is, and will likely remain, a complex and ceaselessly changing terrain. Those instructors who desire to realize the pedagogical possibilities of social media learning activities may often find themselves autodidacts regarding the constraints and affordances of social media platforms, current and yet to come. Faculties and administrations concerned with equity of labor will need to determine how such ongoing labor can be kept visible to promotion-and-tenure committees and count toward institutional "load."[37]

There is far more diversity in religious and theological higher education than could be reflected in a one-size-fits-all guide to netiquette and best practices for the use of social media in learning. Goals for learning and formation differ, as do practices. Religious studies and theology persistently call for the analysis, understanding and, sometimes, promotion of worldviews perceived as offensive and even immediately threatening to enrolled participants and to persons in their lives. Educators considering the use of social media for learning will do well to explicate first their principles and practices for facilitating acceptance, reciprocity and trustworthiness in the classroom and the closed LMS. They can then proceed to the necessary work of determining how they carry these principles into the more public-facing and public-engaged, interconnected and ever-changing terrain of social media discourse.[38]

Notes

1. Grant P. Wiggins and Jay McTighe, *Understanding by Design*, expanded 2nd ed. (Alexandria, VA: Association for Supervision; Curriculum Development, 2005), 35–55.
2. Ibid., 128–30, 135–136.
3. Paulo Friere, *Pedagogy of the Oppressed: 30th Anniversary Edition* (New York: Bloomsbury, 2014), 72; Eileen M. Daily, "The Promise of Mobile Technology for Public Religious Education," *Religious Education* 108, no. 2 (2013): 119–120; Megan Poore, *Using Social Media in the Classroom: A Best Practice Guide*, 2nd ed. (Los Angeles: Sage, 2016), 6, 10.
4. "The more constructivist educational technology activities . . . correlate[] with higher test scores": Mark Warschauer, "Addressing the Social Envelope: Education and the Digital Divide," in *Education and Social Media: Toward a Digital Future*, eds. Christine Greenhow, Julia Sonnevend, and Colin Agur (Cambridge: MIT Press, 2016), 39.
5. Seymour Papert and Idit Harel, *Constructionism: Research Reports and Essays, 1985–1990* (Westport, CT: Ablex Publishing Corporation, 1991).
6. Daily, "Promise of Mobile Technology," 120–121.
7. David Lee and Howard Newby, *The Problem of Sociology: An Introduction to the Discipline* (London: Unwin Hyman Ltd., 1983), 43; Mark K. Smith, "Community," in *The Encyclopedia of Informal Education*, 2001, http://infed.org/mobi/community.
8. Michael Walzer, *On Toleration* (New Haven, CT: Yale University, 1997), 11; Robert D. Putnam, *Bowling Alone: The Collapse and Revival of American Community* (New York: Simon & Schuster, 2001), 19; Smith, "Community."
9. Jonathan A. Obar and Steven S. Wildman, "Social Media Definition and the Governance Challenge: An Introduction to the Special Issue," *Telecommunications Policy* 39, no. 9 (2015): 745–750.
10. Charles Arthur, "What Is the 1% Rule?" July 2006, www.theguardian.com/technology/2006/jul/20/guardianweeklytechnologysection2; George Veletsianos, *Social Media in Academia: Networked Scholars* (New York: Routledge, 2016), 65–68.
11. "Teachers in theological and religious studies are distinctly positioned to grapple with . . . practices of identity formation, media literacy, and embodiment [in networked learning]": Whitney Bauman et al., "Teaching the Millennial Generation in the Religious and Theological Studies Classroom," *Teaching Theology & Religion* 17, no. 4 (2014): 301.
12. Daily, "Promise of Mobile Technology," 126.
13. "Focus on issues, not technologies": Veletsianos, *Social Media in Academia*, 114.
14. G. Brooke Lester, "'Essential Questions' Twitter Chats," *Teaching Theology & Religion* 17 (2014): 224.
15. Glenn Fleichman, "Cartoon Captures Spirit of the Internet," *New York Times*, December 2000, www.nytimes.com/2000/12/14/technology/cartoon-captures-spirit-of-the-internet.html.
16. Jillian C. York, "A Case for Pseudonyms" (Electronic Frontier Foundation, July 2011), www.eff.org/deeplinks/2011/07/case-pseudonyms; Nicole Lee,

"Google Plus Finally Lets You Use Any Name You Like (Update: Well, Almost)," July 2014, www.engadget.com/2014/07/15/google-plus-finally-lets-you-use-any-name-you-like/.

17 "What Names Are Allowed on Facebook?" (Facebook, n.d.), www.facebook.com/help/112146705538576.
18 A hashtag is any string of letters beginning with a # sign (for example, #babystories); Twitter (and now, too, Facebook, GNU Social, and Mastodon) uses hashtags as a convenient convention for search terms.
19 Veletsianos, *Social Media in Academia*, 39, 41–43.
20 Dave Cormier, "The CCK08 MOOC-Connectivism Course, 1/4 Way," October 2008, http://davecormier.com/edblog/2008/10/02/the-cck08-mooc-connectivism-course-14-way/.
21 Minhtuyen Mai, Adam Poppe, and Christine Greenhow, "Social Media and Education on a Massive Scale: The Case of MOOCs," in *Education and Social Media*, eds. Christine Greenhow, Julia Sonnevend, and Colin Agur (Cambridge: MIT Press, 2016), 209–10; Chris Parr, "Mooc Creators Criticise Courses' Lack of Creativity," October 2013, www.timeshighereducation.com/news/mooc-creators-criticise-courses-lack-of-creativity/2008180.article.
22 Dave Cormier, "Rhizomatic Learning: The Community Is the Curriculum," 2014, https://courses.p2pu.org/en/courses/882/content/1796/.
23 Examples of connected courses include ETMOOC by Alec Couros et al., http://etmooc.org/orientation/; Rhizomatic Learning by Dave Cormier, https://courses.p2pu.org/en/courses/882/rhizomatic-learning-the-community-is-the-curriculum/; MOOC MOOC by Sean Michael Morris and Jesse Stommel, www.moocmooc.com/; Connected Courses by Alec Couros, Jim Groom, Alan Levine et al., http://connectedcourses.net/; and OOTLE15 through OOTLE17, G. Brooke Lester, http://ootle17.net.
24 RSS (Real Simple Syndication) is the mechanism by which content is passed from one place on the Internet to another; for example, RSS feeds can place Twitter content on a blog post or collect content from several different blogs into a single web page for easy reading.
25 For broader reflections on "distributed learning," see Chris Dede, "Social Media and Challenges to Traditional Models of Education," in *Education and Social Media*, eds. Christine Greenhow, Julia Sonnevend, and Colin Agur (Cambridge: MIT Press, 2016), 106–108.
26 "An increasingly large number of people are 'learning how to learn' in ways that stress their own passion, interest, and agency": Mary Hess, "A New Culture of Learning: Implications of Digital Culture for Communities of Faith," *Communication Research Trends* 32, no. 3 (2013): 14.
27 An excellent guide to institutional self-inventory in this regard is Steve Delamarter, "Theological Educators and Their Concerns about Technology," *Teaching Theology & Religion* 8, no. 3 (2005): 131–143.
28 Veletsianos, *Social Media in Academia*, 103–108.
29 *Mansplaining* describes a man condescending to explain to a woman something in which she is an expert, has already demonstrated knowledge or is likely to know. (Derivative terms are endless and include, for example, *whitesplaining* and *ablesplaining*.) A *sea lion* harasses persistently in a carefully reasoned and polite tone, placing unreasonable burdens of proof on his or her interlocutor. (The term originates from a comic by David Malki: http://wondermark.com/sea-lion-verb/.) *Doxxing* (or *doxing*) is to publish somebody's personal information online, especially home or work addresses, as an implicit or explicit invitation to others to harm the victim.

30 Tressie McMillan Cottom, "Twitter's New @Replies Re-Design Isn't Just Stupid; It's Really Stupid," October 2016, https://medium.com/@tressiemcphd/twitters-new-replies-re-design-isn-t-just-stupid-it-s-really-stupid-c471ca254f0a.
31 Hamza Shaban, "Mark Zuckerberg Vows to Remove Violent Threats from Facebook," August 2017, www.washingtonpost.com/news/the-switch/wp/2017/08/16/mark-zuckerberg-vows-to-remove-violent-threats-from-facebook/?utm_term=.cd9b9a75264d.
32 Julia Carrie Wong, "Tech Companies Turn on Daily Stormer and the 'Alt-Right' After Charlottesville," August 2017, www.theguardian.com/technology/2017/aug/14/daily-stormer-alt-right-google-go-daddy-charlottesville.
33 Sarah Jeong, "Mastodon Is Like Twitter without Nazis, so Why Are We Not Using It?" April 2017, https://motherboard.vice.com/en_us/article/783akg/mastodon-is-like-twitter-without-nazis-so-why-are-we-not-using-it.
34 Caitlin Dewey, "The Only Guide to GamerGate You Will Ever Need to Read," October 2014, www.washingtonpost.com/news/the-intersect/wp/2014/10/14/the-only-guide-to-gamergate-you-will-ever-need-to-read/.
35 *Furries* refers to a kind of fandom oriented toward appreciation of fictional anthropomorphized mammals (as in, for example, Richard Adams's *Watership Down* or in anime-type animation.
36 Allie Hart, "Mourning Mastodon," April 2017, https://medium.com/@alliethehart/gameingers-are-dead-and-so-is-mastodon-705b535ed616; Jon Pincus, "Mastodon: 14 Perspectives on a Breakthrough Month," May 2017, https://medium.com/a-change-is-coming/mastodon-14-perspectives-on-a-breakthrough-month-521ce46baa71.
37 Veletsianos, *Social Media in Academia*, 17–19.
38 Cf. Steve Delamarter et al., "Technology, Pedagogy, and Transformation in Theological Education: Five Case Studies," *Teaching Theology & Religion* 10, no. 2 (2007): 64–79.

Bibliography

Arthur, Charles. "What Is the 1% Rule?" July 2006. www.theguardian.com/technology/2006/jul/20/guardianweeklytechnologysection2.

Bauman, Whitney, Joseph A. Marchal, Karline McLain, Maureen O'Connell, and Sara M. Patterson. "Teaching the Millennial Generation in the Religious and Theological Studies Classroom." *Teaching Theology & Religion* 17, no. 4 (2014): 301–322.

Cormier, Dave. "The CCK08 MOOC-Connectivism Course, 1/4 Way." October 2008. http://davecormier.com/edblog/2008/10/02/the-cck08-mooc-connectivism-course-14-way.

———. "Rhizomatic Learning: The Community Is the Curriculum." 2014. https://courses.p2pu.org/en/courses/882/content/1796/.

Cottom, Tressie McMillan. "Twitter's New @Replies Re-Design Isn't Just Stupid; It's Really Stupid." October 2016. https://medium.com/@tressiemcphd/twitters-new-replies-re-design-isn-t-just-stupid-it-s-really-stupid-c471ca254f0a.

Daily, Eileen M. "The Promise of Mobile Technology for Public Religious Education." *Religious Education* 108, no. 2 (2013): 112–128.

Dede, Chris. "Social Media and Challenges to Traditional Models of Education." In *Education and Social Media*, edited by Christine Greenhow, Julia Sonnevend, and Colin Agur, 95–112. Cambridge, MA: MIT Press, 2016.

Delamarter, Steve. "Theological Educators and Their Concerns About Technology." *Teaching Theology & Religion* 8, no. 3 (2005): 131–143.

Delamarter, Steve, Javier Alanís, Russell Haitch, Mark Vitalis Hoffman, Arun W. Jones, and Brent A. Strawn. "Technology, Pedagogy, and Transformation in Theological Education: Five Case Studies." *Teaching Theology & Religion* 10, no. 2 (2007): 64–79.

Dewey, Caitlin. "The Only Guide to GamerGate You Will Ever Need to Read." October 2014. www.washingtonpost.com/news/the-intersect/wp/2014/10/14/the-only-guide-to-gamergate-you-will-ever-need-to-read/.

Fleichman, Glenn. "Cartoon Captures Spirit of the Internet." *New York Times*. December 2000. www.nytimes.com/2000/12/14/technology/cartoon-captures-spirit-of-the-internet.html.

Friere, Paulo. *Pedagogy of the Oppressed: 30th Anniversary Edition*. London: Bloomsbury, 2014.

Hart, Allie. "Mourning Mastodon." April 2017. https://medium.com/@alliethehart/gameingers-are-dead-and-so-is-mastodon-705b535ed616.

Hess, Mary. "A New Culture of Learning: Implications of Digital Culture for Communities of Faith." *Communication Research Trends* 32, no. 3 (2013): 13.

Jeong, Sarah. "Mastodon Is Like Twitter Without Nazis, So Why Are We Not Using It?" April 2017. https://motherboard.vice.com/en_us/article/783akg/mastodon-is-like-twitter-without-nazis-so-why-are-we-not-using-it.

Lee, David, and Howard Newby. *The Problem of Sociology: An Introduction to the Discipline*. London: Psychology Press, 1983.

Lee, Nicole. "Google Plus Finally Lets You Use Any Name You Like (Update: Well, Almost)." July 2014. www.engadget.com/2014/07/15/google-plus-finally-lets-you-use-any-name-you-like/.

Lester, G. Brooke. "'Essential Questions' Twitter Chats." *Teaching Theology & Religion* 17 (2014): 224.

Mai, Minhtuyen, Adam Poppe, and Christine Greenhow. "Social Media and Education on a Massive Scale: The Case of MOOCs." In *Education and Social Media*, edited by Christine Greenhow, Julia Sonnevend, and Colin Agur, 209–216. Cambridge, MA: MIT Press, 2016.

Obar, Jonathan A., and Steven S. Wildman. "Social Media Definition and the Governance Challenge: An Introduction to the Special Issue." *Telecommunications Policy* 39, no. 9 (2015): 745–750.

Papert, Seymour, and Idit Harel. *Constructionism: Research Reports and Essays, 1985–1990*. New York: Ablex Publishing Corporation, 1991.

Parr, Chris. "Mooc Creators Criticise Courses' Lack of Creativity." October 2013. www.timeshighereducation.com/news/mooc-creators-criticise-courses-lack-of-creativity/2008180.article.

Pincus, Jon. "Mastodon: 14 Perspectives on a Breakthrough Month." May 2017. https://medium.com/a-change-is-coming/mastodon-14-perspectives-on-a-breakthrough-month-521ce46baa71.

Poore, Megan. *Using Social Media in the Classroom: A Best Practice Guide*. 2nd ed. Thousand Oaks, CA: SAGE, 2016.

Putnam, Robert D. *Bowling Alone: The Collapse and Revival of American Community*. New York: Simon & Schuster, 2001.

Shaban, Hamza. "Mark Zuckerberg Vows to Remove Violent Threats from Facebook." August 2017. www.washingtonpost.com/news/the-switch/wp/2017/08/16/mark-zuckerberg-vows-to-remove-violent-threats-from-facebook/?utm_term=.cd9b9a75264d.

Smith, Mark K. "Community." *The Encyclopedia of Informal Education.* 2001. http://infed.org/mobi/community.

Veletsianos, George. *Social Media in Academia: Networked Scholars.* New York: Routledge, 2016.

Walzer, Michael. *On Toleration.* New Haven: Yale University, 1997.

Warschauer, Mark. "Addressing the Social Envelope: Education and the Digital Divide." In *Education and Social Media: Toward a Digital Future*, edited by Christine Greenhow, Julia Sonnevend, and Colin Agur, 29–48. Cambridge, MA: MIT Press, 2016.

"What Names Are Allowed on Facebook?" *Facebook*, n.d. www.facebook.com/help/112146705538576.

Wiggins, Grant P., and Jay McTighe. *Understanding by Design.* Expanded 2nd ed. Alexandria, VA: Association for Supervision; Curriculum Development, 2005.

Wong, Julia Carrie. "Tech Companies Turn on Daily Stormer and the 'Alt-Right' After Charlottesville." August 2017. www.theguardian.com/technology/2017/aug/14/daily-stormer-alt-right-google-go-daddy-charlottesville.

York, Jillian C. "A Case for Pseudonyms." *The Electronic Frontier Foundation.* July 2011. www.eff.org/deeplinks/2011/07/case-pseudonyms.

8 Blended Learning in Religious Education
What, Why and How

Anthony Sweat

Introduction

In the fall of 2014, I was lost. Standing in front of a religion class of 200 students at Brigham Young University with my khaki slacks and V-neck sweater, I may have looked the part of a professor with a PhD in education, but I sensed my teaching was going a little awry. I had just finished giving a 25-minute, fast-paced, PowerPoint introduction on the historical background to a chapter of scripture—who it was for, how it came about, the context of the time, what certain words may have meant in the original lexicon—all in an attempt to help my religion students dive more deeply into the religious text. I said, "With that background, let's get to the chapter. Are you ready?"

Are you ready? Really? More like, are you awake? Is anyone with me? Processing their stares, I asked myself, "Why do we bring hundreds of students together in a class anyway? It is just to disseminate information? Wouldn't it be better to explain this material *before* class and then use our time together to analyze, answer and apply the concepts?" I turned my gaze and stared off blankly into the distance as I dialoged in my mind, letting my internal professorial epiphany play out in front of everyone. Now, all 200 sets of eyes *were* with me. *Is he having a breakdown?*, the students may have wondered. *Is his PowerPoint frozen? Why has he stopped?* After a moment of personal reflection and a bolt of sudden clarity, I let out a sigh and said, "You didn't come here to have me give you all this information, did you?" My class did not answer the rhetorical question. Their expressions gave any needed reply. "You came here to have an experience with the information." Their heads nodded in agreement, like an unspoken hallelujah. In the fall of 2014, I was found.

The purpose of this chapter is to share how, based on this experience and others, I adjusted my religion course using a model commonly known as "blended learning," or the "flipped classroom" approach. In 2014, I flipped one of my religion courses, creating over 140 blended-learning videos that provide class lecture content outside of the classroom. This chapter focuses on blended learning—traces the historical factors that gave rise to it, defines it, analyzes its benefits and drawbacks, explores its theoretical advantages and provides practical guidelines regarding how it may be approached in religious education.

The Rise of Blended Learning

On the *Today Show* in 1994, host Bryant Gumbel turned to cohost Katie Couric and said, "I wasn't prepared to translate that, as I was doing that little tease—that little mark with the 'a' and then the ring around it [gestures his fingers in a circle motion indicating the @ sign]." "At" says another co-anchor. "See, that's what I said," replies Gumbel, "Katie said she thought it was 'about.'" "'Around,' or 'about,'" Couric clarifies as she motions her fingers in the @ sign. "I had never heard it said" retorts Gumbel, "I've seen the mark, but never heard it said, and then it sounded stupid when I said it, 'at NBC.'" On-screen, a header and Internet address appears displaying the words *Internet Address, violence@nbc.ge.com*. Gumbel, confused, asks, "I mean, what is 'internet' anyway?" Couric answers, "Internet is that massive computer network, the one that is becoming really big now." "How do you mean? What do you, like, write to it like mail?" Gumbel probes bewilderedly. "No, a lot of people use it in communicating," Couric clarifies. Then, with a smile, she asks an off-air producer, "Allison [Davis], can you explain what 'internet' is?"[1]

Twenty years later, that exchange about the Internet has become a classic video, ironically, on the Internet. Back in 1994, however, "Internet" was not an everyday word like it is now. Although the information superhighway was buzzed about and used in primitive forms by advanced techies for many years prior to 1994, it was just coming into use in mainstream culture. Since then, it has become a defining invention of our times and a great disruptive influence in multiple fields. The Internet and the information age have changed countless aspects of daily life, from how we shop to how we connect with friends, even how we catch a ride in a foreign city. It has, and should, fundamentally change how we educate, even in religious education.

Prior to the Internet's advent, obtaining information was more difficult since it was often centralized. A person had two general choices: go to a library to obtain a physical book or go to a physical location to be present with a teacher who would disseminate his or her expertise. For hundreds of years, most campus universities have centered on this model—great books and expert teachers—as the prototypical way to give information and educate students. With the advent of the personal computer and the Internet, that began to change. Innovating educators started placing educational content online for consumers. Suddenly, anyone with an Internet connection could learn about a wide variety of subjects. No need to go to the library to get a book, just Google it! (Which, admittedly, has introduced a new set of educational needs on evaluating reliable information.)

When YouTube launched in 2004, it created a major outlet to "broadcast yourself" (as their company tagline invites) to others around the world, decentralizing the necessity of physical proximity to, for example, give a lecture.[2] A math tutor no longer had to come to your home or help you in her classroom; she could video the instruction and send it out for free to learners across the globe, instantly, individually and independently. Instructional videos and screencasts—where a teacher's computer screen or whiteboard is filmed as they teach—were born.

Salman Khan popularized this form of instruction, perhaps more than anyone, starting with a simple service of making math tutorials for his cousin and uploading them to the Internet. Since then, he founded the Khan Academy, which offers thousands of free instructional videos on various topics. Khan Academy learning videos have been viewed over 1 billion times by more than 40 million students across the world, bringing Internet-based education into the popular mainstream.[3] Bill Gates, cofounder of Microsoft, insightfully said that the Khan Academy "has turned the classroom—and the world of education—on its head."[4] Many others have followed suit. Today, anyone with Internet access anywhere can get online and find websites, blog posts, podcasts, tutorials, lectures and instructional videos, broadly disseminating knowledge on a variety of subjects. Simply put, a brick-and-mortar campus where an expert teacher and physical books reside and wherein students must physically gather to learn is becoming outmoded, outdated and unnecessary, and may even be less educationally effective. Entities that do not change with and adapt to disruptive technologies[5] quickly become obsolete. Just ask Blockbuster Video. Education is no exception, including religious education.

The Rise of Online Education

Because of the expansion of the Internet, online education has grown rapidly, and that growth will likely continue. In their 2015 annual report on the status of online education in America, Allen and Seaman stated that nearly 70 percent of higher-education institutions report online education is critical to their long-term direction. Nearly one-third of all higher-education students have taken an online course as part of their course work. However, 26 percent of academic leaders believe that online learning produces inferior outcomes compared to face-to-face education, and only 58 percent rate online learning outcomes as equal to face-to-face education.[6] The US Department of Education's 2010 meta-analysis of over 1,000 empirical studies of online learning, however, concluded, "Students in online learning conditions performed modestly better than those receiving face-to-face instruction."[7] Not only does online learning seem to produce equal if not slightly better academic outcomes than traditional face-to-face learning but also it appeals to students because of its flexibility and accessibility. Students can learn on their own time, place

112 *Anthony Sweat*

and pace, allowing them to more easily participate in education while balancing other responsibilities.

Strictly educating online, however, has also presented challenges. Online classes, in general, have higher dropout rates than traditional courses, with one study finding the attrition rate seven times higher.[8] Online classes can create feelings of isolation, disconnectedness and distance between the teacher and the learner,[9] minimizing communities of learning, social interaction and collaboration.[10] Despite the effectiveness of online learning, face-to-face, teacher-led learning environments are highly valued and preferred by many students.[11] A computer screen, it seems, cannot easily nor equally replicate interaction, discussion, collaboration and human connectedness. For many, the ideal is to combine both the informational benefits of online education and the unique social learning advantages of face-to-face instruction.

Defining Blended Learning

Enter "blended learning." Blended learning can have many definitions, but herein I use Bonk and Graham's widely cited description that *blended learning* "combine[s] face-to-face instruction with computer-mediated instruction."[12] As opposed to online-only education, a blended-learning model delivers 30–79 percent of its content online [13] and the other portion in class, combining the benefits of Internet-distributed information with face-to-face in-class instruction (Figure 8.1).

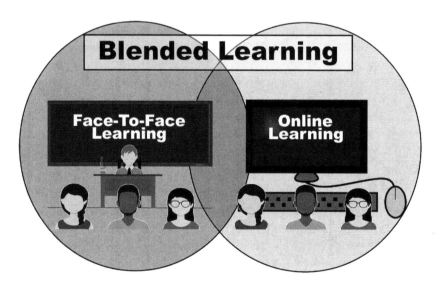

Figure 8.1 Blended Learning Intersects Benefits of Face-to-Face and Online Learning

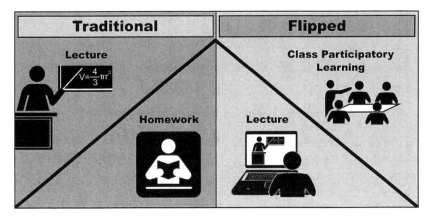

Figure 8.2 Flipped Learning Uses the Internet to Disseminate Information and Then Brings Students Together Face-to-Face to Participate With the Information

A major question in a blended-learning environment is which learning activities students do via the Internet and which they do in class. Herein is where blended learning often overlaps with the educational term called a "flipped" classroom. *Flipped learning* is where you flip the instructional approach: instead of using class time to disseminate information and then sending students home to make sense of it, you flip the order—using the Internet to disseminate the information outside of class and then bringing students together in class time to practice, analyze, discuss, criticize and so on (Figure 8.2).

Using a math example, a traditional classroom approach explains the quadratic equation in class and then sends students home to practice it. A flipped model uses the Internet to deliver the quadratic equation and then brings the students together in class with a teacher to practice and make sense of it. In a religious education example, the teacher would use the Internet to deliver information, such as the context and background of a scriptural chapter, and then use in-class time to analyze, synthesize and apply it. (This has been my approach since 2014.) Practical advantages to a flipped approach include time for students to better process information prior to class and more in-class time with the teacher to participate with the material.

Research on Blended Learning

While blended learning has many potential benefits, the overall data on this relatively new educational phenomenon is mixed. Several studies have compared the learning outcomes obtained by students in a blended-learning environment versus a traditional one. Some studies, such as Hsu and Hsieh's 2011 study with nursing students, report no differences in academic gains in a blended versus nonblended environment.[14] Others, such as Vernadakis et al.'s 2011 study report the opposite, with blended-learning environments producing greater outcomes than traditional ones when learning skills such as Microsoft PowerPoint.[15] Wong, Tatnall and Burgess's 2014 study of accounting students concludes that face-to-face methods were perceived by students as more effective in producing positive student learning outcomes than online options (such as recorded lectures).[16] However, a 2013 meta-analysis by Means, Toyama, Murphy and Marianne wherein 45 studies were analyzed on 50 academic outcomes concluded that online education performed "modestly better than those receiving face-to-face instruction" and that the most statistically significant gains were in those studies "contrasting blended learning with traditional face-to-face instruction."[17] As Torrisi-Steele and Drew summarized in their 2013 meta-analysis of 827 blended-learning research articles, the overall results are inconclusive, and "effective blended learning practices evidently still requires significant scholarly research."[18]

Blending and Bloom's Taxonomy

One potential benefit to a blended or flipped classroom approach is how it better implements Bloom's taxonomy of cognitive domains, an influential and highly used hierarchy of educational goals and objectives. Originally produced in 1956 by lead author Benjamin Bloom[19] and revised in 2001 by Anderson and Krathwohl,[20] the taxonomy classifies lower and higher orders of cognitive outcomes. On the base of the pyramid rests the factual "Remember" and interpretive "Understand." Tiers three, four and five are "Apply," "Analyze" and "Evaluate," wherein the learner can put ideas into practice, break materials into parts to see how they relate and critique or judge based on defined standards. On the highest tier sits "Create," wherein a student can put things together on his or her own in a unique way to create a new product.

In traditional education, face-to-face instructional time is often spent on the base levels of Bloom's pyramid, discussing information students should remember and understand. In a blended-learning environment, the teacher uses time outside of class to impart knowledge-level information via the Internet and preserves face-to-face, in-class time for more participatory, higher-level learning—the apply, analyze, evaluate and create levels of the taxonomy (Figure 8.3).

Thus, theoretically, a blended-learning model better supports in-class active and/or collaborative learning—wherein students participate in meaningful learning activities that cause them to think about what they are doing.[21] Blended learning can help solve the problem of time: in-class time is not used to cover material, but to make sense of it and

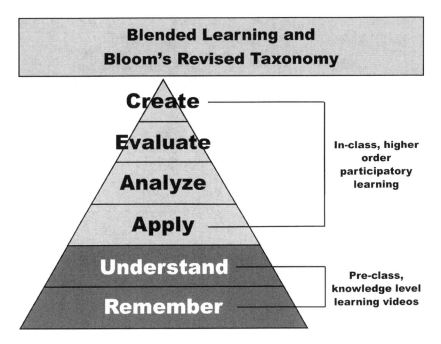

Figure 8.3 Blended Learning Implemented Through the Lens of Bloom's Revised Taxonomy

do something with it. Blended learning has the potential to answer the modern question I posed at the beginning of this chapter: why do we still bring students together face-to-face with a teacher? With blended learning, students can learn the factual information outside of class through a video, podcast or other e-learning methods (which, as opposed to merely reading an article, can implement more powerful learning tools such as audio, images and video) and then meet face-to-face with a teacher and other students to clarify, question and collaborate. It's a win-win.

Blended-Learning Videos

A key to implementing a blended-learning approach is the delivery of knowledge-level content to students outside of class via the Internet. Depending on your field of study, there may already exist excellent, easily available, previously created learning videos that you can incorporate into your curriculum—no need to reinvent the wheel. A quick YouTube search can bring up a surprisingly high quantity and quality of results. Search the name of an expert you admire, and there is most likely a video or podcast of that expert presenting on a subject.

As previously mentioned, the Khan Academy has created thousands of easily obtainable learning videos on a wide array of subjects narrated by various experts. Within two minutes of being on their website, I found quality videos teaching about the protestant reformation, the five pillars of Islam, Hindu scripture and a video giving an overview of Judaism, among other religious subjects. TED Talks, wherein leading scholars and experts give 10- to 20-minute presentations on powerful ideas, have become another useful source of available learning videos, although—as their acronym (Technology, Entertainment and Design) suggests—content directly related to religious education is limited.

This brings us to a key point: what if there are no learning videos on a particular subject? What if they are done poorly? What if the information presented is disagreeable? What if the videos' outcomes don't align with your religious or academic outcomes? Thus some educators employing a blended-learning approach create their own video content. The most prevalent way includes creating a screencast video that records PowerPoint slides or other images displayed on the teacher's computer screen while simultaneously recording the teacher's voice (or sometimes their image) narrating the content on the screen. I took this approach in creating learning videos for my religion class. I prepared a PowerPoint describing knowledge-level content (that previously I would have given in class), recorded my computer screen and voice narration teaching those PowerPoint slides and images and then uploaded the video to our university learning management system for the course. There are many screencast software options available for free and for purchase, some simple and some more sophisticated and complex. For my videos, I use Camtasia Studio because of its user-friendly interface and enhanced options.

Data on Creating Effective Videos

For both beginners and experts alike, creating a screencast instructional video can be an intimidating experience. Like all new processes, a steep learning curve will probably follow those who pursue it. I speak from experience. Having never created a screencast prior to 2014, in the following calendar year, I created 140 blended-learning videos on Latter-day Saint (Mormon) history and doctrine, and some are better than others. After creating and implementing these videos in my semester-long course, I surveyed 317 students and asked them questions that provide insight into creating quality blended videos and their educational effectiveness.[22] The students sampled had an average age of 21 and were strong academically (average incoming freshman had a high school grade point average of 3.8 and an ACT of 28) but were not particularly diverse (6 percent international, 16 percent ethnic minority). With caution while applying these findings to other populations, I share the following data

Video Length

One of my first questions asked students to choose one of four options as the ideal length for a blended-learning video. In their responses, 58 percent selected four to six minutes and 32 percent selected one to three minutes. No students selected ten minutes or more. This is a key finding, indicating that students preferred shorter videos to longer ones. When asked, "What should be the maximum length of time of a pre-class learning video," 41 percent selected seven to nine minutes. In follow-up interviews, students indicated they would prefer two five-minute videos compared to one ten-minute video. When posting the videos for the students to watch prior to class, students also indicated a preference to have the video length listed (i.e., "5:16") so they knew how long to expect the video to be.

Accountability

Another key question related to whether or not students actually watch the pre-class learning videos. Some teachers fear that if they shift the delivery of key information outside of class, they cannot ensure that students learn it. One way to mitigate this concern is to attach some sort of an assessment with the learning video, such as a quiz—a practice I followed in my flipped religion course. I asked the survey question: "How often would you have watched the pre-class learning video if no pre-class quizzes were associated with it?" On a Likert scale, 12 percent said never, 24 percent said rarely, 28 percent said sometimes, 24 percent selected often and 11 percent responded with always. Thus nearly two-thirds of students would never or only sometimes watch learning videos if no sort of assessment or grading incentive were attached. It should be noted that accountability quizzes do not need to represent a large point value; students reported that simply holding them accountable with any course points was enough incentive to ensure that they would watch the videos.

Viewing Device

How are students consuming these videos? On their laptops, PCs, smartphones or tablets? This question was key to determining the quality or resolution of the videos and the size of text displayed on the screen. If students are primarily watching the videos on a small smartphone, then lower quality resolution with higher font sizes are necessary. The opposite is true if videos are primarily consumed on a larger screen computer or laptop. Of the students sampled, 90 percent responded they watch them on a laptop and 7 percent on a desktop PC. Only 1 percent reported watching the videos on a smartphone. Thus higher resolution videos are recommended and relatively smaller text may be used when creating learning videos.

Rewatching Videos

One key benefit of blended-learning videos is the option for students to rewatch it if they missed or did not understand key points, whereas an in-class lecture generally cannot be redone. Therefore, another important question was whether students actually rewatched videos. Again on a Likert scale, 34 percent of students reported they sometimes rewatched videos and 6 percent reported they often did so (40 percent total). Videos seem to enhance relearning of information more so than traditional lectures or even assigned readings. (When was the last time 40 percent of students said they reread an assigned reading?)

Background Music

Audio is one benefit of learning videos, as compared to traditional readings or lectures. To enhance videos, some are produced with background music, often instrumental. Only 12 percent of respondents said they preferred videos with background music, while 62 percent said they preferred none (26 percent had no opinion). In follow-up interviews, participants reported that background music sometimes competed with the voice narration or made it harder to concentrate for certain learners, creating a distraction.

Visual Elements

During many of the learning videos, I used various visual elements to keep the viewer's attention and emphasize certain learning queues. For example, I highlighted text, drew or hand wrote concepts, zoomed in or out on the screen for emphasis, inserted video or visual images and so on. Of all the visual elements, students indicated that images (e.g., pictures, paintings) and videos were the most useful visual elements (55 percent selected this option). The next highest selected was highlighting text (20 percent).

Corner Teacher Image

Some screencast software allows a picture in picture mode, where the main computer screen is recorded but a small corner window is inserted that uses the computer's webcam to simultaneously display the teacher talking. Is it preferable to see this corner image of the teacher talking together with the content on the screen or just see the content on the screen without the teacher's image? Perhaps with encouragement not to pursue a TV or modeling career, 68 percent of students responded they do not want to see the corner webcam image of the professor talking during the presentation. Only 6 percent said it was preferred (26 percent had no opinion). One benefit to this dose of personal aesthetic humility is that it makes it easier to create blended-learning videos by limiting self-conscious and distracting aspects of webcam recording. If you desire your image to be part of the video, I'd recommend occasional full-screen cuts to you talking and then cutting back to the on-screen content.

Video Effectiveness

All the effort to organize a blended-learning course and to create or link to e-content and learning videos is perhaps pedagogically unnecessary if it does not enhance learning. In a meeting wherein I presented the concept of blended learning, one academic administrator responded with, "Why not just have them read an article to get the information? Why all the trouble to create videos?" It is an important question and one I wanted my students to weigh in on. The survey asked,

> Some claim that assigning pre-class videos for students to watch is no more effective (and may be less effective) than assigning pre-class readings for students to read. How much do you agree with the following statement: In general, a pre-class reading is just as or more effective than a pre-class video.

On a five-point Likert scale (strongly agree to strongly disagree) 27 percent of students strongly disagreed with that statement, and 50 percent disagreed. Only 7 percent agreed, and 4 percent strongly agreed (12 percent neither agreed nor disagreed). Thus 77 percent of students in this sample reported that pre-class learning videos were more educationally effective than an assigned reading. In follow-up interviews, students reported that the combination of text, imagery, movement and audio enhanced learning more than the static text in a reading. While this finding must be used with caution, the effort to put information into video content does seem to be warranted in certain contexts, particularly with Millennial audiences. Videos speak the language of a digitally native generation.

In-Class Time

As discussed earlier in this chapter, another key element supporting blended learning is that theoretically it opens in-class, face-to-face time to participatory forms of learning. Students answered the following question:

> Part of the theory behind pre-class learning videos is that it frees in-class time for "higher-level" learning, such as discussion, analysis, questions, instead of using in-class to dispense facts. How much do you agree with the following statement: In-class time was more useful because of the content provided in pre-class videos.

On a five-point Likert scale, 46 percent strongly agreed with that statement and 43 percent agreed. Only 4 percent strongly disagreed or disagreed. This was among the most lopsided finding of all the survey questions, indicating that the use of blended-learning videos seems to enhance the in-class experience rather than diminish it.

Learning Outcomes

Finally, although research is mixed related to learning outcomes in blended environment, student responses in my flipped religion course indicated positive outcomes. When asked, "How effective do you feel the pre-class videos were in contributing to your learning about the content in the course of study," 46 percent of students rated it "extremely effective" and 45 percent selected "very effective." Only 2 percent selected "not effective" or "slightly effective."

While not controlling for other factors, when comparing my overall course ratings between the semester where I did not use blended learning to the semester I implemented blended learning, my overall course ratings improved from a 7.3 out of 8.0 to a 7.7 out of 8.0, supporting the responses in this survey that indicate flipping the class was an effective pedagogical intervention.

Getting Started With Blended Learning

While blended learning or flipped course design may not be the approach you wish to pursue in your religious education environment, for those who are intrigued, I have included a form called "Template to Structure a Blended-Learning Video" (see Appendix). This template guides you through key steps to creating your own learning videos, summarized as follows:

1. Begin by asking yourself, "What information will my students learn out of class and what will they *do* in class?" This is a key question to differentiate video content and face-to-face instruction.
2. Center in on your learning outcomes for the video. Write down what you want your students to know or remember from the video.

This will guide your video content and be useful in creating your assessments. I recommend no more than three to five stated learning outcomes and some sort of quiz or accountability measure on those outcomes.
3. For each outcome, write down the main concepts you will discuss and the text/quotes, writings, animations, images, music or zooms you will add to increase visual interest. In essence, do a rough storyboard of what you want the video to look like.
4. Create a PowerPoint slide presentation to accompany your visual and textual elements you created in the previous step.
5. Use a screen-capture software on your computer to record your screen as you click through your visuals and discuss the PowerPoint. Use a high-quality USB microphone or headset in a quiet room to record your audio, since quality audio matters as much as video.

While you probably will not need to use all five steps after you become accustomed to the process, this deliberate five-step mapping may be helpful as you create your first videos. After making a few videos, give them to your students and seek their feedback. Find out what did and did not work, and then modify your approach based on the information you receive as you create additional videos. A best-practice idea for a potential first blended-learning video is to create a syllabus video where you introduce the class and explain the syllabi content. Think of the valuable in-class time that one video alone may save!

Conclusion

As we continue to search for effective ways to incorporate technology into teaching and learning, blended learning is an approach that should warrant the consideration of serious religious educators. The advent of the Internet has placed technological tools to disseminate information in our hands that were unfathomable to previous generations of educators. The Internet's ability to provide information should not be viewed as a competition to educators but as a complementary tool to accomplish our aims. Although research on the effectiveness of blended learning is mixed, and creating learning videos involves time and a steep learning curve, there are many reasons to pursue its approach. Blended learning can allow religious educators to better maximize in-class time for higher-order, student-centered collaborative learning activities. It can provide students more time to process information and come prepared to class to intelligently discuss, question, analyze and put learning into practice. Students can watch and rewatch lectures at their own time and pace. Blended learning also speaks to the language of a digital generation, better incorporating audio, images and visuals to the learning process as opposed to just written text.

While there is never one silver bullet in making education effective (because of the multiplicity of variables that comprise excellence in teaching), incorporating a blended-learning approach in my core religious education class has paid positive dividends, as some of the survey data shared in this chapter indicates. Because of the technology available via the Internet, blended learning has provided me with an answer to the quandary about why we still bring students together with a teacher in a physical classroom. A student e-mailed me toward the end of the semester and said, "The pre-class learning videos were awesome, and I learned a lot. It was nice to have class time spent mostly answering questions and explaining concepts instead of just giving historical background." Another commented, "I think every class should do this." Perhaps not every class should, given varied educational constraints and contexts; however, if you find yourself somewhat lost or amiss in your current religious education approach—as I found myself—it is my hope that this chapter on blended learning has given you some theories, research and practicable guidelines that may help you find better religious education.

Notes

1 "1994: 'Today Show': 'What Is Internet Anyway?'" accessed June 6, 2017, www.youtube.com/watch?v=UlJku_CSyNg. Transcript by the author.
2 I acknowledge that traditional television broadcasts also play a large role in providing educational content. The primary disruption that YouTube and the Internet (such as blogs) have provided, however, is that anyone can produce and publish content to the public. Content creation and production has become decentralized.
3 Statistics from www.khanacademy.org and www.youtube.com/user/khan academy, accessed July 27, 2017.
4 Bill Gates, "Salman Khan-Time 100," *Time Magazine*, April 18, 2012, http://content.time.com/time/specials/packages/article/0,28804,2111975_2111976_2111942,00.html.
5 The phrase "disruptive technology" was coined by Harvard Business School professor Clayton Christensen in his 1997 best-selling book *The Innovator's Dilemma: When New Technologies Cause Great Firms to Fail* (Cambridge, MA: Harvard Business Review Press, 1997), 41, 191.
6 Elaine Allen and Jeff Seaman, *Grade Level: Tracking Online Education in the United States* (Babson Park, MA: Babson Survey Research Group and Quahog Research Group, 2015), 5, www.onlinelearningsurvey.com/reports/gradelevel.pdf.
7 US Department of Education, *Evaluation of Evidence-Based Practices in Online Learning: A Meta-Analysis and Review of Online Learning Studies* (Washington, DC: US Department of Education, 2009), IX, www2.ed.gov/rschstat/eval/tech/evidence-based-practices/finalreport.pdf.
8 Belinda Patterson and Cheryl McFadden, "Attrition in Online and Campus Degree Programs," *Online Journal of Distance Learning Administration* 12, no. 2 (2009): 3, www2.westga.edu/~distance/ojdla/summer122/patterson112.html.
9 James Bowers and Poonam Kumar, "Students' Perceptions of Teaching and Social Presence: A Comparative Analysis of Face-to-Face and Online

Learning Environments," in *Blended Learning: Concepts, Methodologies, Tools, and Applications*, ed. Mehedi Khosrow-Pour (Hershey, PA: IGI Global, 2017), 1532.
10 Doris Bolliger and Fethi Inan, "Development and Validation of the Online Student Connectedness Survey (OSCS)," *International Review of Research in Open and Distance Learning* 13, no. 3 (2012): 41–65.
11 Phillipa Mitchell and Pip Forer, "Blended Learning: The Perceptions of First-Year Geography Students," *Journal of Geography in Higher Education* 34, no. 1 (2010): 77–89.
12 Curtis Bonk and Charles Graham, *The Handbook of Blended Learning: Global Perspectives, Local Design* (San Francisco: Pfeiffer, 2006), 5.
13 Allen and Seaman, *Grade Level*, 7.
14 Li-Ling Hsu and Suh-Ing Hsieh, "Effects of a Blended Learning Module on Self-reported Learning Performances in Baccalaureate Nursing Students," *Journal of Advanced Nursing* 67, no. 11 (2011): 2435–2444.
15 Nikolas Vernadakis, Panagiotis Antoniou, Maria Giannousi, Eleni Zetou, and Efthimis Kioumourtzoglou, "Comparing Hybrid Learning with Traditional Approaches on Learning the Microsoft Office Power Point 2003 Program in Tertiary Education," *Computers & Education* 56, no. 1 (2011): 188–99.
16 Lily Wong, Arthur Tatnall and Stephen Burgess, "A Framework for Investigating Blended Learning Effectiveness," *Education + Training* 56, no. 2 (2015): 233–251.
17 Barbara Means, Yukie Toyama, Robert Murphy and Marianne Baki, "The Effectiveness of Online and Blended Learning: A Meta-Analysis of the Empirical Literature," *Teacher College Record* 115, no. 3 (2013): 2.
18 Geraldine Torrisi-Steele and Steve Drew, "The Literature Landscape of Blended Learning in Higher Education: The Need for Better Understanding of Academic Blended Practice," *International Journal for Academic Development* 18, no. 4 (2013): 380.
19 Benjamin Bloom (ed.), *Taxonomy of Educational Objectives: The Classification of Educational Goals: Handbook I: Cognitive Domain* (New York: Longman, 1956).
20 Lorin Anderson and David Krathwohl, *A Taxonomy for Learning, Teaching, and Assessing: A Revision of Bloom's Taxonomy of Educational Objectives* (New York: Longman, 2001).
21 Michael Prince, "Does Active Learning Work? A Review of the Research," *Journal of Engineering Education* 93, no. 3 (2004): 223–213. This article is an excellent, short, readable review of the literature of the positive statistical effects of active learning.
22 Anthony Sweat and Kenneth Alford, "Getting Started with Blended Learning Videos," *The Teaching Professor* 29, no. 10 (2015): 5, 7.

Bibliography

Allen, Elaine, and Jeff Seaman. *Grade Level: Tracking Online Education in the United States*. Babson College, MA: Babson Survey Research Group and Quahog Research Group, 2015.
Anderson, Lorin, and David Krathwohl. *A Taxonomy for Learning, Teaching, and Assessing: A Revision of Bloom's Taxonomy of Educational Objectives*. New York: Longman, 2001.
Bloom, Benjamin, ed. *Taxonomy of Educational Objectives: The Classification of Educational Goals: Handbook I: Cognitive Domain*. New York: Longman, 1956.

Bolliger, Doris, and Fethi Inan. "Development and Validation of the Online Student Connectedness Survey (OSCS)." *International Review of Research in Open and Distance Learning* 13, no. 3 (2012): 41–65.

Bonk, Curtis, and Charles Graham. *The Handbook of Blended Learning: Global Perspectives, Local Design.* San Francisco: Pfeiffer, 2006.

Bowers, James, and Poonam Kumar. "Students' Perceptions of Teaching and Social Presence: A Comparative Analysis of Face-to-Face and Online Learning Environments." In *Blended Learning: Concepts, Methodologies, Tools, and Applications*, edited by Mehedi Khosrow-Pour, 1532–1550. Hershey, PA: IGI Global, 2017.

Christensen, Clayton. *The Innovator's Dilemma: When New Technologies Cause Great Firms to Fail.* Cambridge, MA: Harvard Business Review Press, 1997.

Hsu, Li-Ling, and Suh-Ing Hsieh. "Effects of a Blended Learning Module on Self-reported Learning Performances in Baccalaureate Nursing Students." *Journal of Advanced Nursing* 67, no. 11 (2011): 2435–2444.

Means, Barbara, Yukie Toyama, Robert Murphy, and Marianne Baki. "The Effectiveness of Online and Blended Learning: A Meta-Analysis of the Empirical Literature." *Teacher College Record* 115, no. 3 (2013): 1–47.

Mitchell, Phillipa, and Pip Forer. "Blended Learning: The Perceptions of First-Year Geography Students." *Journal of Geography in Higher Education* 34, no. 1 (2010): 77–89.

Patterson, Belinda, and Cheryl McFadden. "Attrition in Online and Campus Degree Programs." *Online Journal of Distance Learning Administration* 12, no. 2 (2009): 1–11.

Prince, Michael. "Does Active Learning Work? A Review of the Research." *Journal of Engineering Education* 93, no. 3 (2004): 223–213.

Sweat, Anthony, and Kenneth Alford. "Getting Started with Blended Learning Videos." *The Teaching Professor* 29, no. 10 (2015): 5, 7.

Torrisi-Steele, Geraldine, and Steve Drew. "The Literature Landscape of Blended Learning in Higher Education: The Need for Better Understanding of Academic Blended Practice." *International Journal for Academic Development* 18, no. 4 (2013): 371–383.

US Department of Education. *Evaluation of Evidence-Based Practices in Online Learning: A Meta-Analysis and Review of Online Learning Studies.* Washington, DC: US Department of Education, 2009. www2.ed.gov/rschstat/eval/tech/evidence-based-practices/finalreport.pdf.

Vernadakis, Nikolas, Panagiotis Antoniou, Maria Giannousi, Eleni Zetou, and Efthimis Kioumourtzoglou. "Comparing Hybrid Learning with Traditional Approaches on Learning the Microsoft Office Power Point 2003 Program in Tertiary Education." *Computers & Education* 56, no. 1 (2011): 188–199.

Wong, Lily, Arthur Tatnall, and Stephen Burgess. "A Framework for Investigating Blended Learning Effectiveness." *Education + Training* 56, no. 2 (2015): 233–251.

Appendix
Template to Structure a Blended Learning Video

1. Consider what your overall learning goals are for this class/unit. Ask yourself: "What information will my students *learn* out of class, and what will my students *do* in class with that information they've learned?"

Learn out of Class	Do in Class

2. Write your knowledge-level outcomes for this video (Bloom's "Remember," "Understand")
   Students will be able to [action verb such as remember, explain, identify, memorize] . . .

   - Learning outcome #1: _____
   - Learning outcome #2: _____
   - Learning outcome #3: _____
   - Learning outcome #4: _____

3. For each learning outcome you listed above in step #2, write down the main concepts you will discuss, the text/quotes, writing, animations, images, music, zooms, etc. to add visual interest.

	Outcome #1	Outcome #2	Outcome #3	Outcome #4
Main Concepts				
Text/Quotes				
On-screen Writing				
Animations/Callouts				
Images/Videos				
Music/Sounds				
Zooms/Highlights				

4. Create a PowerPoint with the elements you listed in step #3. Each outcome you mapped out above should take 1–2 minutes each.
5. Using a screen-capture recording software, record your screen as you click through your visuals and discuss the PowerPoint. Use a high-quality USB microphone or headset in a quiet room to record your audio (audio matters as much as video).

9 Character-izing Gameful Learning

Using Student-Guided Narratives to Motivate, Engage and Inform Learners

Christopher Heard, Steven V. Rouse

Introduction

Since about 2010, gamification—"using game-based mechanics, aesthetics and game thinking to engage people, motivate action, promote learning, and solve problems"[1]—has gained steam worldwide in both commerce and education. On the educational side, the New Media Consortium's annual *Horizon Reports* for 2011–2014 listed gamification as a key "mid-range trend" with a time to adoption of two to three years.[2] Curiously, gamification was absent from the *Horizon Reports* for 2015–2016, perhaps implying that the *Horizon* panel now sees gamification as a practice that is "already here" rather than as an "emerging trend."[3] However, the literature on gamification can be hard to review, interpret and apply. As Karl Kapp has noted,

> There are literally thousands of books, articles, and newspaper reports on the effectiveness of games and gamification. Some of the reporting is based on theoretical underpinnings, some of it is based on opinion, and some of it is based on wishful thinking.[4]

Additionally, the existing literature does not always distinguish carefully between *gamification*, or the use of game mechanics in nongame contexts, usually intended to enhance motivation and engagement, and *gameful learning*, or the use of games and gamelike activities for learning.

Kapp's list might give the inaccurate impression that the books, articles and other reports on gameful learning and gamification give little attention to empirical study. This is not entirely true, although empirical study does seem to have attracted less attention than more theoretical work to date. In part, empirical study of gameful learning and educational gamification is bedeviled by the great variety of activities and approaches that fall under these headings. Any given study can examine only a single practice or small range thereof—a fact that opens up a vast field of research but also impedes researchers' attempts to transfer findings between specific practices.

The present study enriches the existing literature by investigating a gameful learning strategy that has, to the best of our knowledge, received minimal prior attention in published studies: the use of interactive fiction to introduce students to foundational knowledge in a humanistic discipline. A variety of prior studies support the notion that such an approach could have positive effects on student learning, engagement and motivation. Drawing inspiration from these studies, we devised the intervention and assessment thereof described in our methodology section that follows. The results presented thereafter suggest that our specific assignment design failed to meet these aspirations.

Background to the Present Study

Gameful Learning and Gamification

Kapp's review of six meta-analyses and several more specialized research projects spans the mid-1990s to 2011 and strongly informed our own research design.[5] In general, the meta-analyses Kapp reviewed found that "instructional games can provide effective learning for a variety of learners for several different tasks in the domains of higher declarative knowledge, procedural knowledge, and higher retention."[6] Kapp also reported that "games and simulations yielded better attitudes toward learning when compared to traditional teaching methods and seem to facilitate motivation across different learner groups and learning situations."[7] These summary statements, converted (back) into hypotheses and given more specificity, form the central questions of our research (see the following).

However, these optimistic summary statements rest on a quite variegated body of data. Robert Hays's meta-analysis of over 100 treatments of gameful learning (including 48 empirical studies) revealed that "the empirical research on the effectiveness of instructional games . . . includes research on different tasks, age groups, and types of games." This "fragmentation" of the research literature led Kapp to warn, "We should not generalize from research on the effectiveness of one game in one learning area for one group of learners to all games in all learning areas for all learners."[8] More recently, Dicheva et al. narrowed a field of over 1,500 works on gamification down to 34 peer-reviewed empirical studies of specific gameful interventions in education.[9] From these studies, the researchers extracted 11 game design principles and 7 game mechanics that have received significant study, specifically: goals and challenges, personalization, rapid feedback, visible status, unlocking content, freedom of choice, freedom to fail, storyline/new identities, onboarding, time restriction and social engagement.

The systematic mapping of research done by Dicheva et al. provides other researchers with an up-to-date orientation to research published since Kapp. According to Dicheva et al., several studies have examined the impact of "freedom of choice." However, here too fragmentation is evident, as Dicheva et al. included in this category such varied practices as selecting a writing/response medium, choosing assessment types, selecting between different assignments, choosing the order and pace of assignments and customizing assignment weights and deadlines. None of the studies Dicheva et al. cited in this connection used interactive fiction or a similar medium to help students engage with course content; rather, they provided for student choice at a higher level of course organization.

The inclusion of storytelling among Dicheva et al.'s list of game design principles would seem more promising, but further investigation belied this hope. Storytelling actually appears only in Dicheva et al.'s tables; the authors did not discuss this design principle in their narrative and did not include it in their short list of five "most used gamification design principles."[10] Of the three sources to which Dicheva et al. pointed for storytelling as a game design principle, one is theoretical,[11] one is itself a literature review[12] and one is Kapp, bringing us full circle.

Kapp's reviews of Thomas Malone's and Mark Lepper's models of motivation in gaming and education particularly influenced our experimental design. Based on empirical studies of children's responses to selected games, Malone[13] identified *challenge*, *fantasy* and *curiosity* as key elements by which games activate intrinsic motivation. According to Malone, challenge requires "goals whose attainment is uncertain."[14] Clear, personally meaningful goals motivate players best and good games provide feedback that helps players measure their progress. The uncertainty of outcomes can be achieved in various ways, among which Malone highlighted variable difficulty levels, hidden information and randomness.[15]

Citing a simple dictionary definition of fantasy, Malone defined "a fantasy-inducing environment as one that evokes 'mental images of things not present to the senses or within the actual experience of the person involved.'"[16] Malone distinguished between extrinsic fantasies, such as trivia games in which correct answers advance players around a baseball diamond, and intrinsic fantasies, where "problems are presented in terms of the elements of the fantasy world, and players receive a natural kind of constructive feedback" within the fantasy world.[17] Malone considered intrinsic fantasies to be "both (a) more interesting and (b) more instructional than extrinsic fantasies."[18]

Finally, Malone claimed, "Environments can evoke a learner's curiosity" if they are "neither too complicated nor too simple with respect to the learner's existing knowledge. They should be novel and surprising, but not completely incomprehensible."[19] Malone suggested stimulating curiosity by "present[ing] just enough information to make [learners'] existing knowledge seem incomplete, inconsistent, or unparsimonious.

The learners are then motivated to learn more, in order to make their cognitive structures better-formed."[20]

Lepper's model[21] overlaps with Malone's in emphasizing challenge and curiosity but recasts Malone's notion of fantasy as *contextualization* to better clarify that the imagined environment need not include fantastic elements but could be a mundane functional simulation.[22] Additionally, Lepper distinguished learners' *control* over learning activities as a fourth important element of motivation in gameful learning.[23] Dicheva et al. echoed this emphasis under the label "freedom of choice," as previously discussed.

Fiction and Role-Playing in Biblical Studies Pedagogy

It is not typical for biblical scholars to compose fictional narratives for pedagogical purposes, but a few notable exceptions provide precedent for the current investigation. Philip Davies's *First Person: Essays in Biblical Autobiography* presents fictional autobiographical sketches of biblical characters, while his *Yours Faithfully: Virtual Letters from the Bible* and Bruce Longenecker's *The Lost Letters of Pergamum* consist of imaginative letters from biblical or parabiblical characters.[24] These works convey scholarship to their readers indirectly by embedding scholarly findings and speculations into fictive worlds that overlap with the socio-historical world implied in biblical narratives, consistent with Dicheva et al.'s storyline design principle. However, since these works do not give the reader a role within the fictive world, they lack the new-identities dimension of that principle.

Both principles do, however, operate in the Reacting to the Past (RTTP) pedagogy in which students compete in role-immersion games based on historical events. RTTP games do not simply re-enact the past but respond meaningfully to student choices, thus turning students into stakeholders in the games' outcomes. Students win RTTP games by achieving outcomes that prominent individuals or groups actually or plausibly pursued in connection with the games' central events. To date, only one RTTP game—*The Josianic Reform: Deuteronomy, Prophecy, and Israelite Religion* by David Tabb Stewart and Adam Porter—draws students into a biblical narrative, although several others touch on biblical themes or include biblically based argumentation.[25] Despite the many benefits reported by faculty using RTTP games,[26] the games accommodate larger classes with difficulty. For example, the aforementioned "Josiah game" accommodates 12 to 31 students;[27] most games are designed for 18 to 25 students.[28] Professors can clone some generic roles to accommodate a few more students, but adjusting RTTP games for larger classes can present difficulties that some faculty, especially those new to RTTP, may find insuperable.

Context

Pepperdine University's Seaver College is a Christian liberal arts college enrolling approximately 3,300 degree-seeking undergraduates. The general education curriculum requires students to take an introductory Old Testament course (REL 101), an introductory New Testament course (REL 102) and an applied theology course (REL 301), in that order. When this study originated, one of us (Heard) was typically teaching 4 to 6 sections of REL 101 with average enrollments of 48 to 52 students. As early as fall 2009, those REL 101 courses already incorporated elements of gamification; by fall 2011, a gamified course structure was in place that would persist until summer 2017, encompassing the study period of fall 2015–summer 2016. The gamified course structure had three basic components:

- During *Harvests* (homework assignments), students "reaped new knowledge" by completing preparatory activities such as reading biblical and supplemental texts, watching explanatory videos and completing reading comprehension quizzes. Importantly, prior to the experimental intervention, Harvest instructions were delivered to students in a "declarative" format, a straightforward communication between professor and student.
- During *Workshops* (class meetings), students "crafted learning artifacts" by engaging in active learning projects, usually in groups. These projects occupied the majority of classroom time and were designed to require application of the foundational knowledge students gained during the Harvests.
- During *Battles* (unit examinations), students individually reviewed the foundational knowledge gained in Harvests and undertook new applications similar to, but on a smaller scale than, the Workshop activities.

Although this structure was developed several years before the publication of Dicheva et al.'s mapping study, that later study provides a useful framework for summarizing the key game mechanics already incorporated into the course before the experimental intervention, as shown in Table 9.1.

Experimental Intervention

Assignment Redesign

Among other factors, criticisms of gamification as a mere patina of superficial features on top of otherwise unchanged experiences led to a desire for more gameful experiences at the level of individual assignments.[29]

Table 9.1 Course Elements Gamified Prior to Experimental Intervention

Design Principle	Mechanic
Goals/challenges	Frequent reward-yielding activities
Personalization	Accrual grading, achievement levels
Rapid feedback	Auto-grading of most activities
Visible status	
Unlocking content	
Freedom of choice	
Freedom to fail	Option to repeat selected activities
Storyline/new identities	Scope and sequencing
Onboarding	Looser requirements for early units
Time restriction	Timed/time limited activities
Social engagement	Peer extra credit awards

Figure 9.1 Larry Croft and Deanna Jones Invite the Student/Player Into the HARDIS

The format chosen was interactive fiction, in the manner of the *Choose Your Own Adventure* stories pioneered by Edward Packard in the 1970s. This choice was inspired in large part by RTTP (although RTTP itself was not used because of scalability concerns) and guided by Malone's and Lepper's principles, initially mediated to us by Kapp.

In keeping with Malone's and Lepper's principle of contextualization (Lepper) or fantasy (Malone), 6 out of 18 canonically based Harvest assignments for REL 101 were recast as interactive fiction adventures in which students would imaginatively join biblical investigators Lawrence "Larry" Croft and Deanna Jones (loosely based on Lara Croft from the *Tomb Raider* video game series and Indiana Jones from *Raiders of the Lost Ark* and its associated media properties) on their travels through time, space, literature and imagination in a vehicle called the HARDIS (an acronym for "Historical and Religious Discoveries in Scripture," riffing on Dr. Who's TARDIS). In keeping with Lepper's principle of control, students determined their own paths through the material. For example, the second such assignment begins as follows:

> It's a lovely evening as you stroll back up the hill from Alumni Park toward Pepperdine's central campus. The whole "movie in the park" thing turned out to be pretty fun—like an old-time drive-in but without the automotive smells and other distractions. Tonight the SGA showed the 1998 animated film *The Prince of Egypt*, which you thoroughly enjoyed even though you saw it a dozen times when you were a little kid.
>
> Lost in thought, you almost fail to notice the strange blue door that suddenly fades into existence in the outer wall of Tyler Campus Center, right where no blue door should be. But the gentle hum and slight glow of rainbow colors are enough to catch your attention. You definitely remember this door. It's the door to the HARDIS (an acronym for "Historical and Religious Dimensions in Scripture"), the strange vehicle that carries biblical researchers Deanna Jones and Larry Croft into the worlds behind, inside, and in front of the Bible.
>
> As you begin to wonder what Larry and Deanna are doing here, the HARDIS's door bursts open, and Deanna comes rushing toward you. "Quick, [student's name]," she says breathlessly. "There's no time to lose."
>
> What do you do next?
>
> - Follow Deanna into the HARDIS.
> - Ask Deanna what's going on.

The stories were developed using Twine (freely available at twinery.org), which generates output in the form of standard HTML files. Whereas the classic *Choose Your Own Adventure* books would send readers to certain pages upon making various choices, Twine stories present the choices as hyperlinks that players can click. If a student were to click "Ask Deanna what's going on" at the end of the previous example, the screen would refresh and present the student with new choices.

> "The ark of the covenant has gone missing," Deanna replies, somewhat frantically. "Come on, we're going to need your help to find it."
> How do you respond to this news?
>
> - "That's terrible! Let's get going."
> - "How can the ark of the covenant be missing? Wasn't it destroyed a long time ago?"
> - "What exactly *is* this 'ark of the covenant'?"

Each choice the student makes thus branches into additional choices. At certain points within the adventure, students are redirected toward primary or secondary sources relevant to the putative exploration. This design also kept the foundational content of the new narrative-style assignments consistent with the foundational content of the older declarative-style versions of the same assignments. For example, if a student were to click on "What exactly *is* this 'ark of the covenant'?" in the story segment earlier, the next story segment displayed would read:

> "The ark of the covenant was a special decorated box that played an important role in Israelite and Judean religion," Larry explains, his gravelly voice lending an air of gravitas to this simple statement. Handing you a sci-fi gizmo with a digital copy of the Common English Bible glowing on the screen, Larry continues, "The best way to get up to speed is to read about it in the Torah."
>
> Please take a moment to read the following biblical passages narrating events in the life of Moses:
>
> - Exodus 25:1–22
> - Exodus 37:1–9
> - Numbers 10:33–36
>
> In addition, please read 2 Samuel 6, which narrates events from the life of King David, hundreds of years after Moses, and the sidebar on p. 532 OT entitled "The Lord's Chest." After you've read those passages, continue the story.

Tracking mechanisms of various kinds were used to help students monitor their progress through the stories. These mechanisms varied with different stories. In the Exodus story, for example, students "found" different parts of the ark of the covenant and its contents—the box, the lid, the poles, the Ten Commandments tablets and so forth—in different parts of the story. In the Judges story, a map derived from Joshua

13–24 gradually gained colored shading as students advanced through the scenario.

Hypotheses

Based on the considerations outlined in the literature review earlier, we hypothesized the following:

> H1. Students will self-report more motivation for narrative assignments than for declarative assignments.
> H2. Students will self-report more engagement with narrative assignments than with declarative assignments.
> H3. Students will self-report more learning from narrative assignments than from declarative assignments.

Materials

To test these hypotheses, students in three successive semesters (spring 2016, summer 2016 and fall 2016) were surveyed. The survey first presented various questions about demographic characteristics of the respondents. Next, the survey included modified items from the well-known Intrinsic Motivation Inventory (IMI) developed by Richard Ryan and Edward Deci.[30] In keeping with the research questions, items from the standard Interest/Enjoyment and Effort/Importance subscales were combined into a Motivation subscale, items from the standard Perceived Choice and Relatedness subscales were combined into an Engagement subscale, and items from the Perceived Competence and Value/Usefulness subscales were combined into a Learning subscale. All questions were administered twice: once with respect to the declarative-style homework assignments and once with respect to the narrative-style homework assignments. In this fashion, the data generated eight scales for analysis (Table 9.2).

Table 9.2 Study Scales and Subscales

Short Designation	Assignment Type	Subscales Included
D	Declarative	All
DM	Declarative	Motivation
DE	Declarative	Engagement
DL	Declarative	Learning
N	Narrative	All
NM	Narrative	Motivation
NE	Narrative	Engagement
NL	Narrative	Learning

Participants

The survey was completed by 98 respondents, students enrolled in four different sections of REL 101 across three semesters (fall, spring and summer). The sample included both female (61 percent) and male (39 percent) respondents, and included respondents who self-identified as White (58 percent), East Asian (17 percent), Latino or Hispanic (12 percent), Black (4 percent), Middle Eastern (3 percent), Pacific Islander (2 percent) and South Asian (1 percent). One percent chose not to disclose their race. Although 81 percent of the respondents considered the United States or Canada their home, other respondents reported that East Asia (10 percent), Latin America (4 percent), Africa (2 percent), Eastern Europe (1 percent) and South Asia (1 percent) were home, and 1 percent opted not to respond. The respondents reported birth years ranging from 1992 to 1998, with one participant opting not to respond; of those responding, the median birth year was 1996, and the modal birth year was 1997 (36 percent). Christian respondents composed the largest religious affiliation at 78 percent, but the sample also included nonreligious participants (19 percent), Jewish participants (2 percent) and a participant who chose not to respond (1 percent). The majority of the respondents (60 percent) indicated that they had previously experienced faith-based study of the Bible (for example, in a church or synagogue), but the majority (68 percent) also indicated that they had no previous experience with academic study of the Bible.

Results

Scale Refinement

Internal consistency estimates were obtained for all scales, and these are presented in Table 9.3. Because some of these reliability estimates were problematically low (falling significantly below the preferred minimum alpha coefficient of 0.70), individual item statistics were examined, and three items (items 10, 15 and 20) had poor psychometric performance on the IMI both for the declarative and narrative units. Thus these six items negatively affected all scales except the motivation subscale for both direct instruction (DM) and narrative instruction (NM). When these six items were removed, internal consistency estimates increased. The final reliability estimates and the scale means and standard deviations are provided in Table 9.3.

Comparison Across Educational Modes

Paired-samples *t*-tests evaluated the differences in IMI scale scores for the declarative (D) and narrative (N) educational units. The difference between scores on the learning subscales for both direct instruction (DL)

Table 9.3 Descriptive Statistics for IMI Scales

Scale	Initial Reliability	Final Reliability	Mean	SD
D	0.78	0.87	75.09	10.30
DM	0.70	0.70	25.46	3.99
DE	0.46	0.73	19.61	3.86
DL	0.64	0.79	30.12	4.55
N	0.83	0.90	73.83	12.19
NM	0.76	0.76	24.64	4.57
NE	0.31	0.69	20.48	3.81
NL	0.75	0.85	28.70	5.75

Table 9.4 Comparison Across Educational Modes

Comparison Across Educational Modes

	Paired Differences						
			95% CI				
Comparison	Diff	SD	Lower	Upper	t	df	p
D–N	1.37	13.13	−1.26	4.00	1.03	97	0.305
DM–NM (H1)	0.82	4.51	−0.09	1.72	1.79	97	0.076
DE–NE (H2)	−0.87	4.79	−1.83	0.09	−1.79	97	0.076
DL–NL (H3)	1.42	6.32	0.15	2.69	2.22	97	0.029

	Paired Differences					
		95% CI				
Comparison	Difference	Lower	Upper	t	df	p
D–N	1.37	−1.26	4.00	1.03	97	0.31
DM–NM (H1)	0.82	−0.09	1.72	1.79	97	0.08
DE–NE (H2)	−0.87	−1.83	0.09	−1.79	97	0.08
DL–NL (H3)	1.42	0.15	2.69	2.22	97	0.03

and narrative instruction (NL) was statistically significant, with higher scores obtained for the declarative units. This result contradicts hypothesis 3, which predicted that students would report learning more from the narrative units. However, statistically significant differences were not observed between D and N, between DM and NM or between the engagement subscales for both direct instruction (DE) and narrative instruction (NE). These data, summarized in Table 9.4, do not support hypotheses 1 and 2, and contradict hypothesis 3. In other words, students showed no greater motivation or engagement for narrative assignments than for

Table 9.5 Gender Differences on IMI Scales

Scale	Women M (SD)	Men M (SD)	t	p	d	r
D	74.72 (9.81)	75.95 (11.13)	0.57	0.57	0.12	0.06
DM	25.57 (3.77)	25.29 (4.36)	−0.33	0.74	−0.07	0.03
DE	19.22 (3.86)	20.24 (3.83)	1.28	0.20	0.26	0.13
DL	29.93 (4.18)	30.42 (5.14)	0.52	0.61	0.11	0.05
N	74.80 (11.55)	72.29 (13.16)	−0.99	0.32	−0.20	0.10
NM	24.72 (4.25)	24.53 (5.10)	−0.20	0.84	−0.04	0.02
NE	21.12 (3.46)	19.47 (4.14)	−2.12	0.04	−0.43	0.21
NL	28.97 (5.68)	28.29 (5.92)	−0.57	0.57	−0.12	0.06

declarative assignments and actually perceived that they learned more from declarative than from narrative assignments.

Gender Differences

Independent samples *t*-tests evaluated the differences between women and men on the IMI scale scores, and the results are provided in Table 9.5. Women obtained a significantly higher score on NE than men. No other comparisons were statistically significant. Our survey instrument, however, does not provide us with insight into *why* this distinction manifested.

Discussion

In our experiment, delivering foundational information via interactive fiction scenarios failed to motivate or engage students better than delivering the same information via declarative prose (whether in written or video formats). Moreover, students reported learning more from declarative prose than from interactive fiction scenarios. Similarly, in a study whose results were published after ours was already in progress, Andreas Lieberoth reached the "overall conclusion that making something look like a game makes it seem more fun, but other motivational variables remain largely unchanged."[31] Our results are consistent with Lieberoth's—a correspondence made more interesting by the fact that both studies used variations of the IMI and hence can be inferred to measure similar things. Several explanations for these results occur to us for the results our study yielded. These are not mutually exclusive, and other explanations are likely possible.

Perhaps the pervasively, if shallowly, gamified environment in which we intervened experimentally may have already generated the benefits one could reasonably expect from gamification in this context. As noted earlier, the course in which we implemented this experiment was already gamified to a significant degree, though only at the level of course structure and terminology, not at the level of individual assignments (refer again to Table 9.1). Lieberoth found that "adding a 'shallow' game coating to an otherwise serious activity [affected] enjoyment and face-value appreciation of the activity as gamelike—not engagement in a broader sense"—and that "good game mechanics are a nicety that may sometimes be psychologically secondary to the more shallow signals conveyed by the game artifacts themselves."[32] This possibility could be tested by implementing interactive fiction assignments in a course that featured no other aspects of gamification.

Perhaps the scenarios themselves were simply poorly designed. They were certainly early drafts, which did not change substantially across the three semesters in which they were deployed. Additionally, several of them were incomplete in certain respects but had to be deployed as they were to meet externally mandated schedules (such as fitting within a single semester). Playtesting through multiple iterations is a key feature of game design, and our study participants were reacting to the first iteration of each scenario. One known issue is the "scavenger hunt" quality of the scenarios in their current form. For example, one scenario invited students to ask whether the biblical story of Israel's exodus from Egypt (a) represents a garbled memory of the expulsion of the Hyksos from Egypt in the mid-sixteenth century BCE, (b) commemorates (perhaps with varying degrees of accuracy) a historical event that occurred in the mid-fifteenth century BCE, (c) commemorates a historical event that occurred in the early thirteenth century BCE or (d) narrates a completely fictional event. In order to collect all the data needed to participate fully in the subsequent class session, students needed to explore *each* of the possible branches. Thus students could not really succeed by "choosing their own adventures"; rather, they had to "choose all of the adventures" to be prepared for subsequent course material. Were we to deploy these scenarios again, we would seek to rectify this design flaw.

Perhaps the design of the study also contributed to the scenario design flaw just described. In order to make meaningful comparisons between the declarative and narrative units, the narrative units featured assessments identical in format and delivery to the declarative units—that is, Yield Reports (quizzes) at the end of each Harvest and Battle (tests) after every third Harvest. Indeed, the Battles mixed questions about the declarative units and questions about the narrative units without distinction. As mentioned, this design facilitated the study itself; however, it created something of a mismatch between the narrative assignments and the assessments that followed them. Lieberoth reported a similar experience.[33] Although Kapp's research suggests that story-based games can effectively teach declarative knowledge,[34] this seems to work best when that knowledge is used to make progress within the game itself, rather than merely collected within the game for use outside the game, as on a quiz.

In sum, we hypothesized that reconfiguring homework assignments as interactive fiction in a *Choose Your Own Adventure* mode would increase student motivation, engagement and self-reported learning compared with assignments that simply presented information in a declarative, textbook-style mode, but the students themselves told us otherwise. Our specific narrative assignments, at any rate, did not motivate or engage students better than declarative assignments, and students thought they learned more from our declarative assignments than from our narrative assignments. While our study was only an initial exploration whose results must be considered preliminary rather than definitive, our results do suggest that delivering basic factual/declarative knowledge through interactive fiction is not an especially promising form of gameful learning.

Notes

1 Karl M. Kapp, *The Gamification of Learning and Instruction: Game-Based Methods and Strategies for Training and Education* (San Francisco: Pfeiffer, 2012), 10.
2 Larry Johnson et al., *2011 Horizon Report* (Austin: New Media Consortium, 2011); Larry Johnson et al., *NMC Horizon Report: 2012 Higher Education Edition* (Austin: New Media Consortium, 2012); Larry Johnson et al., *NMC Horizon Report: 2013 Higher Education Edition* (Austin: New Media Consortium, 2013); Larry Johnson et al., *NMC Horizon Report: 2014 Higher Education Edition* (Austin: New Media Consortium, 2014).
3 Larry Johnson et al., *NMC Horizon Report: 2015 Higher Education Edition* (Austin: New Media Consortium, 2015); Larry Johnson et al., *NMC Horizon Report: 2016 Higher Education Edition* (Austin: New Media Consortium, 2016).
4 Kapp, *The Gamification*, 76.
5 Ibid., 75–103.
6 Ibid., 101.
7 Ibid., 102.
8 Ibid., 81. Cf. Andreas Lieberoth, "Shallow Gamification: Testing Psychological Effects of Framing an Activity as a Game," *Games and Culture* 10, no. 3 (2015): 244, who urges, "More studies should try to break clusters of game elements down to individual functional units."
9 Darina Dicheva et al., "Gamification in Education: A Systematic Mapping Study," *Educational Technology & Society* 18 (2015): 75–88.
10 Ibid., 79.
11 Sebastian Deterding et al., "From Game Design Elements to Gamefulness: Defining 'Gamification,'" in *Proceedings of the 15th Annual International Academic MindTrek Conference: Envisioning Future Media Environments*, eds. Artur Lugmayr et al. (New York: ACM, 2011), 9–15.
12 Fiona Fui-Hoon Nah et al., "Gamification of Education: A Review of Literature," in *HCI in Business*, ed. Fiona Fui-Hoon Nah (Cham, Switzerland: Springer, 2014), 401–409.
13 Thomas Malone, "Toward a Theory of Intrinsically Motivating Instruction," *Cognitive Science* 5, no. 4 (1981): 333–69; introduced to us by Kapp, *The Gamification*, 55–57.
14 Malone, "Toward a Theory," 356 (italics removed from original).
15 Ibid., 358–359.

16 Ibid., 361.
17 Ibid., 361.
18 Ibid., 361.
19 Ibid., 363.
20 Ibid., 363.
21 Mark R. Lepper, "Motivational Considerations in the Study of Instruction," *Cognition and Instruction* 5, no. 4 (1988): 289–309; introduced to us by Kapp, *The Gamification*, 57–58.
22 Kapp, *The Gamification*, 58.
23 Ibid., 57–58.
24 Philip R. Davies, *First Person: Essays in Biblical Autobiography* (New York: Sheffield Academic Press, 2002); Davies, *Yours Faithfully: Virtual Letters from the Bible* (London: Equinox, 2004); Bruce Longenecker, *The Lost Letters of Pergamum: A Story from the New Testament World* (Grand Rapids: Baker Academic, 2003).
25 David Tabb Stewart and Adam Porter, *The Josianic Reform: Deuteronomy, Prophecy, and Israelite Religion, Instructor's Manual*, version 3.0, 2008, http://reacting consortiumlibrary.org/games-in-development. The "Josiah game" has not yet been formally published. For published Reacting games that engage religious, and sometimes specifically biblical, issues, see Mark C. Carnes and Michael P. Winship, *The Trial of Anne Hutchinson: Liberty, Law, and Intolerance in Puritan New England* (New York: Norton, 2013); Frederick Purnell Jr., Mark C. Carnes, and Michael S. Pettersen, *The Trial of Galileo: Aristotelianism, the "New Cosmology," and the Catholic Church, 1616–1633* (New York: Norton, 2014); Marsha Driscoll, Elizabeth E. Dunn, Dann Siems, and B. Kamran Swanson, *Charles Darwin, the Copley Medal, and the Rise of Naturalism, 1861–1864* (New York: Norton, 2014).
26 Mark C. Carnes, *Minds on Fire: How Role-Immersion Games Transform College* (Cambridge, MA: Harvard University Press, 2014).
27 Stewart and Porter, *The Josianic Reform*, 22.
28 Nicolas W. Proctor, *Reacting to the Past Game Designer's Handbook*, 3rd ed. (New York: Reacting to the Past, 2013), 99–100.
29 Ian Bogost, "Gamification Is Bullshit," (paper, *For the Win: Serious Gamification*, Philadelphia, PA, August 8–9, 2011), and subsequently published at http://bogost.com/blog/gamification_is_bullshit.shtml; see now Bogost, "Why Gamification Is Bullshit," in *The Gameful World: Approaches, Issues, Applications*, eds. Steffen P. Walz and Sebastian Deterding (Cambridge: MIT Press, 2015), 65–79. See also Sarah Smith-Robbins, "'This Game Sucks': How to Improve the Gamification of Education," *EDUCAUSE Review* (January/February 2011): 58–59.
30 Richard Ryan and Edward Deci, *Intrinsic Motivation Inventory*, http://self determinationtheory.org/questionnaires.
31 Lieberoth, "Shallow Gamification," 241; Lieberoth's study also used the Intrinsic Motivation Inventory.
32 Ibid., 244.
33 Ibid., 243.
34 Kapp, *The Gamification*, 169.

Bibliography

Bogost, Ian. "Gamification Is Bullshit." Paper presented at For the Win: Serious Gamification, Philadelphia, PA, August 8–9, 2011. www.bogost.com/blog/gamification_is_bullshit.shtml.

———. "Why Gamification Is Bullshit." In *The Gameful World: Approaches, Issues, Applications*, edited by Steffen P. Walz and Sebastian Deterding, 65–79. Cambridge: MIT Press, 2015.

Carnes, Mark C., and Michael P. Winship. *Minds on Fire: How Role-Immersion Games Transform College*. Cambridge: Harvard University Press, 2014.

———. *The Trial of Anne Hutchinson: Liberty, Law, and Intolerance in Puritan New England*. New York: Norton, 2013.

Davies, Philip R. *First Person: Essays in Biblical Autobiography*. New York: Sheffield Academic Press, 2002.

———. *Yours Faithfully: Virtual Letters from the Bible*. London: Equinox, 2004.

Deterding, Sebastian, Dan Dixon, Rilla Khaled, and Lennart E. Nacke. "From Game Design Elements to Gamefulness: Defining 'Gamification.'" In *Proceedings of the 15th Annual International Academic MindTrek Conference: Envisioning Future Media Environments*, edited by Artur Lugmayr, Heljä Franssila, Christian Safran, and Imed Hammouda, 9–15. New York: ACM, 2011.

Driscoll, Marsha, Elizabeth E. Dunn, Dann Siems, and B. Kamran Swanson. *Charles Darwin, the Copley Medal, and the Rise of Naturalism, 1861–1864*. New York: Norton, 2014.

Lepper, Mark R. "Motivational Considerations in the Study of Instruction." *Cognition and Instruction* 5, no. 4 (1988): 289–309.

Lieberoth, Andreas. "Shallow Gamification: Testing Psychological Effects of Framing an Activity as a Game." *Games and Culture* 10, no. 3 (2015): 229–248.

Longenecker, Bruce. *The Lost Letters of Pergamum: A Story from the New Testament World*. Grand Rapids: Baker Academic, 2003.

Malone, Thomas. "Toward a Theory of Intrinsically Motivating Instruction." *Cognitive Science* 5, no. 4 (1981): 333–369.

Nah, Fiona Fui-Hoon, Qing Zeng, Venkata Rajasekhar Telaprolu, Abhishek Padmanabhuni Ayyappa, and Brenda Eschenbrenner. "Gamification of Education: A Review of Literature." In *HCI in Business: First International Conference, HCIB 2014, Held as Part of HCI International 2014, Heraklion, Crete, Greece, June 22–27, 2014, Proceedings*, edited by Fiona Fui-Hoon Nah, 401–409. Cham, Switzerland: Springer, 2014.

Proctor, Nicolas W. *Reacting to the Past Game Designer's Handbook*. 3rd ed. New York: Reacting to the Past, 2013.

Purnell, Frederick, Jr., Mark C. Carnes, and Michael S. Pettersen. *The Trial of Galileo: Aristotelianism, the "New Cosmology," and the Catholic Church, 1616–1633*. New York: Norton, 2014.

Ryan, Richard, and Edward Deci. *Intrinsic Motivation Inventory*. http://selfdeterminationtheory.org/questionnaires.

Smith-Robbins, Sarah. "'This Game Sucks': How to Improve the Gamification of Education." *EDUCAUSE Review* (January/February 2011): 58–59.

Stewart, David Tabb, and Adam Porter. *The Josianic Reform: Deuteronomy, Prophecy, and Israelite Religion. Instructor's Manual*. Version 3.0. 2008. http://reactingconsortiumlibrary.org/games-in-development.

Part III
Using Technology to Expand Your Classroom

10 Technology Twist on the Visiting Professor

Gerald L. Stevens

The Background Narrative

A little background narrative will set the context for this chapter. For the last three decades, I have been professor of New Testament and Greek at New Orleans Baptist Theological Seminary, where I focus on Greek grammar, Pauline studies (including the book of Acts) and apocalyptic literature. My most recent publications have been *Revelation: The Past and Future of John's Apocalypse*,[1] *Acts: A New Vision of the People of God*,[2] and *Stevens Greek Workbook: A Companion to the Accordance Module*.[3] I mention my recent publications because each derives directly from my classroom work and is tightly integrated into my classroom lectures. In fact, the content of these books is the composite of my notes, class handouts and illustrations from class presentations. Thus my entire teaching career has been focused almost exclusively on the classroom experience.

The classroom experience has changed radically since I entered the teaching profession. These changes are powered mainly by personal computers and the Internet, in tandem with a plethora of personal electronic devices. IBM was on the front side of this wave of electronic innovation by introducing the first personal computer to the American public in August 1981, three months after I walked across the stage with my doctoral degree. Named the IBM Personal Computer model 5150, with IBM CGA monitor model 5153, IBM PC keyboard and IBM 5152 printer/paper stand, the system ran PC DOS 1.0 CP/M-86, powered by an Intel 8088 chip running at 4.77 MHz. Memory ranged from 16 KB up to 256 KB—unbelievably primitive by today's standards.[4] For example, at its June 2017 World Wide Developers Conference, Apple Corporation announced a new iMac model, the iMac Pro, that will have 18 core Xeon processors providing 22 teraflops of GPU performance to facilitate real-time 3-D rendering and VR content creation on a display capable of a billion colors, stored on a 4 TB hard drive and presented with 128 GB of memory. This new iMac Pro's memory is *half a million times more* than the original IBM PC!

Only a decade after the first IBM PC hit the market, software developers saw a great opportunity for its use in business and education markets through a new genre called "presentation" software. This software facilitated sales pitches in the business industry and lectures in the educational world. Presentation software effectively combined three technologies into one. The first technology was the slide projector, which allowed users to present 35 mm translucent photographic slides one slide at a time. The Kodak Company led the way through its Kodak Carousel Projector, popularized in the 1960s with its round tray holding 80–140 slides.[5] The second technology was the film projector, a large and heavy mechanical device looping a continuous roll of film from one spool to another across a projection lamp, which later morphed into the filmstrip projector and then the analog videotape cassette read by a VCR machine. The personal computer transformed this analog film world into digital bits and bytes, enabling video to make the technological leap from analog to digital, leaving behind massive spools of tape and miles of VCR cassettes. The third technology was the ubiquitous bullet-point lecturing device called an overhead cell projector, perfected at 3M in the 1960s by Roger C. Appledorn.[6] This static system used transparent sheets of cellulose acetate manually placed on a glass surface with a lamp underneath shooting bright light up to an angled reflecting mirror on an extension arm, magnifying an enlarged image onto a projection screen.

Formerly, each system required its own proprietary mechanical device for implementation in the classroom. With the computer, all three systems (images, movies and bullet points) were amalgamated into one box, which was incredibly powerful and liberating. In combination with an LCD projection system to broadcast the result to a crowd, computers with their presentation software represented a quantum leap in using technology in the classroom. Back in 1994, I was the first professor at my institution to abandon Kodak carousel slide projectors, cumbersome VCR machines and the overhead cell system altogether to implement a computer using presentation software in my classroom. In fact, my first sabbatical leave was granted to accomplish this very objective. The world of the classroom never has been the same. Extremely powerful and inspiring great creativity for presenting lectures, presentation software has been a pedagogical game changer and is the backbone of my class lectures today. Yet I would acknowledge that presentation software most certainly is not the be-all and end-all of the classroom experience.

The Foreground Need

Presentation software does not suffice for all pedagogical strategies in the classroom. The problem with the extraordinary opportunities afforded by computer presentation software is that the system pedagogically is still static. The information is "burned in"—that is, fixed in some static way on the "slides," even those including video, such as I offer regularly to my students. The video might show a taped interview of a scholar on a question or topic, but the conversation is one way. Students have no interactivity with the scholar, and educators know full well that interactivity is one way to supercharge the learning experience. Even with all the great presentations I have cooked up—lectures so rich in multimedia of all kinds they take gigabytes of storage for one file—I saw a need for classroom interactivity. I did not want a taped lecture of a scholar; I wanted that scholar in my classroom. I was well aware that a live presentation and question-and-answer period with a visiting scholar infuses a session with interest and affords significant pedagogical gains with higher student motivation and engagement.[7]

In a way, I already have been bringing myself into the classroom as a sort of "surrogate" visiting professor by incorporating my own on-location videos shot as I have traveled extensively in Europe, Turkey and the Middle East in my research at archeological sites, museums and areas of interest following New Testament backgrounds on Paul and the early church. Within these videos, I have integrated still images gathered during my travels that enhance the video discussion. Over the years, I have developed hundreds of these three- to five-minute "video vignettes" that students find interesting and informative and can access anytime online outside of class, not just during my lecture presentations in class. For added benefit, I can even initiate my own question-and-answer follow-up after any one of these videos, which proffers the ambiance of the visiting professor and helps to bring some element of interactivity into the classroom experience. One example of a video vignette I produced that is available online gives an overview of the miraculous preservation of 276 passengers and crew in the story of Paul's storm and shipwreck on the island of Malta told in Acts 27:14–44.[8]

While these lectures can be multimedia rich, and even in themselves offer something of the "visiting professor" feel, they lack the full effect of a genuine "visiting professor" experience—a new voice, a new personality, a new world of experience and knowledge brought into the classroom that by nature vivifies student interest and motivation.

The difficulties in facilitating this type of activity in the classroom are expense and logistics. For example, normally one does not have the desired expert nearby, and paying travel and board expenses can overwhelm the available resources. On occasion, an institutional special event may have a roster of scholars that includes a specialist in an area that pertains to a scheduled lecture. An instructor can take advantage of this opportunity by inviting the specialist to present in a class if he or she is available. Logistically, however, this may be difficult if the institutional event conflicts with the class schedule. Another downside of trying to piggyback on an institutional event is that the event timing rarely coincides with the class syllabus for that semester. As a consequence, any potential presentation, while probably worthwhile, may not be pedagogically timely.

Fortunately, technology has advanced to reproduce better the classroom experience of a genuine visiting professor through videoconferencing that facilitates distance learning. The key is wireless access, whether Internet or cellular. Distance learning through technology has been part of institutional endeavors for some time now. Our own institution uses compressed, interactive video. Using a high-speed data link, an instructor can pipe video streams to students in two or more locations, with video from those locations streamed back to the main campus classroom. This type of video streaming, however, requires a dedicated infrastructure of expensive technology, T1 video lines[9] and personnel to manage the system.

Another innovation that bridges the distance for students remote to a main campus is an online learning system, such as Blackboard, which we have incorporated into our online learning strategy at our institution. Again, however, this resource requires a decided institutional investment into a technology infrastructure, along with personnel to manage the system. In the main, these types of technology resources are expensive and personnel heavy. Not all institutions can afford such technology venues. Educators strapped for resources need inexpensive video for classroom purposes.

The Technology Twist

Inexpensive videoconferencing in its many forms is the technology twist that opens up a world of interactivity in the classroom. One group of options that bridges the distance gap and to which almost everyone has access is inexpensive social media platforms. Most social networks, including Snapchat, Instagram, Facebook and Skype, have invested heavily in elements such as messaging and videoconferencing. Skype, for example, started out as a simple peer-to-peer chat service that grew to include video in 2006 but has evolved into a multifaceted, content-rich, real-time information-sharing social platform.[10] Almost everyone who has a portable electronic device—whether phone, tablet or computer—has a Skype, Facebook, Instagram or Snapchat account. More and more, these modern social media venues are offering the basic technology needed for videoconferencing.

Another inexpensive option for videoconferencing at the institutional level is a dedicated videoconferencing service. Such services are far more flexible and less cumbersome than institutional online learning platforms such as Blackboard, which really does not actually facilitate genuine videoconferencing. One example of a dedicated videoconferencing solution is BlueJeans.[11] The BlueJeans system offers plans that are far less expensive and much more easily accessed than online learning systems because the BlueJeans operation is focused on offering only one service: videoconferencing. Several other options are available on this growing list of venues with platforms for live videoconferencing using the Internet and cellular networks.

These inexpensive videoconferencing options were the inspiration for an experiment I conducted built on the paradigm of the visiting scholar. I used the BlueJeans videoconferencing technology to "pipe in" a visiting scholar from the other side of the world to my classroom to present a topic pertinent to our lecture series and to interact with students after his presentation.[12] This technology twist overcomes the major hurdles identified earlier, such as availability of the scholar, expense of the technology, schedule coordination issues when piggybacking on an institutional event and timeliness of the topic in terms of the class syllabus.

The Immediate Occasion

The following description provides a basic overview of the experiment. The seminary class I was teaching was a Greek exegesis of Paul's letter to the Romans in the New Testament. At this particular time in the semester, March 2016, we were studying the meaning of the Greek term *hilastērion* that Paul uses to describe the work of Christ in Romans 3:25. I had heard a presentation related to this crucial term at the annual meeting of the Society of Biblical Literature (SBL) by Dr. Mark Wilson entitled, "HILAS-TERION and Imperial Rhetoric: A Possible New Reading of Romans 3:25." I wanted my class to explore with Dr. Wilson the possibilities of the imperial rhetoric echoing behind Paul's use of this term, giving possible nuance to Paul's meaning. The only problem was that Dr. Wilson lives in Antalya, Turkey.

Professor Wilson directs the Asia Minor Research Institute based in Antalya, a seaport city on the southern Mediterranean coast of Turkey.[13] Dr. Wilson is in demand as a researcher, author, lecturer and tour guide. He is a specialist on first-century Roman roads, especially in Turkey (ancient Asia Minor), and is consulted regularly by the cartographers who produce the Bible maps in various editions of English Bibles. His most recent publication is *Biblical Turkey: A Guide to the Jewish and Christian Sites of Asia Minor*.[14] I had met Dr. Wilson previously, having consulted him in planning several of my own trips to Turkey to research historical background related to the seven churches of Revelation and the missionary journeys of Paul.

Months before the class began, I invited Dr. Wilson to use his SBL presentation as the basis for a revised presentation suitable for my class. He had prepared a PowerPoint pdf handout of his slides beforehand and made this file available through Dropbox. The file included the basic points of his discussion and his illustrations. Students downloaded the pdf of his slides to their computers prior to the class session, which

150 *Gerald L. Stevens*

enabled them to follow the lecture during the actual class session. We streamed both his PowerPoint presentation and a live video of Dr. Wilson through an LCD projector for the session. An eight-hour time differential between Antalya and New Orleans put our class at 8:00 a.m. in New Orleans and Dr. Wilson at 4:00 p.m. in Turkey, so we were able to bridge the time gap effectively.

Dr. Wilson developed his ideas on a possible background to the meaning of the Greek term *hilastērion* in Romans 3:25 based on inscriptions recently found in archeological excavations in the Roman theater at ancient Metropolis in western Turkey near the village Yeniköy in Torbali. This ancient city is not a familiar name to Bible students, since the city never is mentioned in the Bible, but was well known in its day. Metropolis was just north of the famous ancient city of Ephesus, which offers a possible connection to the Pauline mission. According to Acts, Paul spent several years in ministry in Ephesus on his third missionary journey, which is said to have affected the entire province (Acts 19:10). One could conjecture that Metropolis, only 19 miles north of Ephesus, was likely in the orbit of Pauline influence at this time. Metropolis also would have been a city through which Paul likely passed on his way out of Ephesus to Macedonia (Acts 20:1).

Key to the history of Metropolis was its alignment with Antony and Cleopatra against Octavian in the decisive battle of Actium in 31 BC, which Octavian won. This victory finally consolidated the entire Roman world, east and west, under one Roman general, effectively ending two centuries of Roman civil wars during the fading years of the Roman Republic and marking the turning point toward the formation of what became known as the Roman Empire. While advantageous in the larger picture for the peace of Rome, at the local level in Asia Minor the results of Actium were disastrous. Octavian's victory put most cities of Asia Minor at great disadvantage and in serious political jeopardy. These cities unfortunately had joined league with Antony and Cleopatra.[15] After these two allies' forces were utterly destroyed in this decisive naval engagement, Antony and Cleopatra committed suicide, leaving Asia Minor holding the bag for war reparations and repercussions. Immediately after the battle of Actium, Octavian stationed himself in Ephesus for several months.[16]

This move was quite deliberate. His temporary relocation represented a savvy political strategy to force obeisance to the victor among civic leaders throughout Asia Minor. A resident of Ephesus, Octavian received supplicant delegations from cities of Asia Minor, including Metropolis, whose aristocrats and civic leaders pleaded mercy and pledged fealty to the new ruler. Normally, the conquered could be expected to be vanquished, leaders executed and aristocratic families humiliated into slavery. Quite unexpectedly, however, Octavian was magnanimous. Contrary to all expectations, he made peace by reconciling with his former political enemies. Octavian applied his brilliant administrative skills toward reorganizing the imploding fragments of the Roman Republic and used his vaunted political savvy with both the Roman Senate and the Roman people to lay the foundations of what would became the Roman Empire. Later, the Roman Senate gave him the honorific name Augustus for his many accomplishments—the name by which he is known to this day.

This Roman history provides necessary background for understanding Dr. Wilson's hypothesis about inscriptions recently discovered in the 1990s in the theater at Metropolis. Interestingly, Dr. Wilson points out that these newly uncovered imperial dedicatory altars characterize Octavian as the *hilastērion* of Asia Minor. The meaning of *hilastērion* in this context is something on the order of the "reconciler" of Asia Minor. Thus this designation for Octavian in the altar inscriptions in a quite literal way seems to follow the actual history of the cities of Asia Minor in the time period of the inscriptions because the inscriptions refer to Octavian as Caesar, not by his later famous name of Augustus or as emperor.

The potential connection to Paul is the inscription term *hilastērion*. In a letter written to the Romans in the heart of the empire in Rome shortly after Paul was in Ephesus, a possible allusion to this imperial usage could be behind Paul's own use of *hilastērion* for Jesus in Romans 3:25. The traditional understanding for Paul's use is the well-known Old Testament association of *hilastērion* with the mercy seat in the temple, translated as "place of mercy" or "act of mercy" within the Jewish sacrificial system. However, with these newly revealed inscriptions at Metropolis, another possible nuance has surfaced—a direct, political nuance based on recent Augustan imperial history—that also could be echoed in Paul's use in this letter to the Romans.[17]

The Classroom Presentation

For the class session innovating a technology twist on the visiting professor, Dr. Wilson and I agreed on a 25- to 30-minute live PowerPoint presentation over the Internet by Dr. Wilson, followed by a fifteen minute question-and-answer period in which Dr. Wilson would be on-screen in front of the students. Dr. Wilson would be able to see the students and focus on those asking questions. As mentioned, I decided to use the institution's BlueJeans technology for the presentation, which allowed me to have a technician in the class to troubleshoot any technical problems that might arise during the actual session. My goal was to maximize the odds for a successful experience for this experimental foray into classroom pedagogy. Fortunately, no significant technical problems occurred.

As an alternative, I could have set up the event as a simple Skype session, although the live PowerPoint presentation would have had to have been configured differently. If monetary or other constraints had not allowed for the use of BlueJeans, each student could have downloaded a copy of the PowerPoint presentation onto their computers from Dropbox or other sources. Each student then could run the PowerPoint presentation on their own computers and advance to the next slide in sequence at Dr. Wilson's direction. [18]

With either Skype or BlueJeans, we can bridge the distance of time and continents on our own schedule and in a quite timely fashion without much cost and with fairly simple logistics to bring students face-to-face with an expert in the field. After Dr. Wilson's presentation, the students were given a chance to interact and ask questions.

Word of the presentation spread on campus because I had announced the special session to the class well in advance to help prepare them for the event. Admittedly, I had intended the event to be pretty much exclusive to the class, since I was conducting a pedagogical experiment to explore its effectiveness as a classroom tool. To be honest, I was not completely confident the technology would be as functional as desired and might fail to deliver the desired effect. Perhaps subconsciously I had lowered my own expectations so as not to be disappointed should the experiment fall short of the goal. Students on campus calculated differently. I was surprised to receive requests from students not enrolled in the class to join in the event. I allowed them to attend but made clear the question-and-answer session primarily was for class members.

I mention this unexpected attendance development to provide anecdotal evidence that the visiting-scholar concept is still a draw for classroom pedagogy even today. I suspect the reason lies in the promise of real-time interactivity for the students within a classroom setting, which seems to confirm that classroom interactivity increases interest and motivation. Another indicator of interest is that I had perfect attendance for class for that day, which any educator automatically marks as significant by default.

The Q&A Session

Educators who pause in a lecture to allow for questions know the disappointment of that "awkward silence." Usually, that silence means the students are not engaged. We could assume that the lecture to that point was brilliant and skillfully answered every question, but that would be a faulty assumption in too many cases. What I have noted over the years is that a visiting professor almost always gets questions. This effect is another sign of the naturally positive effect of interactivity in the classroom, most especially when the interactivity is person to person.

Following Dr. Wilson's live presentation, the questions were immediate, brisk, broadly distributed across the class and thought provoking. Students were synthesizing the content in a much more intentional way, processing new thoughts and challenging old assumptions about the "meaning" of a Pauline phrase. In seminary, we often "theologize" the scriptural text and lose sight of its inherent historical context and the natural resonances for the ancient audience that are latent in that context. The original Roman audience hearing Paul's letter to the Romans for the first time probably did not hear with Reformation ears. Realizing this contextual reality is a genuine "aha" moment for many students. Having a visiting scholar piped into the classroom to introduce this possibility to the students in a real-time experience ripe for mental processing is a pedagogical achievement that a "static" lecture, even one packed full of multimedia, might not have.

Dr. Wilson also seemed to be energized by the question-and-answer session. He had the opportunity to disabuse students of bad assumptions, fill in gaps in historical information, clarify pertinent points and process new thoughts for himself. He provided a valuable integration of his scholarly knowledge and experience with the educational level of students in a seminary classroom. After the event, I reflected on how Dr. Wilson was adept in both using technology and teaching a class. I was reminded that an obvious criteria for a visiting professor should be to find not only an expert in the field but also someone skilled in technology and teaching.

The Developing Story

After the class session's success, both in my estimation and in the eyes of my students, the thought occurred to me to propose a paper to the Academic Teaching and Biblical Studies section at the annual meeting of the SBL in San Antonio since the theme that year was "Teaching the Bible with Technology." My proposal was accepted, and I presented an overview of my experimental "visiting professor" event.[19] In that presentation, I used video of the actual class session rather than simply describing the event. The video had been shot at my request by our technology support team on campus because I had anticipated possible future demonstration of the event to inspire other faculty on our campus to think innovatively about easy ways to incorporate more interactive technology into the classroom. While I cannot show video of the actual class session in this printed venue, my narrative with its illustrative online links has been detailed sufficiently enough to provide a concrete formulation of the background, foreground, planning and execution of this event.

I would conclude that the experience was a success for the purposes of this particular class. Overwhelmingly positive student feedback, although only anecdotal, seems to reinforce this conclusion. We had excellent participation during the actual class session, and follow-up discussions were animated and sustained. Students continued to process the experience and incorporate new horizons of understanding Romans for the rest of the semester. These post-event indications are constituent ingredients to deep learning results that become more than cognitive but even affective and behavioral.

I realize that several factors favored the implementation of my idea. I already knew the scholar I intended to invite into the classroom. My institution already had a license for the videoconferencing platform I used for the event. I already knew exactly what the presentation was going to involve since I had heard the essence of the presentation in another venue. The class itself had good corporate personality with intelligent and motivated students, so I was confident the visiting-scholar concept would meet the expectations of this particular class. Granted all these factors, I am persuaded that piping in a "visitor" (of whatever type is appropriate to the class and its goals) increases learning on the simple pedagogical principle of interactivity.

Conclusion

My goal in this chapter was to provide a narrative of my experiment with a technologically driven idea for my classroom. Even more creative ways can be used to bring the outside world into our classrooms using videoconferencing. For example, our institution, in conjunction with Israeli antiquities authorities, conducts an annual archeological excavation at Tel Gezer in Israel, which was used as a fortress in the kingdom of Solomon. This excavation has had quite notable success. The premier find is the largest and oldest monumental water system ever discovered in the Ancient Near East, now potentially dated to the Middle Bronze Age using the recently discovered Canaanite gate at Tel Gezer.[20] The excavation is only halfway through the tunnel, which has required removing 550 tons of rock mud. Interesting artifacts from the Canaanite period include a rare scarab and silver pendant discovered incidentally in a storeroom. With this in mind, I can imagine bringing an Israeli authority who is live on-site in Tel Gezer into the classroom in New Orleans through videoconferencing to describe an excavation find.

I think we should be more innovative in considering ways in which modern technology, which continues to expand and offer ever more powerful opportunities, may bridge the obstacles to accomplishing classroom interactivity. I am thinking here particularly of developments in the software fields of 3-D and VR. Who would have dreamed of the power resident today in the tablet or smartphone clutched in a child's hands back in the heady days of the fall of 1981 when the first personal computer for individual consumers was introduced? With this chapter, I hope to inspire educators to think innovatively about ways of using videoconferencing tools for class purposes, whether through visiting professors, live demonstrations, live interactivity with active archeological fieldwork or one of many other possibilities that go beyond the now traditional concepts of presentation resources for the classroom.

Notes

1. Gerald L. Stevens, *Revelation: The Past and Future of John's Apocalypse* (Eugene, OR: Pickwick, 2014).
2. Gerald L. Stevens, *A New Vision of the People of God* (Eugene, OR: Pickwick, 2016).
3. Gerald L. Stevens, *Stevens Greek Workbook: A Companion to the Accordance Module* (Eugene, OR: Pickwick, 2017).
4. See Paul E. Ceruzzi, *A History of Modern Computing*, 2nd ed. (Cambridge: MIT Press, 2003).
5. See Allan T. Kohl, "Revisioning Art History: How a Century of Change in Imaging Technologies Helped to Shape a Discipline," *VRA Bulletin* 39, no. 1, art. 2, http://online.vraweb.org/vrab/vol39/iss1/2; cf. Meghan Bogardus Cortez, "Kodak Carousel Projectors Revolutionized the Lecture," *EdTechMagaine.com*, September 26, 2016, https://edtechmagazine.com/higher/article/2016/09/kodak-carousel-projectors-revolutionized-lecture.
6. "A Century of Innovation: The 3M Story," *3M Company*, http://multimedia.3m.com/mws/media/171240O/3m-coi-book-tif.pdf.
7. Motivation researchers have studied the value of student engagement; see Jochem Thijs and Maykel Verkuyten, "Students' Anticipated Situational Engagement: The Roles of Teacher Behavior, Personal Engagement, and Gender," *The Journal of Genetic Psychology* 170, no. 3 (2009): 268–286. The significant role of engagement in academic achievement has been covered by Andrew J. Martin, "The Student Motivation Scale: A Tool for Measuring and Enhancing Motivation," *Australian Journal of Guidance and Counseling* 11 (2001): 1–20.
8. Available online at http://drkoine.com/movies/4jr/Malta06-ShipwreckSalvationMiracle.mp4.
9. A T1 data line is simply a twisted pair of copper wires originally developed for the Bell telephone system. Consumer telephone lines can transmit data across a twisted-pair line at only 56 Kbps, but T1 twisted-pair lines can transmit data at 1.544 Mbps, a speed that facilitates high-speed data transmission, Internet access, voice and videoconferencing.
10. Skype rolled out a major redesign update in June 2017 and was completely rebuilt by its programmers from the ground up. The paradigm shift is to a mobile-first, cloud-first strategy. Social media is being integrated thoroughly into the interface to customize the platform to an individual user's own personal networks.
11. The BlueJeans commercial site is available at www.bluejeans.com.
12. I used the BlueJeans system because our institution has contracted with this service. However, I am confident that other ubiquitous venues such as Skype or Apple's FaceTime on Mac and iOS could produce a similar result.
13. In the Bible, this bustling metropolis is the ancient port of Attalia in the ancient Pamphylia-Lycia region bordering southern Galatia. The author of Acts mentions Attalia at the end of Paul's first missionary journey on the return to Antioch.
14. Mark Wilson, *Biblical Turkey: A Guide to the Jewish and Christian Sites of Asia Minor* (Istanbul: Ege Yayinlari, 2010).
15. Plutarch, *Antony*, 56.1; Plutarch. *The Parallel Lives*. Translated by Bernadotte Perrin et al. 28 vols. LCL. Cambridge: Harvard University Press, 1914–1969.
16. Dio Cassius, *Roman History*, trans. Ernest Carey, LCL (Cambridge: Harvard University Press, 1914), 51.4.1.
17. For an overview of the Metropolis inscriptions as a possible subtext for Romans 3:25, see the streaming video on my website at http://drkoine.com/movies/3mj/MetropolisInscriptions.mp4.

18 Skype is undertaking a major rebuild of their entire platform, so more media-rich presentation interactivity might be available in the future.
19 Gerald L. Stevens, "Technology Twist on the Visiting Professor" (presentation, Society of Biblical Literature Annual Meeting, San Antonio, TX, 2016).
20 Daniel Warner and Eli Yanni, "Archeological Views: One Thing Leads to Another," *Biblical Archeology Review* 43, no. 3 (May/June 2017): 26–27, 56–57.

Bibliography

3M Company. *A Century of Innovation: The 3M Story.* 2002. http://multimedia.3m.com/mws/media/171240O/3m-coi-book-tif.pdf.

Cassius, Dio. *Roman History.* Translated by Ernest Carey, LCL. Cambridge: Harvard University Press; London: William Heinemann, 1914.

Ceruzzi, Paul E. *A History of Modern Computing.* 2nd ed. Cambridge: MIT Press, 2003.

Cortez, Meghan Bogardus. "Kodak Carousel Projectors Revolutionized the Lecture." *EdTechMagaine.com.* September 26, 2016. https://edtechmagazine.com/higher/article/2016/09/kodak-carousel-projectors-revolutionized-lecture.

Kohl, Allan T. "Revisioning Art History: How a Century of Change in Imaging Technologies Helped to Shape a Discipline." *VRA Bulletin* 39, no. 1, article 2. http://online.vraweb.org/vrab/vol39/iss1/2.

Martin, Andrew J. "The Student Motivation Scale: A Tool for Measuring and Enhancing Motivation." *Australian Journal of Guidance and Counseling* 11 (2001): 1–20.

Plutarch. *The Parallel Lives.* Translated by Bernadotte Perrin et al. 28 vols. LCL. Cambridge: Harvard University Press, 1914–1969.

Stevens, Gerald L. *Acts: A New Vision of the People of God.* Eugene, OR: Pickwick, 2016.

_____. *Revelation: The Past and Future of John's Apocalypse.* Eugene, OR: Pickwick, 2014.

_____. *Stevens Greek Workbook: A Companion to the Accordance Module.* Eugene, OR: Pickwick, 2017.

_____. "Technology Twist on the Visiting Professor." Paper presented at the Society of Biblical Literature Annual Meeting, San Antonio, TX, 2016.

Thijs, Jochem, and Maykel Verkuyten. "Students' Anticipated Situational Engagement: The Roles of Teacher Behavior, Personal Engagement, and Gender." *The Journal of Genetic Psychology* 170, no. 3 (2009): 268–286.

Warner, Daniel, and Eli Yanni. "Archeological Views: One Thing Leads to Another." *Biblical Archeology Review* 43, no. 3 (May/June 2017): 26–27; 56–57.

Wilson, Mark. *Biblical Turkey: A Guide to the Jewish and Christian Sites of Asia Minor.* Istanbul: Ege Yayinlari, 2010.

11 Taming the MOOS
Massive Online Open Seminars in Religion

Phyllis Zagano

Introduction

The developing body of knowledge regarding online education argues both its benefits and its dangers. Some argue that online education has a place within the larger landscape of education,[1] while others argue that the online process is a money-saving (and ultimately destructive) attempt to automate education.[2] Added to these perspectives are considerations of massive online open courses (MOOCs), which often do not bear credit and which create unique challenges. So why consider offering an online course? Further, why consider offering a MOOC?

Ample research demonstrates that online courses serve the scientific and mathematical communities well, both because of the nature of the materials and the opportunity for students to continue reviewing materials at liberty.[3] The same perspective views online language arts courses positively, in large part owing to the opportunities for repetition.

Online teaching in the social sciences and the humanities often does not have such obvious benefits, although the addition of online components to classroom-based courses and the creation of "blended" courses show educational promise. For example, the addition of online documentary films to a history course or recordings of readings of poetry by individual poets to a literature course engenders interesting perspectives in classroom discussion. Of course, the documentary or the poetry reading can be shown in the classroom with the students present, and for shorter recordings, the immediacy of the moment can stimulate engaging discussion, but each may be equally effective in the wholly online or blended environment as additional readings.

Less so than the blended course, the fully online course in the social sciences or the humanities has both supporters and detractors. Even they who argue there is no substitute for classroom-based education do not argue against online education when it provides a public service to relatively underserved communities and others that are otherwise unable to access education. Further, even if online education efforts are viewed solely as added benefits to classroom-based education, or as efforts to provide education to underserved populations, then online courses in the humanities and social sciences gain status.

Moving beyond online education to fully open courses, the sort of MOOCs that garner hundreds or even thousands of people, one can appreciate their social service component. That is, the courses can open an avenue to education not otherwise available. From the perspective of the educational institution, the MOOC can be seen as a "loss leader" to showcase faculty and is presented free of charge to a potential classroom-based audience.

Arguments against MOOCs are plentiful, mainly involving finances and direction of resources. Lack of revenue to support free online efforts militates against paying faculty and support staff to develop and teach a free credit-bearing course. Further, the creation of MOOCs is an expensive undertaking.[4]

Against these latter criticisms, it can be argued that some applications for free online courses stress neither budgetary nor faculty resources, while simultaneously offering colleges and universities a wider online presence. These applications provide faculty the opportunity, under the umbrella of the university, to present the fruits of their research across geographical boundaries in a longer and more structured format than a one-off lecture, while coincidentally offering the university the opportunity to showcase faculty research.

Conceptualizing the Hofstra Massive Online Open Seminar: The MOOS

The varied considerations—both pro and con—led to my approaching Hofstra University with a plan for a noncredit online event that I called a Massive Online Open Seminar (MOOS), which offered me the opportunity to present my own research in a relatively lengthy (30 day) structured format. The project was intentionally labeled a "MOOS" as opposed to a "MOOC" insofar as it carried neither credit nor the appurtenances of a credit-bearing course (examinations, papers, grading).

Along with other institutions, Hofstra University, a private, nonsectarian, coeducational university, has not entered the MOOC market. Its 240-acre campus includes 113 buildings that house 35 residence halls and 11 schools or colleges, including schools of law, medicine and business. In addition to offering approximately 2,000 classroom-based courses annually, the university has a robust online presence and offers many distance-learning courses for credit, especially during summer months. Hofstra's College of Liberal Arts and Sciences includes a small Department of Religion, which emphasizes the academic study of religious traditions both historically and comparatively, with occasional online courses.[5]

Hofstra's small religion department has few majors. Within Hofstra's traditional classroom or online world, it would be nearly impossible to fill a credit-bearing course on the history of and current discussion about my research into the ordination of women as deacons in the Catholic Churches, and such a discussion in an introduction to Christianity course would be necessarily short. Yet my own experience of delivering visiting lectures at various colleges and universities around the world demonstrates the fact that the topic is of interest to many individuals, especially given that Christianity claims nearly one-third of the world's population. Christianity's approach toward women has deep and far-reaching implications, and Catholicism's unwillingness to grant women access to any level of clergy is particularly distressing given the long history of ordained women deacons in Christian history.

I posited that many would be willing to undertake a course of study online and that as a non-credit-bearing enterprise the MOOS would be a public service. The project was approved and supported by the dean of the College of Liberal Arts and Sciences and by the university provost to be technically directed and created by Faculty Computing Services.

Pedagogical Challenges

As noted earlier, the use of MOOCs varies among academic disciplines. Newer entries into the MOOC market include at least one course in introduction to world religions, although there are few courses available in religion or theology.[6] While MOOCs in religion and theology are few and far between, they do seem to be increasing. Even so, they face the challenges of online education presented to all humanities and social science courses.

The basic challenge of online teaching—as with any teaching—rests in the quest for effective teaching methodologies in the online environment, and this quest is closely linked to pedagogically sound instructional design no matter whether the course will be massive and open or restricted to a particular university community. In any case, the course or seminar designer has as a goal the creation of an environment in which a majority of participants actively take part in the online event and to consider and assimilate what is presented and discussed. A major challenge in any online education is preparing and encouraging an environment in which the participants interact with the materials and with each other, as well as with the course or seminar leader. In addition, as Mupinga et al. have pointed out, online students often have differing expectations from classroom students.[7] These challenges are redoubled for MOOCs and, in my case, for the MOOS.

Early in the development of online education, professionals identified three keys to solving the problem of effective online education: (1) student participation, (2) interactivity and (3) professor and teaching assistant presence.[8] These three keys, discussed next, remain as challenges to online education, but as the general use of technology increases so will the ease of participation. Further, when considering online education outside the parameters of a given institution, as in the MOOC or MOOS universe, the fact of worldwide acceptance of emerging technologies supports and contributes to the ever-expanding potential student body. Clearly, research has demonstrated that younger persons are much more at ease (especially given the prevalence of social media) conversing with and among individuals they have never met and most likely will never meet.[9] Much of their apparent ease can depend on creation of community so that the online presence of professor, teaching assistants and learners is one of a supportive community rather than an "audience" to various lectures.[10] Massive or contained, large or small, credit bearing or not, every online course shares this challenge. So, the presenting challenge in this project, joining seminar design and creation of content, was to structure the MOOS in a manner that encouraged participation of all: professor, teaching assistants and learners.

Newer developments in online education rightly tend to question the direct transfer of classroom structures and techniques to the online environment and rather provide self-contained learning environments. The general distinction between the two approaches is between whether the online world or the university is the focus. What have come to be called "connectivist MOOCs" or "CMOOKs" create peer learning experiences, where shared interaction between and among participants creates and guides the discussion. In these, participants set their own goals and levels of participation.

Another type of online event, the "xMOOC," is modeled on classroom lectures and behavior, is designed to attract students to the given institution and is often criticized as relying on outdated pedagogy. The xMOOC sets learning goals and include discussion forums that follow a linear learning trajectory, as much as possible mimicking in-person classroom behavior.

Shoenack discusses a development called a "mesoMOOC," which blends the two approaches and generally describes my approach to the MOOS.[11]

My "invented" term for the project at hand—not a MOOC, but a MOOS—demonstrates my intent to blend the interactive and somewhat free-ranging discussion characteristic of the CMOOC with the classroom-type structure of the xMOOC into a type of "mesoMOOC" without evaluation of student performance. The approach allows the greatest access to all, who are then able to participate at their own individual levels.

The natural question arises, if the MOOS includes no way of evaluating student performance, then is it education? I believe it is. The further question is, with no tests or other means of grading student performance, how can the effectiveness of the seminar be judged? Quite simply, it cannot.

Each question approaches the question of the MOOS (as opposed to the MOOC).

However, the pedagogy employed in the seminar echoed that of any other course—online, blended, or face-to-face—and, in large part, employed the blended CMOOC–xMOOC concept of the mesoMOOC. As described next, the best practices of all three "worlds" were employed: careful development and organization of the syllabus, regular and timely communication and facilitating effective discussion boards.[12] The challenge of the two latter—maintaining communication and facilitating discussion—was tied to the large numbers of seminar participants and the relatively small number of teaching assistants in addition to me.

The three critical efforts in course design—careful development and organization of the syllabus, regular and timely communication and facilitating effective discussion boards—were uppermost in selecting and arranging the seminar content.

Seminar Content

The discussion about the ordination of women has been especially contentious within some Christian denominations. The clear history of ordained women deacons in Christianity supports many arguments that women can be sacramentally ordained again, especially given that the extant liturgies for such ordinations clearly include an epiclesis: the invocation of the Holy Spirit required for sacramentality. In fact, several denominations ordain women as deacons; some ordain women as priests and bishops. At least one of the many churches of Orthodoxy, the autocephalous Orthodox Church of Greece, has contemporary history of women deacons, as does the Armenian Apostolic Church. None of the churches of Orthodoxy ordains women as priests or bishops. The Catholic Churches ordain women neither as deacons nor as priests. The question arises in a differing manner within Protestant denominations and the Anglican Communion. The MOOS focused on the Catholic experience.

Leaving aside the discussion of women as priests or bishops, the MOOS addressed women in the ordained diaconate using two texts: *Women Deacons: Past, Present, Future*, which discusses (1) the history of women in the diaconate (East and West), (2) the diaconate as it was restored as a permanent vocation in the Catholic Church after the Second Vatican Council and (3) considerations of how the completely restored diaconate might function and how it might affect the Catholic Churches. The second text, *Ordination of Women to the Diaconate in the Eastern Churches: Essays by Cipriano Vagaggini*, includes English translations from the original Italian of two extremely important essays (one requested by Pope Paul VI) by a noted Eastern liturgist and my introductory essay.[13]

Seminar Content, Structure and Development

The backbone of any online course, indeed any course, is the syllabus. Here the syllabus developed the objective of creating up to a graduate-level discussion of the Christian history of women in diaconal ministry, through current discussions, to opportunities for the future. Preparations for the thirty-day event, scheduled to open June 9, 2014, began in earnest six months in advance, in January 2014. As discussions progressed, the following questions arose as critical to the seminar content: (1) in the past, who were the women deacons in early Christianity? Were they ordained? What did they do? Why did they disappear? (2) In the present, when was the diaconate rejuvenated? Why? Has there been consideration of women in the diaconate? (3) In the future, what are the obstacles to women in the diaconate? How can these challenges be addressed? What would it mean for women to be ordained?

The plan was to open each week's seminar web pages at the beginning of the week and to offer suggested readings and lectures during each of the first four days of each week. Each day's work represented approximately one hour's work. Each Friday, the discussion board, with a new question or questions, was to open for three days, until the next week's work was opened at the start of the next week. The pattern was to continue, following the four weeks of work and two days of summation and survey. Where possible, an instructor or teaching assistant would join in the discussion boards. Course books were available electronically or in paper from various retailers and online suppliers.

The presenting tasks for course development were (1) develop an annotated bibliography; (2) develop PowerPoint lectures and taped lectures for each section; (3) invite "cameo" comments from cognate scholars; (4) research and select other, previously recorded, content; (5) register with Coursesites.com; and 6) advertise and manage registration. All these required attention prior to the opening of the seminar, which opened the afternoon of June 8, 2014, and "launched" with a Livestream of my June 9, 2014, public lecture in South Pasadena, California.[14]

Each seminar week would be devoted to one topic:

> Week 1) introduction of the topic, week 2) women deacons past, week 3) the diaconate present, week 4) women deacons future, and week 5) two days of conclusions and survey.

While all the work was asynchronous, previous online courses I have taught demonstrate that providing a day-to-day syllabus allows participants to pace themselves and, not incidentally, aids the instructor or seminar leader in choosing and arranging materials.

1. Develop an annotated bibliography. I considered the bibliography the most difficult to prepare yet most useful item to eventually load

to the website. Since seminar participants were projected to come from various backgrounds and locations, many without direct access to major libraries, we prepared annotations in English for the majority of the approximately 120 entries, many of which first appeared in foreign languages and remain untranslated. The bibliography remains posted on my Hofstra web pages at "Research Documents" and has since been updated and published in *Women Deacons? Essays with Answers* (Liturgical Press, 2016).[15] Since the University receives donations on my behalf, I also registered as an Amazon.com affiliate and linked most of the bibliographic materials (in addition to course books) to that program. The Phyllis Zagano Research Fund has received nearly $150 in Amazon fees from book purchases and Amazon referrals, all electronically deposited to Hofstra's bank account and subsequently transferred to the Research Fund maintained by the University's Office for Development and Alumni Affairs.

2. Develop PowerPoint lectures and taped lectures for each section. My coauthors agreed to provide brief (20-minute) lectures on their sections, as well as PowerPoint lectures coordinated to their materials. Following the pattern we used while developing our joint book, first Gary Macy recorded a lecture and a PowerPoint presentation focusing on the history of women in the diaconate and the history of their ordination ceremonies. Then William T. Ditewig, having reviewed Dr. Macy's work, prepared both a lecture and presentation on the diaconate today. Finally, I prepared my materials after reviewing those of Drs. Macy and Ditewig.

3. Invite "cameo" comments from cognate scholars. Coincidental with the preparation of the annotated bibliography and the presentations, and as each week's proposed questions developed, I invited a number of cognate scholars to provide brief (six-minute) commentaries, either video or audio. Six scholars, from Australia, Canada and the United States, provided brief audio or video commentaries. The appendix lists all the individuals who participated in the project.

4. Research and select prerecorded content. To round out the week's work, which moved from reading, to narrated PowerPoint, to lecture, we researched previously recorded online materials and selected one each by Drs. Macy, Ditewig and me, in addition to a few shorter items already posted on the Internet.

5. Register with Coursesites.com. While there are a number of providers, including Coursera, OpenLearning, Class Central, edX and Udacity, Coursesites is a Blackboard product and was recommended by Hofstra's Faculty Computing Services because of my familiarity with Blackboard.[16]

6. Advertise and manage registration. Various online blogs and journals announced the MOOS, and some interested groups directly alerted

their members to the registration period (April 21 through June 10, 2014). Coursesites software can be set to automatically register participants or advise of a request to register. Toward the end of the registration period, a blogger announced the opportunity for those who were opposed to the discussion of the ordination of women to flood registration. The disruption took place over the better part of a day, when I was flying cross country, and required the assistance of Hofstra Faculty Computing Services personnel.[17] Similar disruptions can be expected in open online events that examine neuralgic issues.

The MOOS

The MOOS itself opened Sunday, June 8, 2014, at 4:00 p.m. Pacific Daylight Savings Time, to accommodate participants in Australia, New Zealand, Asia and Europe, where dawn would be breaking well before 8:00 a.m. June 9 in the United States.[18] I followed this pattern throughout the seminar, opening each section by at least 7:00 p.m. Eastern Daylight Savings time on Sundays.

Student use of the materials could be tracked with Coursesites software, and it appeared that significant numbers of students preferred to run through the readings and lectures in one day, although others (perhaps those with work commitments) kept pace with the syllabus.

Discussion board membership was randomly generated by Coursesites software, with approximately 75 persons in each of four boards. Each board had a moderator: two volunteers, my paid research assistant and me. Each board was scanned by a federal work-study undergraduate student, who advised the discussion board moderators of any problems or difficulties. Some participants faced technical challenges; others needed guidance in following the curriculum.

I designed the syllabus to allow discussion on one topic for three or four days before closing and then opening again with a new topic. Participants, however, preferred ongoing discussion boards. Therefore, while the first board opened on the Thursday of the first week, with questions coordinated with the seminar materials, eventually I opened the discussion board with a new question nearly coincidental to the opening of the given week's materials, allowing for longer and deeper discussion of each week's work. While I presented the guiding questions for the seminar week, any of the three teaching assistants and any seminar member could (and did) introduce new threads, creating ongoing substantive discussion over nearly 30 days, including weekends. Discussion board comments ranged from brief insights, interjections or questions to 1,500-word essays and responses to discussion of the topic at hand.

With an average of 300 registrants to start, and three teaching assistants plus me, the discussion board moderation was somewhat understaffed. While a seminar of 75 persons is daunting for anyone, in each case, slightly more than half the number of registrants participated in the discussion boards at any given time, although overall "attendance" (as indicated by Coursesites-generated reports) was greater than 50 percent and, in many cases, as high as 75 percent, discussion board participation eventually dropped as low as 25 percent, a significant number of "lurkers"—at times 50 percent of registrants—remained. Along with the three teaching assistants, I routinely checked my assigned discussion board three times per day. The work-study student continually monitored each discussion board and alerted me and the individual discussion board teaching assistants of any major difficulties.

The decision to assign participants to discussion board groups randomly overtook an original plan to divide them geographically according to the regional groupings of the U.S. Conference of Catholic Bishops' 15 regions, and also overtook plans to include French- and Italian-language sections. Groups were originally projected to be smaller—perhaps 20 or 25 persons—allowing for use of Zoom.us meeting software for live discussions. The numbers of registrants soon made it clear that such a plan, requiring 12 to 15 discussion board sections, would be unwieldy given that the seminar had just one leader and three teaching assistants.

The random assignment of participants to one of the four discussion boards actually worked out well in a different way. Seminar participants later reported the advantages of conversing with persons from around the world—an individual from Alaska, for example, found common ground with someone from Ireland and an individual from New Zealand entered into discussion with someone from Atlanta, Georgia. The usual online "icebreakers" were not used directly; individuals were at first asked to introduce themselves briefly; tell of their location and work, perhaps their training; and why they were interested in the topic. Because of the large numbers involved in the discussion board, participants were also asked to briefly identify themselves at the start of each of their comments—for example, "Mary, pastoral minister, New Zealand."

The substantive nature of many of the interventions and subsequent discussions belied the common belief that "content" materials could not be adapted to online events. While such does not and cannot replicate the classroom experience exactly, in this instance, the exigencies of time and space collaborated to make classroom engagement impossible and online engagement quite possible. Some—perhaps many—of the participants were not familiar with online work and certainly not with discussion boards, but with few exceptions, the conversations did not devolve to the level of ordinary Facebook or chat room irrelevancies. Overall, I found the openness and availability of online "conversations" enhanced the experience for all, a finding supported by Mackness, et al. in other instances.[19]

Survey Results

Comments and questions throughout the seminar, where they digressed from the materials at hand, mostly had to do with the site itself, typically various software problems and difficulties viewing videos. Coursesites apparently operates best through the web browser Google Chrome, although some participants were able to use Firefox. Some participants initially did not have either proper software or powerful enough connectivity to view videos, suggesting that audio tracks of the videos might also be loaded to the site. Some were never able to log in; an additional few could not manage the systems and simply gave up. Here it should be noted that the individuals participating in the seminar were not initially joining it because it was online, but rather because it was on the topic of women in ministry, specifically Catholic women deacons. Many expressed the desire to learn more, combined with the fact that their lack of access to such study and discussion led to their trying out an online event for the first time.

The final days of the seminar included a wrap-up lecture, a segment of a previously recorded radio interview program that summed up the discussion and an article and attendant podcast that also summarized the discussion, as well as a request to participate in the 23-question survey.

The survey instrument was developed along the lines of other survey instruments used for Hofstra and other institutions' online courses, and left significant space for general thoughts and suggestions. Within the 63 completed surveys, participants wrote 13,000 words of comments, in addition to answering the 19 multiple-choice questions and 4 open-ended essay questions.

The largest number of survey respondents was in the 55–65 age range, with none under 25.[20]

The survey itself was at first inadvertently set so that participants could not return to change or complete their answers, and so its results are both skewed and incomplete because some participants did not return to work the survey after the setting was changed, and some were only able to complete part of the survey. Even so, 87.3 percent of respondents reported their knowledge of the subject increased, the majority reporting it "increased greatly," while 7.9 percent reported a "slight" or "somewhat" increased knowledge in the topic, with other insignificant percentages of "no response" reported, most probably the result of initial difficulties with the instrument.

Overall responses to the multiple-choice questions were positive. The responses from approximately 23 percent of the initial registrants or (66 percent of those who completed the seminar) strongly demonstrated appreciation for the major lecturers as well as for the "cameo" comments. The majority of the responses regarding the lecture presentations were that these were either "mostly clear" or "always clear."

The distinction may be attached to whether participants viewed the lectures or commentaries before or after completing the attendant readings. More (90.5 percent) found the *Women Deacons* text useful or very useful than did the Vagaggini text (77 percent). Regarding the optional additional readings, 79.4 percent found them useful or very useful. A total of 76.2 percent of the respondents said they read each book completely, while 73.0 percent reported watching all of the presentations, with the large majority (77.8 percent) reporting that the lecturers and commentators demonstrated an "outstanding" mastery of the subject matter, and 15.9 percent judged the presenters' mastery as "very good."

Responses to the question "I participated in the discussion boards" even though answered by a smaller percentage of participants, echoed the seminar's overall participation rate, with 17.5 percent reporting "no participation," 55.6 percent reporting "some participation" and 22.2 percent reporting "a lot of participation." (Discussion board participation dropped off as the seminar progressed, although it continued to be strong throughout.) Nearly half (49 percent) of the respondents thought the discussion board interaction was either "very good" or "outstanding," while a third reported it to be average and a small percentage (7.8 percent) found it "poor" or "not good."

As for the educational level of the participants, 3.2 percent reported only some college, while the rest who answered the question reported baccalaureate (12.7 percent), master's (54 percent), doctoral or professional (25.4 percent) education. The high percentage of post-baccalaureate participation seems indicative of the levels of interest in the specialized subject matter among persons who have completed other types of formal education in religion and theology.

While the responses were not otherwise broken down as to Eastern or Western Catholic Church members, 92 percent of the respondents reported their religious membership as Catholic.

Nearly 86 percent of the respondents reported they were female, a number that corresponds greatly with a hand count of the total registration.

Similarly, 81 percent of the respondents reported US residency, with 8 percent from Europe and slightly more than 6 percent from Australia/New Zealand, again mirroring hand counts and captured IP addresses of participants. The age range of the respondents is probably representative of the entire registration, with none reporting "under 25" and nearly 10 percent reporting "over 75," with the majority of respondents ages being between 40 and 74.

Conclusions

The argument that MOOCs better fit the pattern and educational objectives of courses in the sciences, technology and languages is a genuine one. Several of the difficulties of teaching a topic within religion that touched on history, literature, social sciences, church law and theology well presented themselves, both in the MOOS' creation and its execution. Further, while the pitfalls of transferring a classroom-type event to the online world are obvious, the challenge to incorporate differing teaching techniques presented itself early on. The challenge led to the valuable incorporation of the several six-minute-long "cameo" comments so generously provided by professors in what turned out to be a successful effort to encourage online conversation and comment.

The use of online education, in the traditional distance learning setting, or in the MOOC or the MOOS environment, presents different challenges depending on the subject matter. Wherever course or seminar content is essentially factual and not subject to interpretation, as in language arts and in introductory mathematics or science, which lends itself more to rote than interpretation, there is little more for the instructor or seminar leader to do beyond correct factual errors. However, the teaching of theology and religion moves well beyond science, technology and languages, to evaluative discussions of the content of a given piece of information, whether historical or doctrinal. The quest for the essential meaning and relative import of whatever information is presented is uppermost. Such a quest was central to this seminar, as historical facts and present realities often collided with each other and with perceptions of the seminar participants. Here the task was not learning as presenting historical facts, but rather learning as evaluative understanding and individual determination. Each was achieved.

Related to these ways of looking at education in theology and religion, the question of participation and formation of community was well and early answered. One unexpected part of the seminar was the enthusiasm of many of the participants who read deeply from the required and recommended readings and who entered fully into discussion board conversations. Many of their postings were graduate-level essays. Alternatively, the uneven preparation of the 292 participants showed somewhat in that some participants eventually became nervous about posting or asking questions given the apparent expertise of some of the participants. However, teaching assistants and other seminar members often jumped in to clarify a point or answer a question (including technical questions regarding site navigation), and there was a genuine evolution of a sense of community as the seminar progressed, as participants shared more individual insights and experiences. This is not to say that each of the four discussion boards evolved in a linear fashion. While each was active, some boards were more active than others, and in at least one case, a participant asked to be moved to another, more active, board.

The sense of community was evident when a woman who neither completed readings nor viewed presentations began posting in an obstreperous and bullying manner, objecting to the content of the seminar (restricted to women deacons and not addressing women priests). Seminar members engaged her defiant attitude and, in at least one case, incorrect information. The seminar community's participation was not sufficient to end the ongoing distraction, and so this person was at first barred from the discussion boards and eventually removed from the seminar. There is no way to effectively screen against such participants, but the uprising among discussants demonstrated their own intent on serious consideration of the topic.

While even I entered the event with a certain amount of skepticism—I have found that completely online teaching of, for example, my course, Mysticism and the Spiritual Quest is difficult and, to my mind, lacking—I was genuinely surprised by the depth and attention to detail, as well as the liveliness of the discussions, among the participants. Many wrote, either in the essay portion of their survey responses or in private e-mails directly to me, that they not only enjoyed the event but also hoped that it would run again. Some asked for the future availability of online seminar discussion boards in French—an early idea I had discarded because of the limited number of volunteer teaching assistants (two) and the one teaching assistant.

The argument that online courses portend a commercialization of education is real, but that does not apply here because of the parameters of the student body and the detailed nature of the topic. Even the research that shows the ability to repeat lectures and demonstrations at will in scientific and mathematical applications of online learning serves to establish in a larger way what I discovered to be true in this iteration of the MOOS. Because participants came from diverse educational and cultural backgrounds, the ability to replay materials at will was helpful to those who needed to catch up, either because of linguistic or content barriers to the topics at hand within the seminar.

However, given the diverse educational and cultural backgrounds of the participants, the development of an active online learning community hit bumps along the information highway in that some participants eventually felt unable to keep up with the levels of discussion, while others simply found other things to occupy their time in the northern hemisphere's summer. (Most participants in the southern hemisphere and in colder regions of the northern hemisphere completed the seminar and continued to post.) Many participants from both the global north and south requested that the seminar remain available, and so the site was left open until July 20, 2014, with significant, although decreasing, attendance.

In general, the MOOS exceeded my expectations in that it demonstrated to me and others involved in specialized research in religion that technology does have an application in teaching theology and religion.

Appendix
Lecturers and Professionals

Sara Butler, MSBT, PhD, Professor Emerita, University of St. Mary of the Lake, Mundelein, Illinois
Paul Carson, Instructional Designer, Hofstra University
Ron Chalmers, Executive Director of Online Learning, Hofstra University
John N. Collins, PhD, Lector Emeritus, Yarra Theological Union, Australia
William T. Ditewig, PhD, Director, Office of the Diaconate, Diocese of Monterey, California and Dean's Executive Professor, Graduate Program in Pastoral Ministries, Santa Clara University, California
Dennis Doyle, PhD, Professor of Religious Studies, University of Dayton, Ohio
Mary Freeman, Teaching Assistant, Rhode Island
Gary Macy, PhD, John Nobili, S. J. Professor of Theology, Department Chair, Director of Graduate Program in Pastoral Ministries, Santa Clara University, California
Alexander Mitchell, Student Assistant, Hofstra University
Carolyn Osiek, RSCJ, PhD, Archivist for the Society of the Sacred Heart, US-Canada Province, St. Louis, Missouri and Charles Fischer Professor of New Testament Emerita, Brite Divinity School, Texas Christian University, Fort Worth, Texas
Carmela Leonforte-Plimack, PhD, Research Assistant, Hofstra University
Amanda Quantz, PhD, Pastoral Ministry Program Director and Assistant Professor of Theology, University of Saint Mary, Leavenworth, Kansas
Susan Roll, PhD, Associate Professor of Liturgy and Sacramental Theology, University of St. Paul, Ottawa, Canada
Anne Southwood, Volunteer Teaching Assistant, Massachusetts
Alexander Smiros, Instructional Designer, Hofstra University
Jackson Snellings, Instructional Designer, Hofstra University
Judith Tabron, PhD, Director of Faculty and Student Computing Services, Hofstra University
David Woolwine, PhD, Associate Professor of Library Services and Reference Librarian, Hofstra University

Monica Yatsyla, Manager of Instructional Design Services, Hofstra University
Phyllis Zagano, PhD, Senior Research Associate-in-Residence and Adjunct Professor of Religion, Hofstra University
Joseph Zona, Instructional Technologist, Hofstra University
Student Assistants at Faculty Computing Services

Notes

1 Gerhard Fischer, "Beyond Hype and Underestimation: Identifying Research Challenges for the Future of MOOCs," *Distance Education* 35, no. 2 (2014): 149–158.
2 Tanner Mirrlees and Shahid Alvi, "Taylorizing Academia, Deskilling Professors and Automating Higher Education: The Recent Role of MOOCs," *Journal for Critical Education Policy Studies* (JCEPS) 12, no. 2 (2014): 45–73; Moshe Y. Vardi, "Will MOOCs Destroy Academia?" *Communications of the ACM* 55, no. 11 (2012): 5.
3 Kimberly F. Colvin et al., "Learning in an Introductory Physics MOOC: All Cohorts Learn Equally, Including an On-Campus Class," *International Review of Research in Open and Distance Learning* 15, no. 4 (2014): 263–282.
4 Jeffrey M. Stanton and Suzan J. Harkness, "Got MOOC? Labor Costs for the Development and Delivery of an Open Online Course," *Information Resources Management Journal* 27, no. 2 (2014): 14–26.
5 Distance Learning Sections during AY 2013–2014: fall 2013, 79; spring 2014, 69; January 2014, 32; summer 2014, 104.
6 "First-Ever HBCU-Created MOOC Offers Context for Understanding World Religions," *PR Newswire*, September 16, 2014, www.prnewswire.com/news-releases/first-ever-hbcu-created-mooc-offers-context-for-understanding-world-religions-275282961.html. The Center for Excellence in Distance Learning (CEDL) at Wiley College announced a new MOOC developed by Dr. Keith Augustus Burton of CEDL member institution Oakwood University: "Understanding World Religions: An Occupational Approach." Free open enrollment is available through canvas.net. Laura S. Nasrallah conducted an online course module on the letters of Paul through HarvardX/edX. From Emory University, Jacob Wright's The Bible's Prehistory, Purpose, and Political Future is on the Coursera platform.
7 Davison M. Mupinga, Robert T. Nora, and Dorothy Carole Yaw, "The Learning Styles, Expectations, and Needs of Online Students," *College Teaching* 54, no. 1 (2006): 185–187.
8 William E. Pelz, "My Three Principals of Effective Online Pedagogy," *Journal of Asynchronous Learning Networks (JALN)* 8, no. 3 (June 2004): 33–46.
9 Tsai Chia-Wen, "How to Involve Students in an Online Course: A Redesigned Online Pedagogy of Collaborative Learning and Self-Regulated Learning," *International Journal of Distance Education Technologies* 11, no. 3 (2013): 47–57.
10 Rita Kop, Helene Fournier, and John Sui Fai Mak, "A Pedagogy of Abundance or a Pedagogy to Support Human Beings? Participant Support on Massive Open Online Courses," *International Review of Research in Open and Distance Learning* 12.7 (2011): 74–93.
11 Lindsie Shoenack, "A New Framework for Massive Online Open Courses (MOOCs)," *Journal of Adult Education* 42, no. 2 (2013): 98–103.

12 These strategies are well discussed by many academics. See, for example, Kristy Motte, "Strategies for Online Educators," *Turkish Online Journal of Distance Education* 14, no. 2 (2013): 258–267; Evrim Baran, Ana-Paula Correia, and Ann Thompson, "Tracing Successful Online Teaching in Higher Education: Voices of Exemplary Online Teachers," *Teachers College Record* 115, no. 3 (2013): 1–41.
13 The two course books were *Ordination of Women to the Diaconate in the Eastern Churches: Essays by Cipriano Vagaggini*, ed. Phyllis Zagano (Collegeville, MN: Liturgical Press, 2013) and Gary Macy, William T. Ditewig, and Phyllis Zagano, *Women Deacons: Past, Present, Future* (Mahwah, NJ: Paulist Press, 2011). Since that time, the first has sold out and the essays are now published in *Women Deacons? Essays with Answers*, ed. Phyllis Zagano (Collegeville, MN: Liturgical Press, 2016).
14 Staff at Holy Family Catholic Church, which hosted the lecture, advised that 46 persons watched the Livestream video; once added to the MOOS, it was viewed by most of the MOOS participants. Approximately 125 persons attended the evening lecture.
15 http://people.hofstra.edu/phyllis_zagano/.
16 None of these providers currently offers a course or courses in religion or theology.
17 The neuralgic nature of some religious and theological discussion can militate against open registration, thereby defeating the principal point of MOOCs and MOOSs—free and open access to education and information.
18 Captured IP addresses of registrants indicate the following distribution of participants: Australia, 14; Belgium, 1; Canada, 10; Chile, 1; China, 4; France, 1; Ireland, 7; Italy, 5; Mexico, 3; New Zealand, 2; Norway, 1; South Africa, 1; United Kingdom, 8; and United States, 234. Some IP addresses were not captured.
19 Jenny Mackness, Sui Fai John Mak, and Roy Williams, "The Ideals and Reality of Participating in a MOOC," in *Proceedings of the 7th International Conference on Networked Learning*, eds. Lone Dirckinck-Holmfeld, Vivien Hodgson, Chris Jones, Maarten de Laat, David McConnell, and Thomas Ryberg (Lancaster, England: University of Lancaster, 2010), 266–275.
20 Age range of survey respondents: under 25: 0 percent; 25–40: 4.8 percent; 40–55: 15.9 percent; 55–65: 36.6 percent; 65–75: 28.6 percent; over 75: 9.5 percent.

12 Welcoming the Stranger to the Conversation

Charlotte Heeg

Not all people who take academic biblical studies courses look forward to having an academic biblical studies discussion. In fact, some may dread it. I have noticed many times that when I, the teacher, am "lecturing," students look alert and interested, but the minute I say, "So, questions? Comments? Critique?" they turn shifty. Their gazes drop, and their shoulders hunch; they don't want to speak up.

I teach academic biblical studies in a congregation and have also been a teaching assistant in academic biblical studies in higher education, so I know that this phenomenon of not wanting to enter into a conversation about critical interpretation is a problem in both environments. Even when people are well acquainted with each other, as in my congregational studies—even when they have no problems launching into casual conversation, or stories or gossip—they flinch when asked to venture their opinions on academic biblical topics.

Since I have long believed that, between private and public theology, there must also be a *conversational* theology where people feel free to share their thoughts, suggestions and conjectures about the biblical texts, I volunteer in my congregation as a teacher of academic biblical studies and a small-group discussion leader. I do this entirely so I can hear what new and interesting thoughts people have about the Bible once they've learned to view it through a historical or literary lens. The persistent unwillingness of individuals to share their views within the group makes me feel forlorn and sometimes exasperated. I have often wished that I had some sort of comic book style technology—a radioactive spider, an extraterrestrial orb, cosmic rays—to transform them instantly from shy learners to confident academic biblical scholars. Recently, I started a new Bible study on the book of Judges, and, perhaps because of the violent nature of the stories, my participants seemed even more terrified than usual at the thought of chatting or theorizing about the biblical texts. In my frustration, it occurred to me that perhaps I should simply use some everyday technology to show them an example of the sort of dialogue I'm looking for: low stakes, provisional, casual. So I asked for volunteers from among the Judges group to watch some online examples of academic biblical studies experts talking in an informal fashion about the Bible and the teaching of the Bible in higher education. About a third of the group—nine women—agreed to participate in my experiment.

My conversational examples came from an introductory open online course on the Old Testament, called Open Old Testament Learning Event 2016—or OOTLE16[1]—designed by Dr. Brooke Lester, assistant professor of Hebrew Scripture and director of Digital Learning at Garrett-Evangelical Theological Seminary in Evanston, Illinois, and coauthor of the book *Understanding Bible by Design: Create Courses with Purpose*.[2] One feature of the course was Dr. Lester presenting a series of live discussions with other professors of the Bible using hour-long "Google Hangouts." Anyone watching was invited to live-tweet along, and afterward the Hangouts were posted to YouTube.

There are about a dozen of these very interesting OOTLE Hangouts posted on YouTube, all featuring Dr. Lester having a conversation with a fellow academic biblical studies scholar or scholars—you can find them by searching OOTLE16 on YouTube—but for my participants I chose to show the three Hangouts featuring Dr. Bryan Bibb,[3] Dr. Nyasha Junior,[4] and Dr. John B. F. Miller.[5]

Since I knew that the Hangouts contained many terms and ideas that would be unfamiliar to my learners, I gave them paper and pens and asked them to write down any questions or comments they had as they watched the video. I also explained that we would be stopping the video approximately every 20 minutes so they could ask questions or offer comments.

I will now present excerpts from the three Hangouts along with comments about how my learners responded to this experience.

* * *

OOTLE16 On Air: Jeremiah and Jerusalem (7th century)
Dr. Bryan Bibb Hangout On Air
March 9, 2016
"This is Mind-Blowing!"

Bryan Bibb is the Dorothy and B. H. Peace Jr. associate professor of Religion at Furman University in Greenville, South Carolina, and the author of *God's Servants, the Prophets*.[6] Bibb's book plays a large part in the discussion; Dr. Lester refers to it several times as he poses questions about subject and approach. In fact, Dr. Lester begins the conversation by expressing his admiration for Dr. Bibb's book, *God's Servants, the Prophets*, and invites Dr. Bibb to talk about his approach in writing the introduction to the pre-exilic prophets. Dr. Bibb responds,

> The idea was, I can't explain every passage in the prophets, and I can't really even do much to explain any key passages in any depth

in a book this size, and so what I had to do was ask myself, what do people need to know minimally when they open the prophets and encounter a passage? And also, what kinds of questions should they be asking themselves when they read it? And what are the things the prophets present as difficulties or as resources for addressing those questions?

Dr. Bibb describes how he wants to convey *principles* that will help any reader of a prophetic text to "uncover" or to "discover" something new in that text. Dr. Lester agrees wholeheartedly with this; I also agree completely. However, my learners' expressions are steadily darkening. They brighten momentarily when Dr. Bibb stresses the importance of "slowing down" in reading—reading the Bible more slowly is an easily comprehensible suggestion. They also enjoy the discussion about openness and curiosity. But Dr. Bibb's remark about the necessity of "minimal, efficient, strategic, limited historical background" causes some frowns.

At this point, I pause the video and invite comments, questions and critiques. And now, only 20 minutes in, I can see that my experiment has already succeeded: there is no hesitation, no sidling and no covert glances at each other. The participants begin speaking at once: it appears they are baffled. Dr. Bibb is a specialist in what? Pre-exilic prophets? Why doesn't he talk about the pre-exilic prophets then? What does that have to do with the seventh century? Is he going to talk about Jeremiah or Jerusalem? Why is he talking about this "idea"? What actually *is* the idea? Is it something in the Bible?

At first, I am at a loss to understand their indignation; then I realize that running across the top of the screen is the heading "OOTLE16 On Air: Jeremiah and Jerusalem (7th Century)." I hadn't even noticed it, but they had and were therefore expecting a discussion about Jeremiah and Jerusalem, not a discussion about principles of historical and literary interpretation. They were expecting the subject matter itself, not "approaches to" the subject matter.

Fortunately, I had equipped myself with Dr. Bibb's book and point out that Dr. Lester had been quoting from the introductory portion where Dr. Bibb lays out his pedagogical presuppositions—and, I was forced to admit, at no point during the discussion does Dr. Bibb teach us anything about Jeremiah, Jerusalem barely gets mentioned and the "7th century" in the heading really ought to read "7th century BCE." This earns me some side-eye.

I provide a brief sketch of the biblical studies categories "pre-exilic," "exilic" and "post-exilic" ("so three time slots?"); Bibb's tripartite division of historical, literary and theological ("three kinds of analysis?"); and his directives about the importance of context, imagination and conversation for historical interpretation ("three steps for interpretation?"). By then the group is mollified and we move on.

However, the discussion we have after the second portion of the video largely revolves around a couple of points made by Dr. Lester: "The Bible is filled with competing voices and competing claims about God," and, "If all you've ever read is the Bible, you're not ready to read the Bible." Dr. Bibb has an assertion as well. "You've got what you need to do this thing."

My participants, as they point out, have read many things besides the Bible; yet they're not sure they can tell the difference between those competing voices; they're not sure they've got what it takes to do "this thing"—biblical interpretation by the methods of academic biblical studies. It still seems to them that no matter how encouraging these professors imagine themselves being toward those not in the know, they nevertheless are presupposing such an enormous amount of knowledge—historical, literary, theological—that undertaking biblical interpretation in the way the good doctors propose is unrealistic and unmanageable.

Fretfully, we move on to the third and final portion of the Hangout. Dr. Lester is now referring to the portion of Dr. Bibb's book titled "Three Moments in Time" in which he says that all the prophetic texts can be understood in relation to the fall of Israel in 722 BCE, the Babylonian Exile beginning 587–586 BCE or the Restoration period in 538 BCE. Dr. Lester says that he thinks this is true not only of the prophetic texts but also of *all* Old Testament texts. He displays for the camera the time line[7] from *God's Servants, the Prophets*, pointing to those three dates. "Almost everything you read in the Hebrew bible is either written, preserved, or edited in light of these three events," he says. Dr. Lester and Dr. Bibb go on to have a rather intricate discussion about the way rhetoric makes use of events, using the example of US history and conversations around race relations and the Black Lives Matter movement, the usefulness of academic biblical study methods for increasing empathy and listening skills and the importance of empathy for translating the Bible. But in regard to any favored translation, Dr. Bibb says flatly, "I don't really like any of them, to be honest." "I know!" Dr. Lester replies, laughing.

The video concludes, and everyone looks at me quizzically. "No scholar likes any translation other than his or her own," I explain. The participants approve of all the bits about empathy—empathy, after all, is a good thing—but what they really want to talk about is "those three dates!" They are struck by Dr. Bibb's and Dr. Lester's assertions that everything in the Old Testament can be related in some way to just three dates. I rehearse the three dates for them again, and one participant says abruptly, "That's mind-blowing!" Everyone agrees. Learning just three dates could allow you to wrap your head around the entire Old Testament? Someone quotes directly from a remark made by Dr. Bibb about a common complaint he hears whenever he teaches in churches: "Why did no one tell me this before?" Another participant also cites Dr. Bibb: "It's that 'minimal and strategic and efficient' thing he was talking about."

And just like that, we're in the middle of a lively discussion about how academic biblical studies can be structured around those three dates.

I learned two things as a result of watching this particular video in company with my group:

First of all, captions matter more to learners than we educators might think. The video caption, "Dr. Bryan Bibb's Suggestions on How to Interpret the Prophetic Texts Using Academic Biblical Studies Methodology," would have been a decidedly long and boring title, but it would have let the participants know what they were in for. (It made me ponder whether it might be better to title courses we usually call "Introduction to the Old Testament" something a little more on the nose, like "Current Techniques for Interpreting the Old Testament.") On the other hand, the group's irritation at the mismatch was what made them eager to speak up, so I have to count the misleading caption as not only a bug but also a feature.

Second, I learned that the canned nature of the dialogues is a plus. When I made the initial decision to ask my learners to watch these videos, I had been thinking about using YouTube as a means of showing them a model of interesting academic conversation, and I considered the YouTube Hangout a mere work-around, a second-best to actual professors talking in the room. Now I had learned that recorded modeling was even better for my purposes. It allowed me to stop the video for necessary questions; plus, I realized that my participants would not have felt as comfortable complaining about the conversation if Dr. Bibb and Dr. Lester had been there in the flesh. It was the complaints and questions that furnished the substance of our conversation. But it was their casual tone that licensed the equally casual conversation we were able to continue in our classroom.

* * *

OOTLE16 On Air: Dr. Nyasha Junior and the Pentateuch
Dr. Nyasha Junior Hangout on Air
April 20, 2016
"Hey, *I'm* a Reception History!"

Dr. Nyasha Junior is assistant professor of Hebrew Bible at Temple University in Philadelphia, Pennsylvania, and the author of *An Introduction to Womanist Biblical Interpretation*.[8]

Of course, I had been wondering what, of all the many things Dr. Lester and Dr. Bibb had discussed the week before and the group members had retained, and I soon learn that what they remember is "those three dates that help you organize everything in the Old Testament!" They had remembered the significance of the dates—although not the dates themselves, as they cheerfully admit to me—and so they ask me to repeat them. I do, and they write them down. The participant who had announced last week that she was going to order Bibb's book tells us she has now gotten the book and is reading it. "It's really good!" she shares.

I introduce that day's video by explaining who Dr. Nyasha Junior is and proudly show them my copy of her book, *An Introduction to Womanist Biblical Interpretation*. I have the video cued up, and the group looks at the Hangout heading, which reads "Dr. Nyasha Junior and the Pentateuch."

"Are they actually going to talk about the Pentateuch?" one participant asks sarcastically. I am pleased because I had learned the week before that nothing bodes better for a good discussion than a little pushback. (As a matter of fact, Dr. Lester and Dr. Junior do not begin to talk about the Pentateuch until about halfway through the video.)

Dr. Lester and Dr. Junior, after some back and forth about Philadelphia and the movies *Rocky* and *Creed*, begin talking about what skills are needed for biblical interpretation. Dr. Lester admits he doesn't quite know what to do with people who want to study the Bible but who don't read much; he fantasizes about sending the people who want to take his biblical studies courses away for ten years of reading:

> When and only when you have found that you have had your perceptions of yourself and of the world and perhaps of God changed by a work of literary fiction or of poetry, then come back and we will do this thing.

Dr. Junior, however, demurs at Dr. Lester's strictures: she wants to assure her participants that they are already equipped: "With students, what I try to do is to help them to see that they already have some of the interpretive skills that I'm looking for; we just need to polish them up." She provides some examples of how students who think they don't know anything about interpretation actually interpret all the time—in reading e-mails, text messages and even course syllabi. Dr. Lester uses the example of the syllabi to segue into asking Dr. Junior how she came to abandon her dissertation topic—Genesis 39, Joseph and Potiphar's wife—to write instead a book about womanist biblical interpretation. Junior says frankly, "I was just sick of it [her dissertation topic] and needed to do something else."

The first third of the video is over, and even though Dr. Junior has not yet defined womanist biblical interpretation—and I know my participants will point out to me that she hasn't—I have promised them I will stop periodically so they can ask questions. I stop the video. "Why doesn't Dr. Junior like it that people assume that she must be a womanist?" they ask immediately. They have never heard of womanist biblical interpretation before. Why are we 18 minutes into the video, and they can see Dr. Junior's book prominently displayed on the shelves behind her head, the very same book that's sitting on the table in our room, and no one has yet said what womanist biblical interpretation is? (And what about the Pentateuch?)

First of all, I assure them that Dr. Junior is going to talk about both what womanist biblical interpretation is and the Pentateuch in the very next part of the video.

I can see that the group is taken with Dr. Junior and is eager to hear her explain womanist biblical interpretation, so I turn the video back on again almost immediately.

Dr. Lester asks Dr. Junior to define womanist biblical interpretation. "Buy the book!" Junior replies, pointing over her shoulder at the copy of *An Introduction to Womanist Biblical Interpretation* and winning a laugh from my group. Pressed by Dr. Lester, she offers a few explanations of what a definition of womanist biblical interpretation might be. Dr. Junior says,

> So for some people, they understand a womanist to be a black woman who's interested in feminism who may choose not to identify herself as a black feminist, but may prefer to use the term "womanist"—for a variety of reasons. That does not do justice to the issue, but that's a brief snippet.

At this point, I see my participants scribbling notes. "But why," asks Dr. Lester, playing devil's advocate, "wouldn't a black woman interested in feminism not just call herself a feminist?" Junior explains, "Feminism itself has a history of excluding women who were not white women, who were not affluent, educated women. So the term itself is already problematic for a number of people." I hear a faint murmur of comprehension: more scribbling.

And now the discussion turns to the Pentateuch. (A small cheer breaks out from my participants.) Dr. Junior proclaims her love of narrative:

> Narrative is the good stuff! It's fun, it's exciting, it's reality TV from biblical texts! It's family drama, baby-mama drama, who doesn't like who, who got kicked out, who slept with whose husband—it's all juicy stuff. The narratives, that's where the action is.

She adds blithely, "People are always shocked and appalled at what's actually in the Hebrew Bible."

Dr. Junior goes on to say that her next book will be a reception history of the story of Hagar (Genesis 16:1–15; 21:8–20). Dr. Lester seems floored by this announcement: "A reception history of Hagar; really?"

Junior explains,

> What I'm interested in looking at is how different communities look at this character as either an insider or an outsider, depending on

how they're trying to use her; how different communities use her to make their arguments about inclusion and exclusion.

It's now time to pause the video. How about Dr. Junior's book on womanist biblical interpretation, they ask—did I like it? Oh, yes, I say; I'm interested in womanist biblical interpretation just because I'm interested in any approach that provides more respect for "boots on the ground" interpretations. Well, how hard is it? Could they read it? I hand my copy over to one questioner, and she reads the first paragraph of the introduction, shakes her head and hands it back with a rueful look. How about reception history? Dr. Junior is writing a history of the different ways people have thought about the story of Hagar? How old is this video? Is that book out yet? No, I say regretfully; I already looked. I have the feeling that if the book were available, Dr. Junior might sell some copies on Amazon that very afternoon.

We talk a little about changes we have seen in our own lives concerning the "reception" of certain biblical texts, such as 1 Corinthians 14:34— "Women should be silent in the churches, for they are not permitted to speak." One participant points out that anybody who's been around long enough and listened to enough sermons becomes a reception history all by him- or herself—"*I'm* a reception history!" However, I can see that they're not so much interested in our discussion as they are in what Dr. Junior has to say next.

In the third part of the video, Dr. Junior and Dr. Lester continue their discussion of how reception history is used in teaching. Dr. Junior describes how, before she has her students read the biblical text, she gets them to unpack what it is they already have in their heads about the narrative: she uses the example of Samson.

> Samson, from the Bible, what do you know? "He was big, he was strong, there was something about this woman, there was some woman, and hair. Something. Something like that." So when we finally sit down and read Samson they say, "Oh my stars, this dude is—he has anger management issues, he's a criminal, he's killing people, he's a terrorist!"

I can see my participants' interest in this. They're sitting up straighter and leaning forward slightly.

When the entire video has ended, the learners ask about two things: reception history and Dr. Junior herself. Do I "do" reception history? Could we do a study on reception history? They like the idea of taking a tour of other biblical interpretations throughout history. Isn't Hagar important to Islam? Could we do a reception history study about Hagar with our neighborhood mosque? Have I ever met Dr. Junior? What was Dr. Junior's website again? I spell it out for the group, who all write it down.

From this session, I learned that an interesting video might make for more learning but a less animated discussion. Approval doesn't necessarily drive people to express themselves. I wonder what, if anything, my learners will retain from watching this video.

I also learned that the casual chattiness of academics in these Hangouts is misleading to my participants. They hear Dr. Junior joking about Samson, and they think her writing will have the same tone. And as an educator who works in a congregation, I regret that it does not: a commentary on Judges that evinced the same cheerful colloquial voice Dr. Junior employs in this Hangout would be a commentary that my participants would buy, read and use.

* * *

OOTLE16 On Air: Dr. John Miller
Dr. John Miller Hangout On Air
April 28, 2016
"You Just Became a Redaction Critic!"

Dr. John Miller is professor of religion and a pre-ministry advisor at McMurry University in Abilene, Texas, and the author of *Convinced That God Had Called Us: Dreams, Visions, and the Perception of God's Will in Luke-Acts* (Brill, 2007).[9]

The participants come piling into the room for this, the last session of Google Hangouts, and their affect is markedly different than it was before the first video—no caution, no suspicion, just cheeriness. One participant reports that she couldn't find Dr. Junior's website, so I find it and show it to her; another tells me that she also got a copy of Dr. Bibb's *God's Servants, the Prophets*, and she has decided that our Adult Education Committee should buy a few more copies to put in the church library. A third marches in and announces, "I remember the term 'reception history' from last week!" A fourth mentions that she wants to buy a study Bible and asks what kind should she get. (I recommend either the HarperCollins or the Oxford.)

The learners look at the video and note that this one is captioned simply "Dr. John Miller." "All right," says one. "Truth in advertising!"

Dr. Lester and Dr. Miller begin by comparing their respective situations. Dr. Lester teaches in a seminary; Dr. Miller is, as he says, "the Bible person in a small department of religion and philosophy." Dr. Lester asks whether Dr. Miller gets much of a chance to talk to scholars from other fields. Dr. Miller says that he does, but they don't wind up talking about their respective fields as much as they talk about their common problems and challenges in teaching itself. He says soberly,

> The "multiple choice test" model of education, and all teachers sort of being motivated to teach to that test, one of the results is you get a

lot of people in this age range who are coming into college who have just had the inquisitiveness stomped out of them. You know, there is no reward for being curious. There is no reward for exploration. Trying to get students to follow a logical thought process is really, really difficult when you have people coming from such disparate backgrounds.

Dr. Lester agrees fervently that the present system of teaching is far from ideal, that as a teacher he is constantly battling a lack of curiosity in his students: "Find out what Lester wants to hear, check off the right answers, and get through so that they can go on to the next thing."

Dr. Miller says ruefully, "How do you incorporate this idea of sort of inspiring curiosity within a classroom structure? Because you know what the model that we're all so inscribed with is; I stand up here and convey information, you sit there and write it down; I ask you a question that is designed to make sure that you understand the information that I've just relayed, you give me an answer that shows me you understand that. Talk about coloring inside the lines."

But Dr. Miller quickly adds—and Dr. Lester quickly agrees—that today's students have more constraints on their time and finances than previous generations.

It's time to stop the video and discuss. Immediately one of my participants asks, "Why are they always complaining about their students not being able to think?" The rest of the group recalls how Dr. Lester had talked about this same issue with Dr. Bibb and Dr. Junior: "They said the students need more curiosity and empathy. He said they didn't read enough." And now here is Dr. Miller saying that a lot of his students can't follow a logical thought process. "Why are they all so bothered by this?"

My participants seem to me to be implying that since it's just Bible study, why are all these professors going on about curiosity, empathy, creativity and logical thinking? I take a deep breath and say, "Because it's academic biblical study, and academic biblical study requires critical reading skills. And Dr. Miller is a narrative critic, so he especially needs people to have the skills to bracket out their own ideas so that they can pay attention to the narrative itself."

I want to demonstrate to them how easy it is to read things into a narrative that aren't actually there, so I ask them to read Luke 3:21–22. We read it aloud, and I ask, "So who baptized Jesus in this narrative?" "John the Baptist," they say, looking puzzled. I tell them to go back one line and read 3:19–20. They are astonished. "John is in prison!"

At this point, we could have completely abandoned the video and launched into a comparison of the different gospel accounts of the baptism of Jesus: that's how interested they are. But I say, "Wait, next Dr. Miller is going to talk about Luke's use of the Holy Spirit in Luke-Acts! But can you see why he needs people to be able to read what's there and not just what they have in their heads?"

"Yes, and I can also see why Dr. Lester cares about people thinking independently," says one of the participants. "Because he teaches in a seminary, and if you go to seminary and all you care about is giving the teacher the answer they want, then as a pastor, won't you just give the congregation the answers they want?"

Everyone agrees that this is an excellent point, and we go on to watch the second third of the video. Dr. Miller talks enthusiastically about "dreams, visions, and messengers" in Luke-Acts:

> What I really love about that is the theological payoff that I find in studying that topic . . . what you have are situations in which people have a dream, or they have a visionary encounter, say with an angel, or whatever, or they hear a voice from heaven; they hear a voice telling them exactly what to do. And then they walk away from that experience and Luke shows them interpreting that experience, processing that experience. I think that's *so* valuable from a theological standpoint.

Dr. Miller goes on to cite Acts 21:4, where different parts of the community, feeling equally inspired by the Spirit, nevertheless have different prescriptions for what Paul should do next. Dr. Lester brings up the nuances of the discernment of prophecy in the Old Testament. And then the documentary hypothesis rears its head: Dr. Lester asks if there are differences in the New Testament, as there are in the Old, between portraying God as "immediate" or as "mediated." Dr. Miller says that in Luke-Acts God seems to be both immediate *and* mediated, and cautions that Christians tend to impute a Trinitarian, and therefore anachronistic, approach to Luke. Dr. Miller concludes this portion of the video with a crack about the excesses of a possible redaction critic who might posit a Holy Spirit source: "Yeah—it's stupid."

We stop the video, and I have to explain, as quickly as possible, the documentary hypothesis—differences between the Jahwist (or Yahwist) and Elohist sources as regards the immediacy of God—what redaction criticism is and why Dr. Miller might legitimately find some aspects of it stupid. During all this, I mention that Mark was the first Gospel written and that redaction criticism shows that Matthew and Luke used Mark. At this point, one of my participants asks about "Q," (the material common to Matthew and Luke that isn't also in Mark) which I apparently mentioned in some past Bible study. I hastily gabble out something about the Saying Source, but now I feel that I am doing too much of the talking; I want to conclude the video and hear what they have to say. "Well, let's finish up!" I say.

In the final third of this, our final OOTLE16 Hangout, Dr. Miller talks about his specialty, narrative criticism and how hard it is to come up with original topics. He and Dr. Lester complain in mock-depressive tones about super-scholars who publish continuously and use up all the good questions. It's a funny exchange, and my participants giggle through it appreciatively.

I turn off the video, and one of my participants, who has been quietly looking through her Bible, looks up and says, "Mark has Jesus being baptized by John. You said Mark is first. So why would Luke change Mark?"

She has clearly been thinking about this ever since I told them about Markan priority. I am thrilled. "You just became a redaction critic!" I say.

The participant looks flummoxed. "I did?"

I say, "You asked why Luke changed Mark, which is exactly the question a redaction critic would ask!" And the group bursts into spontaneous applause.

From this session, I learned that I really should have been providing a handout each week with the various technical terms Dr. Lester and his guests use in these discussions. The participants wanted to talk about "redaction criticism," but they kept confusing that with "reception history" from the week before; also, they weren't sure of the distinction between literary criticism and narrative criticism. So I wrote up a handout of eight of the terms and e-mailed it to my participants; I got many replies to the effect that they were going to print it out and do their best to remember the terms so that we could use them in the Judges study.

It also occurred to me that I could have spread the videos out over a longer period and used them as a springboard to actual Bible study. I could have used Dr. Bibb to introduce a study of prophetic forms, Dr. Junior to talk about Genesis or Judges and Dr. Miller to look at Luke.

On the whole, however, I am very happy with the results of my experiment. Aside from my main goal of greasing the conversational skids, there were several side benefits to my showing these three online videos to my participants: we got a number of excellent ideas for future adult-education Bible studies, we sold a dozen books for Dr. Bibb, we drove some traffic to Dr. Junior's website and we inspired the purchase of at least one study Bible. But of course, my real happy ending was that even though only a third of the participants of my Judges study had volunteered to watch the three videos, the overall conversational tone of the entire Judges group ricocheted from reserved to raucous in just three weeks. The video-viewing learners became noticeably more searching in their use of different interpretive lenses, and the rest of the group followed their lead.

Watching three YouTube videos may not seem a particularly exciting "origin story" for my congregational heroes, but, nevertheless, viewing these videos did quickly transform my participants, if not into amazing super-academicians, at least into model members in the league of biblical learning. If you long to similarly mind-alter your own learners, try showing them these online examples of lively biblical and theological conversation. And may the OOTLE be with you.

Notes

1 G. Brooke Lester. OOTLE17. "Open Old Testament Learning Event 2017," accessed August 12, 2017, http://ootle17.net. This site is slightly revised from its OOTLE16 form.
2 G. Brooke Lester, Christopher M. Jones, and Jane S. Webster, *Understanding Bible by Design: Create Courses with Purpose* (Minneapolis, MN: Fortress Press, 2014).
3 "OOTLE16 On Air: Jeremiah and Jerusalem (7th century)," YouTube video, 1:02:45, posted by "YouTube," March 9, 2016, https://youtu.be/X44ON6SJgUg.
4 "OOTLE16 On Air: Dr. Nyasha Junior and the Pentateuch," YouTube video, 58:09, posted by "YouTube," April 20, 2016, https://youtu.be/04GTINL7tK4.
5 "OOTLE16 On Air: Dr. John Miller," YouTube video, 55:04, posted by "YouTube," April 28, 2016, https://youtu.be/oHYakaJizOs.
6 Bryan Bibb, *God's Servants, the Prophets* (Macon, GA: Smyth & Helwys, 2014).
7 Ibid., 9.
8 Nyasha Junior, *An Introduction to Womanist Biblical Interpretation* (Louisville, KY: Westminster John Knox Press, 2015).
9 John Miller, *Convinced That God Had Called Us: Dreams, Visions, and the Perception of God's Will in Luke-Acts* (Leiden, Netherlands: Brill, 2007).

Bibliography

Bibb, Bryan D. *God's Servants, the Prophets*. Macon, GA: Smyth & Helwys, 2014.
Junior, Nyasha. *An Introduction to Womanist Biblical Interpretation*. Louisville, KY: Westminster John Knox Press, 2015.
Lester, G. Brooke, Christopher M. Jones, and Jane S. Webster. *Understanding Bible by Design: Create Courses with Purpose*. Minneapolis, MN: Fortress Press, 2014.
Miller, John B. F. *"Convinced That God Had Called Us": Dreams, Visions, and the Perception of God's Will in Luke-Acts*. Leiden, Netherlands: Brill, 2007.
"OOTLE16 On Air: Dr. John Miller." YouTube video, 55:04. Posted by "YouTube." April 28, 2016. https://youtu.be/oHYakaJizOs.
"OOTLE16 On Air: Dr. Nyasha Junior and the Pentateuch." YouTube video, 58:09. Posted by "YouTube." April 20, 2016. https://youtu.be/04GTINL7tK4.
"OOTLE16 On Air: Jeremiah and Jerusalem (7th century)." YouTube video, 1:02:45. Posted by "YouTube." March 9, 2016. https://youtu.be/X44ON6SJgUg.

13 Comparing Spiritual Outcomes in Face-to-Face Versus Online Delivery of a Religion Course

John Hilton III, Kenneth Plummer, Ben Fryar, Ryan Gardner

Introduction

Can distance education provide the same benefits as face-to-face instruction? This question has been debated for decades, with some people making arguments on one or the other side and with other people stating that the concept of "which is better" is entirely irrelevant. Such evaluation is not easy; Carol Weiss defined *evaluation* as "the *systematic assessment* of the *operation* and/or the *outcomes* of a program or policy, compared to a set of *explicit* or *implicit standards*, as a means of contributing to the *improvement* of the program or policy."[1] Some who favor distance education might assume that their method of delivery is best, while face-to-face instructors operate under the assumption that their classrooms are the most effective mode of delivery. Both groups inevitably find students who offer confirmatory feedback for these implicit suppositions. However, until an "evaluator [tries] to discover the reality of the program rather than its illusion," no real discussion can take place—a discussion that will, hopefully, lead both groups to learn from each other in a way that will enhance learning in every mode of delivery.[2]

Over the course of 30 years in the field, Terralyn McKee has written generally about the pros and cons of various "generations" of distance education.[3] Her experience shows that while we have made significant progress in improving the quality of distance education in recent decades, we still have much to learn and potential yet to realize. Many comparative studies have been conducted to measure learning styles and outcomes for distance/online students and face-to-face students. For example, Allen, Bourhis, Burrell and Mabry conducted a meta-analysis of student satisfaction studies in distance education and traditional classrooms and found only a slight favoring of traditional classrooms; this slight favoring certainly did not discredit the claims of other researchers that distance education does not detrimentally affect student satisfaction when compared with traditional classroom learning environments.[4] Gros, Garcia and Escofet have recently looked for differences in how online and traditional face-to-face students in multiple disciplines perceive the use of technology in learning.[5] The researchers found that while many students frequently use Internet technologies, teaching methodology is more important than the mode in which it is delivered.

Within the field of distance-based religious education, less work has been done. Broadbent and Brown provided some discussion on assessment and evaluation of student learning outcomes in religious education.[6] Steven Frye wrote regarding how religious organizations have used the wide variety of Internet tools available to them to increase their ability to promote more religious education for adults.[7] While Mary Hess acknowledged that "digital technologies are reshaping how we interact with each other," very little research has been completed in religious education to assess how these technologies are being used in religious education and how or even if those technologies are affecting learning outcomes for students in religious education programs and courses.[8] One of the authors of the present study reviewed over 400 articles in a religious education journal and did not find any on digital technologies in religious education.

Within religious education, teachers have a variety of goals. Walvoord extensively discussed survey data showing that both students and teachers have multiple, and sometimes differing, aspirations for religious education courses.[9] Some educators focus on cognitive aspects, including an emphasis on Bible literacy[10] or using historical lenses.[11] Hella and Wright described the roles of religious educators as teaching about religion and helping students apply religious practices in a way that informs student religiosity.[12]

Certainly, there is room for additional discussion on the purposes of religious education; in the present study, we have adapted the principles asserted by Loving[13] and Csinos[14] that religious education should help students *act* on what they learn in the classroom. We also apply principles from Jeynes, who asserted that clergy and congregations will have better outcomes (in terms of intellectual development and theological accuracy) when they highlight spiritual applications of scripture.[15]

Purpose of the Study

We believe that among other important outcomes, religious education should (1) help students develop a habit of reading sacred literature, (2) improve students' ability to read sacred literature, (3) motivate students to live the principles they learn from sacred literature and (4) feel an overall divine presence and direction. The purpose of the present study was to examine the question of whether distance instruction limits students' abilities to achieve these outcomes. Specifically, we sought to determine whether students taught in face-to-face or distance settings reported higher spiritual and religious outcomes. Moreover, we wanted to determine whether there was a difference in reported outcomes among the teachers of the distance-based courses and the teachers of face-to-face courses.

Methods

Participants

The subjects of this study were college students at Brigham Young University–Idaho (BYU-Idaho). These students were all enrolled in Religion 122, an introductory religion course required for graduation (BYU-Idaho graduates are required to take 14 credit hours of religion courses). This class is designed for and composed of mostly first-year students, but some sophomores, juniors and seniors also enroll. It is vital to note that 99 percent of students at BYU-Idaho are members of the Church of Jesus Christ of Latter-day Saints and as such tend to have largely shared values regarding the purposes of religious education.

Students close to campus had the option of taking this course in a traditional face-to-face setting or at a distance. The distance course was designed through collaboration between instructional designers and BYU-Idaho faculty members. Students in the distance course were assigned to read passages of religious text and commentary and then discuss with peers and the instructor, via discussion boards, what they had learned. Assignments required students to first demonstrate factual knowledge of the assigned passages and then to extrapolate and apply principles from the reading. The instructor facilitated the extrapolation and application through feedback on the discussion boards, journal assignments and a project paper in which students reported on their attempts to improve regarding a specific virtue throughout the semester. The content and assignments in each section of the distance course were identical, with the exception of introductory material provided each week by individual instructors. The vast majority of the distance students (84 percent) were on-campus students who chose to take the distance course. The remaining 16 percent of students were those who were pursuing a degree from a distance.

Students in the face-to-face sections met twice weekly for 50 minutes each class period. While the face-to-face teachers had a great deal more latitude in determining their course design, their assignments concerning scripture study were generally similar in that they required students to read specific chapters before coming to class. Some instructors gave quizzes on the reading, while others had students write about what they were learning.

Students were enrolled in 21 different sections of the same course. Six of these sections were distance, and 15 were face-to-face. A different instructor facilitated each distance section, and the five face-to-face instructors taught from one to five sections of the course. In total, 335 students were enrolled in distance sections, and 614 were enrolled in the face-to-face sections. All instructors used the same chapters from the same religious text as the basis for instruction. Enrollment in the distance classes ranged from 50 to 57 students. Enrollment in the face-to-face classes ranged from 26 to 50 students, with an average of 44 per class.

Although we did not ask students to declare their gender or race, the proportions in these classes tend to mirror the student population because they are required classes. There are more female students than male students (55 percent to 45 percent). The university is not particularly diverse regarding race and ethnicity: of the students, 89 percent are white, 6 percent are Hispanic, 1 percent are American Indian, 1 percent are Asian American and less than 1 percent each are black, Pacific Islander and of unknown ethnicity.

Procedures

All distance sections were surveyed; in addition, face-to-face instructors who were teaching Religion 122 at the time of the study were given the opportunity to participate. Of these 13 face-to-face teachers, 5 chose to participate. Students in both the face-to-face and online sections were notified via the university's LMS of the opportunity to take the study survey. The survey was administered during the last week of the semester.

Instrument

Plummer and Hilton developed an instrument that was shown to be reliable and valid within a limited population sample.[16] Because the population in the present study was similar to Plummer and Hilton's, we used their instrument to measure students' self-reports of their religious and spiritual growth. The instrument consists of 20 items that target 3 religiosity-oriented constructs and one spirituality-oriented construct. The religiosity-related constructs focus on the frequency and the quality of student reading of sacred text, as well as religious practice in the student's personal life. The spirituality-related construct measured the student's spiritual well-being. As Court writes, spiritual aims should be an important part of religious education.[17] While spiritual behaviors cannot be fully measured, we can assess students' self-reports on how religion classes affect their spiritual growth. While some of the items in the survey may seem unusual given their religious nature, they make sense in many contexts, including at BYU-Idaho.[18]

Results

In total, 269 out of 335 distance students completed the survey, for a response rate of 80 percent. Similarly, 520 out of 614 face-to-face students completed the survey, for a response rate of 85 percent. In all, 789 students participated. Our primary research question regarded whether there were different outcomes for in distance sections versus students in face-to-face sections. We considered the question in a variety of ways. First, in order to determine whether there was a difference between distance and face-to-face settings, we compared the combined results of the distance sections with the combined results of the face-to-face sections. Second, we compared the distance section that reported the highest outcomes with the face-to-face section that reported the highest outcomes. ("Highest" outcomes were determined by calculating the average mean score in each section.) We then compared the distance section that reported the highest outcomes with the face-to-face section that reported the lowest outcomes and the distance section with the lowest outcomes to the face-to-face section with the highest outcomes. Finally, to determine whether there were differences within the instructional types, we compared the scores of the highest and lowest distance sections with each other, and we did the same for the face-to-face sections.

Results of Comparing Distance Sections to Face-to-Face Sections

Table 13.1 illustrates the difference between distance and face-to-face sections. The table also includes a measure of the degree of the effect size (Cohen's D); 0.2 to 0.3 is considered a small effect; 0.5 is a medium effect, and above 0.8 is a large effect.[19] Effect sizes lower than a 0.2 for statistically significant results were not recorded.

Regarding the 20 items used in this measure, there were no statistically significant differences between the mean scores of the distance and face-to-face sections.

Comparisons of the Highest and Lowest Distance and Face-to-Face Sections

After determining that there was no overall difference between the sections taught by distance and face-to-face faculty, we determined what kinds of individual differences there were between specific classes in the two types of sections. First, we compared the distance section that reported the highest outcomes with the face-to-face section that reported the highest outcomes. Table 13.2 illustrates the results of this comparison.

Similar to the overall comparison, there was little difference between the highest distance section and the highest face-to-face section. In one instance ("Because of this class, I am using new techniques that help me study the scriptures") there was a statistically significant difference; however, the effect size was small.

Table 13.1 Comparisons of All Distance and Face-to-Face Sections

Survey Item	Mean Difference	T	Significance	Effect Size	Magnitude	Favors
Because of this class, the number of **days** I read per week has increased.	0.029	0.276	0.782			
Because of this class, the number of **minutes** I read per day has increased.	-0.020	-0.196	0.845			
Because of this class, I am more consistent in reading at a set time each day.	0.087	0.762	0.446			
Because of this class, I better understand what I read.	-0.028	-0.321	0.748			
Because of this class, I read more carefully and thoughtfully.	0.013	0.150	0.881			
Because of this class, I am doing better at relating the scriptures to my life.	0.004	0.044	0.965			
Because of this class, scripture study has become more meaningful for me.	0.067	0.739	0.460			
Because of this class, I feel a greater excitement to read the scriptures.	0.013	0.137	0.891			
Because of this class, I am using new techniques that help me study the scriptures.	0.038	0.379	0.704			
Because of this class, I have increased my ability to find insights from the scriptures.	0.041	0.453	0.651			
Because of this class, I find it easier to keep the commandments.	-0.061	-0.645	0.519			
Because of this class, I find it easier to be more Christlike.	-0.137	-1.582	0.114			
Because of this class, I find it easier to resist temptation.	-0.057	-0.609	0.543			
Because of this class, I find it easier to put God first in my life.	-0.095	-1.043	0.297			
Because of this class, I feel closer to the Heavenly Father.	-0.108	-1.319	0.188			
Because of this class, I feel greater spiritual fulfillment.	-0.129	-1.522	0.129			
Because of this class, I feel greater peace with my life.	-0.037	-0.414	0.679			
Because of this class, I feel an increased sense that God is keenly aware of me.	-0.113	-1.308	0.191			
Because of this class, I feel that I have more of an eternal perspective on life.	-0.149	-1.741	0.082			
Because of this class, I feel an increased sense of spiritual direction in my life.	-0.140	-1.610	0.108			

Table 13.2 Comparisons of the Highest Distance and Face-to-Face Means

Survey Item	Mean Difference	T	Significance	Effect Size	Magnitude	Favors
Because of this class, the number of **days** I read per week has increased.	0.084	0.378	0.706			
Because of this class, the number of **minutes** I read per day has increased.	-0.044	-0.201	0.841			
Because of this class, I am more consistent in reading at a set time each day.	0.335	1.309	0.193			
Because of this class, I better understand what I read.	0.002	0.011	0.991			
Because of this class, I read more carefully and thoughtfully.	0.074	0.368	0.714			
Because of this class, I am doing better at relating the scriptures to my life.	-0.056	-0.337	0.737			
Because of this class, scripture study has become more meaningful for me.	0.010	0.054	0.957			
Because of this class, I feel a greater excitement to read the scriptures.	-0.243	-1.149	0.253			
Because of this class, I am using new techniques that help me study the scriptures.	-0.441	-2.221	0.028	0.417	Small	Highest F2F
Because of this class, I have increased my ability to find insights from the scriptures.	-0.156	-0.782	0.436			
Because of this class, I find it easier to keep the commandments.	-0.127	-0.743	0.459			
Because of this class, I find it easier to be more Christlike.	-0.235	-1.558	0.122			
Because of this class, I find it easier to resist temptation.	-0.080	-0.449	0.654			
Because of this class, I find it easier to put God first in my life.	-0.107	-0.754	0.453			
Because of this class, I feel closer to the Heavenly Father.	-0.084	-0.551	0.583			
Because of this class, I feel greater spiritual fulfillment.	-0.221	-1.443	0.152			
Because of this class, I feel greater peace with my life.	0.090	0.559	0.577			
Because of this class, I feel an increased sense that God is keenly aware of me.	0.014	0.085	0.932			
Because of this class, I feel that I have more of an eternal perspective on life.	0.091	0.559	0.577			
Because of this class, I feel an increased sense of spiritual direction in my life.	0.088	0.576	0.566			

We next compared the distance section with the highest results with the face-to-face section with the lowest results. Table 13.3 shows how these two sections compared with each other.

The distance section with the highest mean scores outperformed the lowest face-to-face section on five of the 20 survey items. Four of the five items clustered around scripture study and all had small effect sizes.

Next, we examined the differences between the distance and face-to-face sections with the lowest outcomes. Table 13.4 summarizes the outcome of this comparison.

The face-to-face section with the highest means scores outperformed the lowest distance section. The face-to-face instructor had statistically significant higher outcomes in 18 of the 20 questions; 14 of these had medium effect sizes. The distance section with the highest mean scores outperformed the lowest face-to-face section.

Our final group comparison was between the distance and face-to-face sections with the lowest ratings; there were no statistically significant differences between these two sections.

Comparisons Among Face-to-Face Sections

After establishing that there is a difference in outcomes between the lowest distance and highest face-to-face sections, we examined whether there were differences among the face-to-face sections. Table 13.5 contains the results.

The table shows differences in the means for 14 of the 20 questions with one medium effect size. This finding is not surprising given that face-to-face instructors have wide latitude in their course design. The more interesting question is whether there were meaningful differences in the distance classes, where the instructors are much more restricted regarding the curriculum.

Results of Comparing Within Distance Education

Although all the distance sections followed the same curriculum, was it possible that some instructors did more through discussion boards and other online conversations with students to facilitate positive outcomes? We compared the scores of the three highest- and lowest-rated distance sections. Table 13.6 illustrates the results of this comparison.

For 15 of the survey items, there were statistically significant differences between the high and low sections. Seven items had a medium effect size, with four of those clustering around the concept of feelings of increased spiritual direction. We next compared the highest-two distance sections with the bottom-two distance sections. The results are shown in Table 13.7.

Table 13.3 Comparisons of the Highest Distance Means and the Lowest Face-to-Face Means

Survey Item	Mean Difference	T	Significance	Effect Size	Magnitude	Favors
Because of this class, the number of **days** I read per week has increased.	0.392	2.087	0.040	0.269	Small	Highest distance
Because of this class, the number of **minutes** I read per day has increased.	0.203	0.893	0.373			
Because of this class, I am more consistent in reading at a set time each day.	0.719	2.882	0.004	0.483	Small	Highest distance
Because of this class, I better understand what I read.	0.270	1.387	0.167			
Because of this class, I read more carefully and thoughtfully.	0.341	1.784	0.076			
Because of this class, I am doing better at relating the scriptures to my life.	0.399	2.071	0.039	0.364	Small	Highest Distance
Because of this class scripture, study has become more meaningful for me.	0.480	2.872	0.005	0.369	Small	Highest distance
Because of this class, I feel a greater excitement to read the scriptures.	0.277	1.283	0.201			
Because of this class, I am using new techniques that help me study the scriptures.	0.350	1.780	0.079			
Because of this class, I have increased my ability to find insights from the scriptures.	0.365	1.900	0.062			
Because of this class, I find it easier to keep the commandments.	0.268	1.525	0.131			
Because of this class, I find it easier to be more Christlike.	0.124	0.652	0.515			
Because of this class, I find it easier to resist temptation.	0.303	1.848	0.068			
Because of this class, I find it easier to put God first in my life.	0.306	1.947	0.055			
Because of this class, I feel closer to the Heavenly Father.	0.328	1.659	0.099			
Because of this class, I feel greater spiritual fulfillment.	0.244	1.260	0.209			
Because of this class, I feel greater peace with my life.	0.572	3.782	0.000	0.470	Small	Highest distance
Because of this class, I feel an increased sense that God is keenly aware of me.	0.365	1.774	0.077			
Because of this class, I feel that I have more of an eternal perspective on life.	0.275	1.406	0.161			
Because of this class, I feel an increased sense of spiritual direction in my life.	0.321	1.617	0.107			

Table 13.4 Comparisons of the Highest Face-to-Face Means and the Lowest Distance Means

Survey Item	Mean Difference	T	Significance	Effect Size	Magnitude	Favors
Because of this class, the number of **days** I read per week has increased.	−0.486	−1.857	0.066	0.519	Medium	F2F
Because of this class, the number of **minutes** I read per day has increased.	−0.665	−2.794	0.006	0.392	Small	F2F
Because of this class, I am more consistent in reading at a set time each day.	−0.570	−2.081	0.040	0.474	Small	F2F
Because of this class, I better understand what I read.	−0.546	−2.538	0.012	0.549	Medium	F2F
Because of this class, I read more carefully and thoughtfully.	−0.641	−2.764	0.007	0.632	Medium	F2F
Because of this class, I am doing better at relating the scriptures to my life.	−0.699	−3.004	0.004	0.432	Small	F2F
Because of this class, scripture study has become more meaningful to me.	−0.514	−2.302	0.023	0.598	Medium	F2F
Because of this class, I feel a greater excitement to read the scriptures.	−0.719	−3.254	0.001	0.661	Medium	F2F
Because of this class, I am using new techniques that help me study the scriptures.	−0.822	−3.252	0.002			
Because of this class I have increased my ability to find insights from the scriptures.	−0.704	−2.697	0.009	0.560	Medium	F2F
Because of this class, I find it easier to keep the commandments.	−0.508	−1.975	0.053	0.604	Medium	F2F
Because of this class, I find it easier to be more Christlike.	−0.664	−2.738	0.008	0.516	Medium	F2F
Because of this class, I find it easier to resist temptation.	−0.628	−2.434	0.018	0.666	Medium	F2F
Because of this class, I find it easier to put God first in my life.	−0.726	−2.987	0.004	0.602	Medium	F2F
Because of this class, I feel closer to the Heavenly Father.	−0.656	−2.746	0.008	0.682	Medium	F2F
Because of this class, I feel greater spiritual fulfillment.	−0.768	−3.121	0.003	0.515	Medium	F2F
Because of this class, I feel greater peace with my life.	−0.601	−2.378	0.021	0.604	Medium	F2F
Because of this class, I feel an increased sense that God is keenly aware of me.	−0.700	−2.790	0.007	0.496	Small	F2F
Because of this class, I feel that I have more of an eternal perspective on life.	−0.575	−2.237	0.029	0.513	Medium	F2F
Because of this class, I feel an increased sense of spiritual direction in my life.	−0.579	−2.275	0.027			

Table 13.5 Comparisons Among Face-to-Face Sections

Survey Item	Mean Difference	T	Significance	Effect Size	Magnitude	Favors
Because of this class, the number of **days** I read per week has increased.	0.307	1.709	0.089			
Because of this class, the number of **minutes** I read per day has increased.	0.248	1.416	0.158			
Because of this class, I am more consistent in reading at a set time each day.	0.385	1.979	0.049	0.263	Small	High F2F
Because of this class, I better understand what I read.	0.268	1.788	0.075			
Because of this class, I read more carefully and thoughtfully.	0.268	1.763	0.079			
Because of this class, I am doing better at relating the scriptures to my life.	0.455	3.132	0.002	0.427	Small	High F2F
Because of this class, scripture study has become more meaningful for me.	0.470	3.085	0.002	0.363	Small	High F2F
Because of this class, I feel a greater excitement to read the scriptures.	0.519	3.391	0.001	0.414	Small	High F2F
Because of this class, I am using new techniques that help me study the scriptures.	0.790	5.264	0.000	0.596	Medium	High F2F
Because of this class, I have increased my ability to find insights from the scriptures.	0.522	3.525	0.001	0.420	Small	High F2F
Because of this class, I find it easier to keep the commandments.	0.395	2.940	0.004	0.327	Small	High F2F
Because of this class, I find it easier to be more Christlike.	0.360	2.531	0.012	0.334	Small	High F2F
Because of this class, I find it easier to resist temptation.	0.384	2.739	0.007	0.326	Small	High F2F
Because of this class, I find it easier to put God first in my life.	0.413	3.472	0.001	0.363	Small	High F2F
Because of this class, I feel closer to the Heavenly Father.	0.413	3.374	0.001	0.369	Small	High F2F
Because of this class, I feel greater spiritual fulfillment.	0.465	3.882	0.000	0.424	Small	High F2F
Because of this class, I feel greater peace with my life.	0.482	3.518	0.001	0.404	Small	High F2F
Because of this class, I feel an increased sense that God is keenly aware of me.	0.352	2.687	0.008	0.301	Small	High F2F
Because of this class, I feel that I have more of an eternal perspective on life.	0.183	1.449	0.149			
Because of this class, I feel an increased sense of spiritual direction in my life.	0.233	1.912	0.057			

Table 13.6 Comparisons of the Highest and Lowest Distance Section Means

Survey Item	Mean Difference	T	Significance	Effect Size	Magnitude	Favors
Because of this class, the number of **days** I read per week has increased.	0.570	2.011	0.048	0.431	Small	Highest distance
Because of this class, the number of **minutes** I read per day has increased.	0.621	2.144	0.035	0.456	Small	Highest distance
Because of this class, I am more consistent in reading at a set time each day.	0.905	2.854	0.005	0.598	Medium	Highest distance
Because of this class, I better understand what I read.	0.548	2.112	0.038	0.452	Small	Highest Distance
Because of this class, I read more carefully and thoughtfully.	0.714	2.705	0.008	0.626	Medium	Highest distance
Because of this class, I am doing better at relating the scriptures to my life.	0.643	2.518	0.014	0.533	Medium	Highest distance
Because of this class, scripture study has become more meaningful for me.	0.524	2.071	0.042	0.443	Small	Highest distance
Because of this class, I feel a greater excitement to read the scriptures.	0.476	1.793	0.077			
Because of this class, I am using new techniques that help me study the scriptures.	0.381	1.348	0.181			
Because of this class, I have increased my ability to find insights from the scriptures.	0.548	1.899	0.061			
Because of this class, I find it easier to keep the commandments.	0.381	1.356	0.179			
Because of this class, I find it easier to be more Christlike.	0.429	1.628	0.107			
Because of this class, I find it easier to resist temptation.	0.548	2.014	0.047	0.432	Small	Highest distance
Because of this class, I find it easier to put God first in my life.	0.619	2.346	0.021	0.499	Small	Highest distance
Because of this class, I feel closer to the Heavenly Father.	0.571	2.193	0.031	0.468	Small	Highest distance
Because of this class, I feel greater spiritual fulfillment.	0.548	2.035	0.045	0.436	Small	Highest distance
Because of this class, I feel greater peace with my life.	0.690	2.650	0.010	0.558	Medium	Highest distance
Because of this class, I feel an increased sense that God is keenly aware of me.	0.714	2.649	0.010	0.558	Medium	Highest distance
Because of this class, I feel that I have more of an eternal perspective on life.	0.667	2.402	0.019	0.510	Medium	Highest distance
Because of this class, I feel an increased sense of spiritual direction in my life.	0.667	2.421	0.018	0.513	Medium	Highest distance

Table 13.7 Comparisons Between the Highest Two and Lowest Two Distance Sections

Survey Item	Mean Difference	T	Significance	Effect Size	Magnitude	Favors
Because of this class, the number of **days** I read per week has increased.	0.316	1.374	0.172			
Because of this class, the number of **minutes** I read per day has increased.	0.421	1.894	0.060			
Because of this class, I am more consistent in reading at a set time each day.	0.428	1.746	0.083			
Because of this class, I better understand what I read.	0.405	2.027	0.045	0.325	Small	Top-two distance
Because of this class, I read more carefully and thoughtfully.	0.416	2.156	0.033	0.364	Small	Top-two distance
Because of this class, I am doing better at relating the scriptures to my life.	0.568	2.972	0.004	0.471	Small	Top-two distance
Because of this class, scripture study has become more meaningful for me.	0.385	2.024	0.045	0.326	Small	Top-two distance
Because of this class, I feel a greater excitement to read the scriptures.	0.424	2.197	0.030	0.351	Small	Top-two distance
Because of this class, I am using new techniques that help me study the scriptures.	0.228	1.083	0.280			
Because of this class, I have increased my ability to find insights from the scriptures.	0.412	2.020	0.045	0.325	Small	Top-two distance
Because of this class, I find it easier to keep the commandments.	0.567	2.778	0.006	0.443	Small	Top-two distance
Because of this class, I find it easier to be more Christlike.	0.516	2.764	0.007	0.441	Small	Top-two distance
Because of this class, I find it easier to resist temptation.	0.614	3.127	0.002	0.496	Small	Top-two distance
Because of this class, I find it easier to put God first in my life.	0.614	3.245	0.002	0.515	Medium	Top-two distance
Because of this class, I feel closer to the Heavenly Father.	0.403	2.159	0.033	0.348	Small	Top-two distance
Because of this class, I feel greater spiritual fulfillment.	0.483	2.478	0.015	0.398	Small	Top-two distance
Because of this class, I feel greater peace with my life.	0.575	3.071	0.003	0.488	Small	Top-two distance
Because of this class, I feel an increased sense that God is keenly aware of me.	0.548	2.855	0.005	0.455	Small	Top-two distance
Because of this class, I feel that I have more of an eternal perspective on life.	0.523	2.682	0.008	0.428	Small	Top-two distance
Because of this class, I feel an increased sense of spiritual direction in my life.	0.565	2.806	0.006	0.447	Small	Top-two distance

While the contrast between the top-two and bottom-two sections is not as stark as between the one top and one bottom section, the two groups statistically differed on 16 survey items; however, only one statistical difference had a medium effect size.

Discussion

In this study, we sought to determine whether the outcomes differ between students in distance sections and students in face-to-face sections of a religion course. Within our sample and given the limitations discussed next, there were no significant differences between the two groups.

In particular, while there were no overall significant differences, there were differences when comparing the highest and lowest sections in each group. The highest-rated, face-to-face section significantly outperformed the lowest-rated distance section—more so than the highest-distance section outperformed the lowest face-to-face section. Nevertheless, the variance in student outcomes appeared to be more significant in terms of different sections within a single delivery mode. This result could be related to the instructor of an individual section; alternatively, other factors may have made sections within a delivery mode different from each other.

Given that each of the distance sections used the same curriculum and course structure, it is perhaps surprising that there was variance within the distance sections across all constructs. One possible reason is that distance instructors can influence both the mechanical aspects of religiosity (developing habits of studying the scriptures) and a student's choice to follow and connect with a divine influence. Further research may be helpful in determining whether high scores were attributable to the actions of instructors or other factors.

In many instances, a finding of nonsignificance is considered unimportant. However, we believe our finding is practically significant in that little previous research has been published regarding affective religious outcomes in distance education. While some might have a default assumption that outcomes such as "feeling greater spiritual direction" and an increased likelihood to "keep the commandments" are better accomplished in face-to-face settings, this assumption is not supported in the present study.

Limitations and Directions for Future Research

There are many reasons why these results should be interpreted cautiously. Both face-to-face and distance classes have several components, including content, instructor personality, the dynamics of the class and technology problems. This study bundles these factors and does not isolate the delivery mode as the single variable. It is also possible that one population of students perceived the class differently from the outset. For example, if the distance students experienced gratitude for a flexible option or perhaps lowered expectations because the course was online, the students' perceptions might have been altered in a way that affected the results of this study.

There are several additional limitations to this study. First, the face-to-face teachers were not selected at random for participation in this study. Teachers were invited to participate, and they chose whether to do so. Second, the registration system made one distance section available at a time; once that section was filled, another section opened for enrollment. In other words, students who registered early were all in the same section, and students who registered later were in the same section. There were small differences between distance sections regarding the number of off-campus students who registered for the course, and the students taking the distance sections tended to be older than those in the face-to-face sections. These factors may have influenced the overall results. Face-to-face students could choose from any available section; they selected sections based on a variety of factors, likely including the time of day (favoring a time that was convenient for them) and perhaps based on what they had heard about a specific professor. Moreover, it is likely that the students who opted to take the distance course represent a different population than that of the students who elected to take the face-to-face course.

A large weakness in terms of transferability is that this study focused on a religion class at a church-affiliated university where students may already be motivated to read religious material. In addition, the degree to which students at this university seek spiritual outcomes may not be the same as at other universities; we might have obtained different results in other contexts. Thus the results may not be transferrable to religion classes generally.

Future research could address the limitations of this study. Although it is not feasible to assign students randomly to distance or face-to-face versions of a course, future studies could include more sections and teachers in the sample. Moreover, this or similar research should be conducted in a variety of other religious contexts. A particularly interesting approach for future research could be to create different versions of the online course and test whether different course designs result in different outcomes. Such a study would be particularly effective if it examined the perceptions of students of comparable demographics who have taken both online and face-to-face courses so that they can more completely compare them. Moreover, future research should account for demographic factors such as age and gender, which were not examined in this study. Ideally, such a study would also include qualitative interviews to ascertain how students perceive these courses more fully.

Our study's findings lead to several important questions: why was there variance within the two groups (e.g., highest distance section versus lowest distance section)? Did the students who report the highest outcomes have a teacher who did something different than the other teachers did? If so, what? Answers to these questions require follow-up studies to obtain additional information. Future studies should do more to pinpoint specific actions professors take that lead to improved outcomes in religious education. The work of Kuo, Walker, Belland and Schroder might serve as a helpful starting point for identifying which factors in an online learning setting should be more closely examined to find answers to the questions noted earlier.[20] Ideally, teachers whose students report lower scores could implement these teaching strategies and then use the instrument to measure if this implementation leads to improved student ratings. Becoming aware of student outcomes can increase instructors' desire to improve student outcomes. Using the instrument we have discussed may help both face-to-face and distance teachers alter their approaches in order to provide students with a better learning experience.

Appendix A
Survey

Religious Education Survey

Instructor: _____
Class: _____
Section: _____

Do not put your name on this survey

Instructions: The purpose of this survey is to understand better the influence your religion class is having on certain aspects of your life. If you are taking multiple religion classes, please base your answers on the class in which you are taking this survey. In this survey, you should rate the degree to which this class has influenced you in several areas. Please note: it is possible that you are making progress in an area, but not because of any influence that your class has had. For example, imagine you are answering the following item:

Because of this class...	*Strongly Disagree*	*Mostly Disagree*	*Slightly Disagree*	*Slightly Agree*	*Mostly Agree*	*Strongly Agree*
the number of days I read my scriptures per week has increased	O	O	O	O	O	O

- If you are increasing the number of days you read per week, but it is **NOT** in any way because of this class, then you would mark **"Strongly Disagree."**
- If the class is the **PRIMARY REASON** you are increasing your reading frequency then you would mark **"Strongly Agree."**

- Depending on the degree of influence of the class, you may choose one of the middle options: **"Mostly Disagree" "Slightly Disagree," "Slightly Agree"** or **"Mostly Agree"**.
- If you have made **NO CHANGE** or **DECREASED** the number of days you read, then you would mark **"Strongly Disagree."**

Please mark your answers with an "X." Read each item carefully and respond thoughtfully. If you have any questions, please raise your hand

Begin Survey

To what extent do you agree with the following statements about your **SCRIPTURE STUDY?** "BECAUSE OF THIS CLASS:						
	Strongly Disagree	*Mostly Disagree*	*Slightly Disagree*	*Slightly Agree*	*Mostly Agree*	*Strongly Agree*
1. the number of <u>days</u> I read per week has increased."	O	O	O	O	O	O
2. the number of <u>minutes</u> I read per day has increased."	O	O	O	O	O	O
3. I am more consistent in reading at a set time each day."	O	O	O	O	O	O

To what extent do you agree with the following statements about your **SCRIPTURE STUDY?** "BECAUSE OF THIS CLASS:						
	Strongly Disagree	*Mostly Disagree*	*Slightly Disagree*	*Slightly Agree*	*Mostly Agree*	*Strongly Agree*
4. I better understand what I read."	O	O	O	O	O	O
5. I read more carefully and thoughtfully."	O	O	O	O	O	O
6. I am doing better at relating the scriptures to my life."	O	O	O	O	O	O

To what extent do you agree with the following statements about your **SCRIPTURE STUDY?**
"BECAUSE OF THIS CLASS:

7. scripture study has become more meaningful for me."	O	O	O	O	O	O
8. I feel a greater excitement to read the scriptures."	O	O	O	O	O	O
9. I am using new techniques that help me study the scriptures."	O	O	O	O	O	O
10. I have increased in my ability to find my own insights from the scriptures."	O	O	O	O	O	O

To what extent do you agree with the following statements?
"BECAUSE OF THIS CLASS I FIND IT EASIER TO:

	Strongly Disagree	*Mostly Disagree*	*Slightly Disagree*	*Slightly Agree*	*Mostly Agree*	*Strongly Agree*
11. keep the commandments."	O	O	O	O	O	O
12. be more Christlike."	O	O	O	O	O	O
13. resist temptation."	O	O	O	O	O	O
14. put God first in my life."	O	O	O	O	O	O

"BECAUSE OF THIS CLASS I FEEL:						
	Strongly Disagree	*Mostly Disagree*	*Slightly Disagree*	*Slightly Agree*	*Mostly Agree*	*Strongly Agree*
15. closer to the Heavenly Father."	O	O	O	O	O	O
16. greater spiritual fulfillment."	O	O	O	O	O	O
17. greater peace with my life."	O	O	O	O	O	O
18. an increased sense that God is keenly aware of me."	O	O	O	O	O	O
19. that I have more of an eternal perspective on life."	O	O	O	O	O	O
20. an increased sense of spiritual direction in my life."	O	O	O	O	O	O

	Not carefully at all	*Somewhat Carefully*	*Very Carefully*
21. How carefully did you respond to these statements?	O	O	O

Thank you for your help

Notes

1 Carol H. Weiss, *Evaluation: Methods for Studying Programs and Policies*, 2nd ed. (Upper Saddle River, NJ: Prentice Hall, 1998), 4.
2 Ibid., 49.

3. Terralyn McKee, "Thirty Years of Distance Education: Personal Reflections," *The International Review of Research in Open and Distance Learning* 11, no.2 (2010): 100–109.
4. Mike Allen, John Bourhis, Nancy Burrell, and Edward Mabry, "Comparing Student Satisfaction with Distance Education to Traditional Classrooms in Higher Education: A Meta-analysis," *American Journal of Distance Education* 16, no. 2 (2002): 83–97.
5. Begoña Gros, Iolanda Garcia, and Anna Escofet, "Beyond the Net Generation Debate: A Comparison of Digital Learners in Face-to-Face and Virtual Universities," *The International Review of Research in Open and Distance Learning* 13, no. 4 (2012): 190–210.
6. Lynne Broadbent and Alan Brown (eds.), *Issues in Religious Education* (New York: Routledge, 2002).
7. Steven B. Frye, "Religious Distance Education Goes Online," *New Direction for Adult and Continuing Education* 133 (2012): 13–22.
8. Mary E. Hess, "2010 Presidential Address: Learning Religion and Religiously Learning Amid Global Cultural Flows," *Religious Education* 106, no. 4 (2011): 360.
9. Barbara E. Walvoord, *Teaching and Learning in College Introductory Religion Courses* (Malden, MA: Blackwell, 2008).
10. Nel Noddings, "Critical Thinking in Religious Education," in *Education and Hope in Troubled Times: Visions of Change for Our Children's World*, ed. H. Svi Shapiro (New York: Routledge, 2010), 147–156.
11. Rob Freathy and Stephen Parker, "The Necessity of Historical Inquiry in Educational Research: The Case of Religious Education," *British Journal of Religious Education* 32, no. 3 (2010): 229–243.
12. Elina Hella and Andrew Wright, "Learning 'About' and 'From' Religion: Phenomenography, the Variation Theory of Learning, and Religious Education in Finland and the UK," *British Journal of Religious Education* 31, no. 1 (2009): 53–64.
13. Gregory D. Loving, "The Religious Experience Project: Bringing an Experiential Dimension to Teaching Religion," *Teaching Theology and Religion* 14, no. 3 (2011): 249.
14. David M. Csinos, "'Come, Follow Me': Apprenticeship in Jesus' Approach to Education," *Religious Education* 105, no. 1 (2010): 45–62.
15. William H. Jeynes, "The Need for Changes in the Nature of Christian Seminary Education," *Christian Higher Education* 11, no. 2 (2012): 69–80.
16. John Hilton III and Kenneth Plummer, "Examining Student Spiritual Outcomes as a Result of a General Education Religion Course," *Christian Higher Education* 12, no. 5 (2013): 331–348.
17. Deborah Court, "Religious Experience as an Aim of Religious Education," *British Journal of Religious Education* 35, no. 3 (2012): 251–263.
18. Hilton and Plummer, "Examining Student Spiritual Outcomes," 331–348.
19. Jacob Cohen, *Statistical Power Analysis for the Behavioral Sciences*, 2nd ed. (Hillsdale, NJ: Lawrence Erlbaum Associates, 1988).
20. Yu-Chun Kuo, Andrew E. Walker, Brian R. Belland, and Kerstin E. E. Schroder, "A Predictive Study of Student Satisfaction in Online Education Programs," *The International Review of Research in Open and Distance Learning* 14, no. 1 (2013): 16–39.

Contributors

Ben Fryar, Brigham Young University-Idaho
Ryan Gardner, Brigham Young University-Idaho
Christopher Heard, Pepperdine University
Charlotte Heeg, Garrett-Evangelical Theological Seminary
John Hilton III, Brigham Young University
Renate Hood, University of Mary Hardin-Baylor
David Kniep, Abilene Christian University
Brooke Lester, Garrett-Evangelical Theological Seminary
Richard Newton, Elizabethtown College
Kyle M. Oliver, Teachers College, Columbia University
Rob O'Lynn, Kentucky Christian University
Kenneth Plummer, Brigham Young University
Steven V. Rouse, Pepperdine University
Kristy L. Slominski, University of Mississippi
Gerald L. Stevens, New Orleans Baptist Theological Seminary
Anthony Sweat, Brigham Young University
Phyllis Zagano, Hofstra University

Index

Actium 150
Alexa.com 84, 85, 86, 88, 89
Alexander, Bryan 98
Amazon 95, 163
analog film 146
AnswerGarden 36, 38, 40
Antony 150
Apple 145
Appledorn, Roger C. 146
artifacts 30, 62, 70, 93, 99
Audacity 29
audio 9, 18, 25, 67–68, 118, 121

backchanneling *see* live-tweeting
Bain, Ken 22
Baker, Kelly J. 5
Bibb, Bryan 174–177
Blackboard 40, 46, 97, 148
blended courses 157
blog/blogging 88–89, 94, 95, 96, 99
Blogger 88
Bloom's Taxonomy 114
BlueJeans 148–149, 151–152

Camtasia Studio 116
Canvas 25, 40, 97
captions 177
Choose Your Own Adventure series 132–133, 140
classroom-based education 157
clickers: benefits of 44–47; defined 35; features of 44; uses of 47–54
CMOOK 160–161
cognitive understanding 35
collaborative learning 114
collaborative note-taking 10
Collins, Jim 8
community 92–93; and acceptance 93, 104; and reciprocity 93, 104; and trustworthiness 93, 104

conceptual understanding 35, 40
conversational theology 173–174
cool media 80
cooperative learning 7
Cormier, Dave 98, 99
course design 161
Coursesites.com 162, 163
cultural expansion 3
curiosity 93, 129–130, 175, 182

Delicious 95
dictation versus note-taking 8
digital: age myths 6; aliens 81; citizenship 80–81; geographies 59, 61, 63, 68, 71; immigrants 6, 7, 80; literacy 7, 62, 64, 69; natives 6, 7, 80, 119; technology 7
digital technologies in religious education 187
digitized media 6
Diigo 95
Discord 95
discussion boards 40, 190
disruptive technologies 111
distance education 186, 188
Downes, Stephen 98
Dropbox 149, 152

effective teaching methodologies 159
ethical reflection 23
evaluation defined 186
Evernote 25, 86–87
experimental intervention 131–138
external referencing 7
extrinsic fantasies 129

Facebook 59, 82–83, 84, 85, 88, 94, 95, 96, 97, 148
face-to-face education 97–98, 100, 111, 112, 114, 186, 188

feedback 6, 25, 35, 52, 39, 40, 44–46, 53, 85, 121, 128, 153, 186
Flickr 59, 69, 70, 96, 96, 99
flipped learning, advantages of 113, 120
Folkways 68
formation defined 92–93

Gamergate 102
gamification defined 127
gamified course structure 131
GarageBand 29
Gates, Bill 111
geophysical context 58, 69
Gmail 89, 102
Godin, Seth 81
Google 83, 89, 86, 97, 110
Google Books 89
Google Cardboard 13, 64, 66
Google Chrome 166
Google Docs 90, 97, 98
Google Earth 63, 65, 66
Google Expeditions 64, 65
Google Groups 95
Google Hangouts 174, 181
Google Lit Trips 66, 70
Google Maps 65–66, 70, 89
Google Scholar 89
Google Slides 89
Google Street View 65–66
Google Translate 69
GoSoapBox 36
Graphics Interchange Format (GIFs) 13, 83
Guided Discovery 19

harassment 100, 101, 102, 103
hilastērion 149–151
historical context 58, 69, 109, 153
history of religion 5, 63, 87
Hofstra massive online open seminar 158, 161–167
hot media 79
HTC Vive 65
Hyatt, Michael 81

IBM 145, 146
icebreaker activities 34, 37
information production 7
Instagram 6, 79, 84–85, 95, 148
instructional videos 111
interactive fiction 128, 129, 133, 140
interactivity 147, 148, 152, 154, 159

Internet 4, 6, 12, 28, 59, 94, 110, 121
intrinsic fantasies 129
iTunes U 29

Josianic Reform, The 130
Junior, Nyasha 174, 177–181

Kahoot 12, 36, 37, 38, 39
Khan Academy 111, 116
knowledge assessment 18–22
Kodak 146
Kraybill, Donald 5

LCD projection 146
learning management system (LMS) 94, 97, 100, 116, 189
Lester, Brooke 174
Let's Go Vote 36
LinkedIn 82
live-tweeting 11, 84
Logan, Dave 81
Long, Kimberly Bracken 26

massive online open course (MOOC) 157, 158, 159, 160, 168
Mastodon 99, 101, 103
mesoMOOC 160–161
message context and content 79
Messenger 98
Metropolis 150, 151
microblogging 89, 95, 99, 102
Millennials 6, 45, 85, 87, 119
Miller, John B. F. 174, 181–184
MOOC 98
Moodle 40, 97
Moretz, Matthew 61
museums 64, 68

narrative versus declarative assignments 140
Netflix 28
new media 58, 61, 62, 63, 68, 69
Notebook Layout 29

Octavian 150–151
online: codes of conduct 99, 100, 102, 103; education 111–112, 157, 158, 168; videos 184
online/blended class 97–98
Open Old Testament Learning Event (OOTLE) 174
overhead cell 146
overhead map view 59, 66

Packard, Edward 132
Pear Deck 36, 39, 40
personal computer 4, 35, 46, 116, 145, 146, 154
personal study 7, 8, 11
photographs/photography 67–68, 69, 79, 84, 96
Pinterest 63, 86–87, 95
place-based annotation tools 69
podcasts: audio 18–19, 24; sample 29; scripts 24; "top-down," 18–19; video 18, 28, 115
Poll Everywhere 11, 12, 35, 37, 38, 39
polls/polling 34, 35, 36, 37, 39
PowerPoint 36, 46, 114, 116, 121, 149–150, 151–152, 162, 163
presentation software 146
professor presence 159–160

Quizlet 36
quizzes 35, 36, 117
Quizzizz 36, 40

Reacting to the Past (RTTP) 130, 132
reception history 180
recorded modeling 177
reflective tasks 27
religious: diversity 58; illiteracy 58; sites 57, 58, 58, 61, 63, 66, 68, 69
Roddenberry, Gene 3, 4
rubric development 20, 23, 24, 28

Sacred Destinations 68, 70
screencasts 111
scriptures 21, 22, 24, 58, 187, 190, 199
Siemens, George 98
Sites in 3D 65
Sites in VR 65
Skype 148, 151, 152
smartphones 4, 6, 7, 9, 29, 117, 154
Smithsonian Global Sound for Libraries 68
SMS Poll 36
Snapchat 28, 85–86, 95, 148
social media: abusive behavior in 96; anonymity of 95; content consumption in 93; as generous 81–82, 83; as influential 81–82, 83; openness of 94, 95; as relational 79–90
Society of Biblical Literature (SBL) 19, 149, 153
sociocultural context 58, 69
Socrative 36, 39
sophisticated contextual understanding 58, 72
SoundCloud 68, 69
storytelling 129
student: anonymity 38; assessment of, behavior 23; feedback 36, 39, 40; freedom of opinion 38; motivation 39, 40; participation 159; retention 34
student-centered learning 41
student response systems 45
subject-matter anxiety 34, 37
surveys 38, 40
Survnvote 36

teaching methodology, perception of 187
technical term handout 184
technology-as-furniture concept 7, 12
TED Talks 116
televisions 4
Tel Gezer 154
Text the Mob 36
textual content 19
theological reflections 26
third screen: devices 5, 11, 12, 13; interactivity 13; teaching 7, 8, 13; technologies 5, 12
3-D 13, 145, 154
3M 146
tribal leadership 81–82
Tumblr 88–89
TurningPoint ResponseWare 36
Twine 133
Twitch 95, 98
Twitter 11, 82, 83–84, 85, 88, 92, 94, 95, 96, 97, 99
2-D 13, 71

Vasudevan, Lalitha 59, 61, 66, 69
VCR 146
video 67–68, 115, 117, 118–119

videoconferencing 148, 149, 154
Vimeo 87–88, 95, 96, 98
virtual reality 58, 63, 64
Voice Memos 19
VotApedia 36

Web 1.0, 93
Web 2.0, 93, 97
web-based response systems 35, 36
Wikipedia 86
Wilson, Mark 149–153

word-cloud response system 37, 38
WordPress 88, 94, 96

xMOOC 160–161

YouCanBookMe.com 9
YouTube 28, 61, 68, 69, 87–89, 94, 95, 96, 98, 99, 111, 115, 174, 177, 185

Zoom.us 165